The Pan American Imagination

New World Studies

J. Michael Dash, *Editor*

Frank Moya Pons and
Sandra Pouchet Paquet,
Associate Editors

The Pan American Imagination

CONTESTED VISIONS
OF THE HEMISPHERE IN
TWENTIETH-CENTURY LITERATURE

Stephen M. Park

University of Virginia Press

Charlottesville and London

University of Virginia Press
© 2014 by the Rector and Visitors of the University of Virginia
All rights reserved
Printed in the United States of America on acid-free paper
First published 2014

9 8 7 6 5 4 3 2 1

Library of Congress Cataloging-in-Publication Data

Park, Stephen M., 1979–
  The pan american imagination : contested visions of the
hemisphere in twentieth-century literature / Stephen M. Park.
    pages cm. — (New world studies)
  Includes bibliographical references and index.
  ISBN 978-0-8139-3665-9 (cloth : alk. paper)
  ISBN 978-0-8139-3666-6 (pbk. : alk. paper)
  ISBN 978-0-8139-3667-3 (ebook)
  1. America—In literature. 2. Literature—20th century—
History and criticism. 3. Pan-Americanism. 4. Transnationalism
in literature. 5. Literature and globalization. I. Title.
PN56.3.A45P37 2014
809'.93327—dc23

                                        2014014774

A book in the American Literatures Initiative (ALI), a collaborative
publishing project of NYU Press, Fordham University Press, Rutgers
University Press, Temple University Press, and the University of Virginia
Press. The Initiative is supported by The Andrew W. Mellon Foundation.
For more information, please visit www.americanliteratures.org.

THE
AMERICAN
LITERATURES
INITIATIVE

For Sofia

Contents

**Women, Migration, and Memories
of Pan Americanism**

Illustrations

Acknowledgments

I COULD NOT HAVE completed this project without the help of many people. First I'd like to thank John Carlos Rowe. His insights and encouragement were crucial at the earliest stages of the writing process, and he continues to be an incomparable mentor. It was from John that I first learned to think about American literature in a larger context; the historical, political, and cultural connections this book traces across the Western Hemisphere first emerged years ago in our many conversations and I cannot thank him enough for his guidance. Beyond his direct contributions to this project and the numerous drafts on which he commented, John has taught me how to be a scholar and a teacher. Even though he is always engaged with several research projects of his own, he makes time for each and every student, displaying a warmth and intellectual generosity that continue to inspire me. Above all, he's been a model for how to think about American literature and simply how to *be* while in academia. Susan McCabe was also a generous reader of this work, and I thank her for continually pushing my reading toward new insights. Her patience and thoughtfulness were always evident in our conversations, even as she unrelentingly challenged key parts of my argument. Roberto Díaz has been a wonderful reader of my work as well. He's offered me great advice and, when I've started to recapitulate the "Northern" perspective of the authors I write about, has nudged me back on track in the kindest way.

Brett Garcia Myhren read through every part of this book (often many times!). Throughout the entire process he not only provided insightful feedback, but he kept me sane. His own hard work has been inspiring, and his dedication to my work has shaped this book in more ways than I could name. I also want to thank Casey Shoop, Jessica Bremmer, and

Michael Cucher for reading earlier drafts of this material; I'm indebted to them for their valuable help.

I would also like to thank the University of Southern California College Commons for a fellowship that sustained my research, as well as USC's English Department for the travel grant that allowed me to visit the home of the Pan American Union. While I was there Stella Villagran and the staff at the Columbus Memorial Library provided immense help with my research on the PAU. This book also benefited from the early feedback I received from Anna Brickhouse, Elizabeth Maddock Dillon, and other scholars at the Futures of American Studies Institute at Dartmouth College.

The staff at the University of Virginia Press was amazing throughout the preparation of this book. Cathie Brettschneider has been a wonderful editor, and I want to thank her for all of her work in shepherding the manuscript into print. The two anonymous readers offered invaluable feedback; this book has benefited greatly from their probing questions and it is much richer for the additions they each suggested.

I owe a debt to my parents, Bill and Louise Park, for reading to me and with me for so many years. It's from them that I learned to love books, and I can't thank them enough for teaching me that it's good to be curious about many things. Finally I'd like to thank Sofia Park, who has lived with this book for so long. Her ideas, questions, and insightful comments have taken this project to places I would have never reached on my own, and she is present on every page. Her love and encouragement enabled me to write this book, and she continues to find new ways of making my life wonderful every day.

An earlier version of chapter 1 appeared in the *Journal of Modern Literature* 34 no. 4 (© 2011 Indiana University Press); an earlier version of chapter 3 appeared in *Modern Fiction Studies;* and an earlier version of chapter 4 appeared in *Comparative American Studies* 10, no. 4 (www. maneyonline.com/cas). I thank the editors for permission to republish this work.

The Pan American Imagination

Introduction

A History of an Idea and Its Institutions

TODAY THE HOUSE OF THE AMERICAS sits unnoticed on a corner of Constitution Avenue in Washington, D.C. Now the ceremonial home of the Organization of American States, it is overshadowed by its more glamorous neighbors, the White House a few blocks to the north and the Washington Monument just across the street. The House of the Americas attracts no attention from the Mall's tourists and very little notice from the State Department. In 1908, however, the scene was far different. Dignitaries from across the Western Hemisphere gathered to lay the cornerstone for a building that would be the new home of the Pan American Union. The PAU, founded in 1889, was finally to have a home worthy of its status. A decade before the League of Nations was founded and nearly forty years before the United Nations, the now forgotten Pan American Union was viewed as so important to the relations between the United States and the rest of the Americas that it was afforded this prime symbolic real estate.

President Theodore Roosevelt gave a dedicatory speech at the ceremony, as did Andrew Carnegie, who had put up most of the one million dollars that would be spent on the building's construction. Perhaps the most telling speech, though, came from Secretary of State Elihu Root. Although Root is now best remembered for his involvement in adding the Platt Amendment to Cuba's Constitution (one of the period's great symbols of U.S. hegemony), on that day in 1908 he captured the spirit of the Pan American Union. Its goals, Root explained, were "to break down the barriers of mutual ignorance between the nations of America by collecting and making accessible, furnishing and spreading, information about every country among the people of every other country in the Union, to facilitate and stimulate intercourse, trade, acquaintance, good understanding, fellowship, and sympathy."[1] The U.S. role in the

Americas during the twentieth century is typically defined by its military and economic dominance of its neighbors. From Roosevelt and his Rough Riders landing in Cuba in 1898 to the military occupations of Haiti, Nicaragua, and the Dominican Republic, just to name a few, Pan Americanism at first blush runs counter to all these images.[2] The utopian rhetoric that promises a transnational partnership of equals seems to come from another era, one that surely did not involve the U.S. military invading nearly half of the PAU's twenty-one member nations. While the supposed fellowship of the American nations is in direct opposition to the imperialist actions of the United States in the twentieth century, these two opposing narratives intertwine and enable one another within the Pan American Union.

I have begun with Root's speech because these narratives can be disentangled by focusing on his aspiration of "collecting and making accessible, furnishing and spreading, information." The Pan American Union itself had little formal power. It had no army, and it could not sign treaties or make international law. What the institution did do, however, was engage in a systematic study of the hemisphere. It organized numerous conferences on science, trade, sanitation, architecture, immigration, and other areas of specialization. And, as Root noted, the PAU had "established a rapidly increasing library of history, travel, description, statistics, and literature of the American nations."[3] It is this act of compiling and organizing knowledge that this book explores. While over the past two decades numerous scholars have taken into account the role that U.S. hegemony played in shaping the cultural relations of the Americas in the twentieth century, this study focuses more specifically on the role that the U.S. "informational empire" played during this period.[4] The early part of the century, from the completion of the House of the Americas in 1910 until the shift of foreign policy on the U.S. entry into World War II in 1941, marked an intense period of interest in Latin America and the Caribbean. The burgeoning field of Spanish American studies saw an increase in archaeological expeditions to the region, along with corresponding exhibits in museums back home. Important archives emerged around this time, including Berkeley's Bancroft Library (in 1905) and the PAU's own Columbus Memorial Library (1890). However, the Pan American imagination was not the product of a single archive or institution. It was instead a way of thinking about and representing the peoples of the Western Hemisphere as part of a knowable, unified whole. The system of knowledge production that grew out of these physical spaces served to frame Latin America and the

Caribbean as objects of study and to organize their people and cultures within U.S.-defined notions of modernity. As much as hemispheric relations in the early part of the twentieth century were shaped by decisions of the state and the pressures of international trade, a nation's status within the U.S. hierarchy of modernity was very much a function of the textual representations of the region.

The Pan American Union therefore is only the most visible element of the larger intellectual project of Pan Americanism. Its rhetoric of cooperation and subtle imperialism are bound together in the body of knowledge it amassed, but in producing and organizing this knowledge about Latin America such contradictions were muted, suppressed from the official record. In order to explore the gaps and contradictions in this knowledge about the region, this study looks at literary texts from the period and explores their relation to Pan Americanism and its system of knowledge production. As Aimé Césaire has famously remarked, "Poetic knowledge is born in the great silence of scientific knowledge."[5] Therefore I have chosen the subjects of this book not only because their work demonstrates inter-American cultural exchange but because they in some way engage the system of knowledge production at the center of Pan Americanism. William Carlos Williams, Alejo Carpentier, Carleton Beals, Walker Evans, José Clemente Orozco, Ana Castillo, and Katherine Dunham, to varying degrees, both internalized and resisted the logic of Pan Americanism that framed Latin America and the Caribbean as objects of study. In each of the works I examine, the archive has been raided and its store of knowledge redeployed in ways that call into question the nature of hemispheric relations.

This book focuses on the visual and textual record of the Pan American era (1910–41) with the hope of sorting out the way representations of Latin America and the Caribbean as well as the U.S. academic discourse around these regions shaped transnational cultural exchange. In addition to illuminating a largely forgotten historical moment, this study also serves as an occasion to reflect on the hemispheric turn in American studies. As much as the U.S. academy has employed this framework in the past two decades—with all of the benefits of multiplicity and accusations of academic imperialism that has entailed—it is worth returning to a period nearly a century ago when U.S. scholars and intellectuals also employed a hemispheric rhetoric. The dominant discourse of Pan Americanism, with its seamless mix of good intentions and condescension, might serve as a cautionary example to present-day scholars who engage in Hemispheric American studies. From the vantage of the North

American university, it can be all too easy to recapitulate the same hegemonic discourse behind the Pan Americanism of the early twentieth century. Looking from North to South and South to North, *The Pan American Imagination* offers not so much a corrective to the structures of power at work in Pan Americanism as an understanding of how literary and scholarly texts enable or undermine those structures of power.

The Hemispheric Turn in American Studies

This project grows out of the relatively recent shift in American studies away from examining the nation-state and reinforcing the tenets of U.S. exceptionalism and toward an approach that takes into account the complex interrelation between the United States and the rest of the hemisphere.[6] It is also important to note, however, the methodological distinctions between the transnational approach, as articulated by Shelley Fisher Fishkin and others, and a hemispheric approach to American studies. Transnational American studies offers potentially limitless lines of inquiry, and indeed the example Fishkin offers is a study of letters written by Chinese laborers building the railroad in the American West to their families back in Guangdong Province.[7] Hemispheric American studies, on the other hand, appears to impose just one more arbitrary boundary; it replaces the political fiction of the U.S. borders with the geographic fiction of the hemisphere. However, since the idea of a hemispheric community has for centuries been promoted by artists and intellectuals, as well as nation-states, a hemispheric approach to American studies is needed to interrogate this same ideology. My intent is not merely to apply a hemispheric frame to our understanding of American literature and culture but instead to explore the history of the hemispheric idea itself.

Pan Americanism was rooted in the assumption that all the regions of the Americas could be spoken for and that the site of that enunciation would be the United States, which positioned its own culture as the model for modernity in the hemisphere. But, as Doris Sommer has noted, the presumption to speak for the Other is predicated upon first knowing the Other.[8] Part of the project of any hemispheric study, including this one, should be to explore the historical and textual absences of the dominant narrative of modernity in the Americas and to reinterpret those narratives from other geographical and cultural localities. This "occluded history," as Kirsten Silva Gruesz has called it, demonstrates that trans-American literary connections are not the product of revisionist work by American studies scholars, but rather such hemispheric connections have been present for centuries, although readers, blinkered by the categories of national identity, have missed these connections.[9]

However, the hemispheric turn, even at its most inclusive, multilingual, and multivocal, is still laden with its own intellectual pitfalls. Because this scholarly approach is centered in the U.S. academy (and largely within American studies and English departments), it has met with the accusations that (1) it recapitulates U.S. imperialism by excluding the voices of scholars from Latin American and Caribbean institutions and by creating another stage on which the inhabitants of the Americas are unable to represent themselves; and (2) within the U.S. university, such a "turn" infringes upon the role of Latin American studies and other disciplines based on the methods of area studies, in terms of both research and teaching responsibilities.[10]

While these concerns must certainly be kept in mind, accusations of intellectual tourism are inevitable when one's work crosses traditional disciplinary boundaries. When a North American scholar endeavors to study the rest of the Americas, there is always a danger that the politics of that scholarly work will reinforce the traditional power relationships of the hemisphere. However, as Anna Brickhouse has reminded us, scholars make conscious intellectual choices as well as unconscious ones, and indeed the rhetorical move of self-critique often becomes a conceit, one that foregrounds the politics (and therefore the conclusions) of the scholarly work rather than the act of scholarship itself.[11]

Though I hope that my own scholarly work amounts to more than tourism, this book does not arrive at a final ruling to condemn or redeem the hemispheric turn. Instead my examination of Pan Americanism is itself a reflection on intellectual tourism, on the power structures of hemispheric study. While some scholars and writers of the time imagined an egalitarian hemisphere in which ideas could circulate, many works certainly recapitulated a North/South hegemony. Yet the rhetoric and realities of Pan Americanism make clear that both of these narratives were intertwined.

A Usable Pan Americanism: Its History and Modern Appropriations

One version of Pan Americanism can be traced back a hundred years earlier, to the postcolonial vision of Simón Bolívar. In the aftermath of their victories over the Spanish Empire, the newly independent Creole leaders sought to cement their new nation-states (and their American identity) by organizing under the banner of the Pan Americanism.

In order to solidify his hemispheric dream, Bolívar organized the 1826 Congress of Panama, which no delegates from the United States attended and to which, had Bolívar had his way, none would have been invited.[12] This Pan American vision has its roots the Creole nationalism of the nineteenth century. The very idea of a cultural bridge between the Anglophone and Hispanophone worlds was a product of its historical and ideological moment, an idea rooted, as Gruesz has pointed out, "in a revolutionary and cosmopolitan Romantic ethos."[13] From our vantage in the early twenty-first century, when the nation-state is increasingly challenged by other critical frameworks of global and local organization, it is important to note that Bolívar's vision was transnational but certainly not *post*national. However, as Bolívar's Congress fell apart amid infighting and as the regions of Central and South America, newly freed from Spanish control, came increasingly under the influence of other European powers, the strong independent nations of the Americas that would form the foundation of a united hemisphere were on shaky ground themselves.

For half a century after the Congress of Panama there was little mention of transnational cooperation in the Americas. However, in 1888 U.S. Secretary of State James G. Blaine reignited the idea of Pan American cooperation by proposing the First International Conference of American States to be held in Washington the following year, thus laying the groundwork for the Pan American era I explore in this study. The Pan Americanism of the early twentieth century was far removed from the vision of Bolívar, though the members of the PAU rarely missed an opportunity to align themselves with his legacy. A visitor to the House of the Americas today finds numerous statues and portraits of the Liberator, and the surrounding neighborhood also features enormous equestrian statues of Bolívar.

As lofty as these associations might seem, in 1888 Blaine's ambitions were thoroughly commercial. He envisioned a strengthened relationship between the United States and Latin America as a way of supplying the increasingly industrialized North with the raw materials of its southern neighbors *and* with a new market in which to sell the resultant products. One journalist who attended the Congress in 1889 was none other than the Cuban nationalist José Martí. By way of explaining the motives for the meeting, Martí writes that the United States had sent an invitation to the other American nations because it was "glutted with unsaleable merchandise and determined to extend its dominions in America."[14] As with so many other issues, Martí's analysis of this nascent Pan Americanism is extremely prescient. He sees through the politicians' talk of cooperation and mutual prosperity to "the marked pressure brought to bear by the companies that solicit subsidies for their ships," and, at base, he sees the United States as "a nation reared in the hope of ruling the continent."[15] Martí's confrontational rhetoric was intended to unmask the otherwise banal nature of the conference. As with much of the PAU's official activities over these decades, this is an informational project whereby governmental and academic institutions collude with corporations to map the development of the Americas. It is the kind of power created by the rhetoric of statesmen and reinforced by the literary representation of the hemisphere. "The fiction of hemispheric solidarity," as the historian Mark Berger has noted, "is shored up by the constant and powerful rhetoric about partnership," and thus, through an elaborate system of representation, U.S. dominance is recontextualized as cooperation.[16] If there was a U.S. dominion in the Americas, it was never a declared one but rather something that would have to be interpreted. There were, however, numerous contemporary critics who saw through the dominant narrative that the PAU promoted.

Martí was not alone in his suspicion of the Pan American Union. While numerous dignitaries, intellectuals, and ruling elites from Latin American and Caribbean nations took a central role in the PAU, to others in the region the term *Pan Americanism* was merely a euphemism for *imperialism*. The promise of hemispheric cooperation, in practice, meant cooperation with the goals of U.S political and business interests, and countries could easily be grouped according to their level of "cooperation." This distinction was discernible if one lived in a "problem" country (such as Nicaragua, where U.S. Marines battled a guerrilla insurgency whose leader, Augusto Sandino, was barred from the PAU conference in 1928) or if one lived in a country under the rule of a dictator who was propped up by U.S. business interests (such as Gerardo Machado's Cuba or Rafael Trujillo's Dominican Republic). While ambassadors to Washington and to the PAU engaged as equals in the organization's diplomatic activities, such pretenses were mostly dropped among the hemisphere's writers and intellectuals.

During the Pan American era there was a countermovement of Pan-Hispanism whereby Latin American intellectuals articulated a version of transnational cooperation that did not include the United States. The Nicaraguan poet Rubén Darío sounded a resounding anti-imperial call in his *Cantos de vida y esperanza* (1905), especially in the invective "A Roosevelt." In that poem Darío challenges the supremacy of U.S.

progress so that Roosevelt, the builder of the Panama Canal and the House of the Americas, becomes instead a "Hunter" who is "primitive and modern, simple and complicated, one part Washington and four parts Nimrod!"[17] As an alternative to Pan Americanism, Darío images a union based on a common Spanish language and Spanish ancestry: "our naive America / with its Indian blood, an America / that still prays to Christ and still speaks Spanish."[18] While Darío appealed to a common heritage, other intellectuals of the period articulated numerous transnational alternatives to Pan Americanism. The Cuban Marxist Julio Antonio Mella attempted to redefine hemispheric cooperation as an anti-capitalist movement. While living in Mexico in 1925, exiled for speaking out against the dictator Machado, who had U.S. support and who would host a major PAU summit in 1928, Mella declared his opposition to Pan Americanism:

> American unity is still forged by Yankee imperialism. The Pan American Union is the International of the future political empire which will have for its only capital Wall Street and for its nobility the kings of each industry. The American unity of which all the elevated spirits dream at this moment is a unity of *our* America, of an America based in social justice, a free America, not an exploited America, a colonial America, or a feudal America of a few capitalist corporations served by a few governments, simple agents of the imperialist invader.[19]

Mella's talk of "elevated spirits" in the face of imperialism as well as his insistence on uniting "*our* America" clearly illustrate Pan-Hispanism's debt to Martí. The work of the Cuban writer and revolutionary was the inspiration for much of the Hispanophone world's opposition to imperialism, especially his famous essay "Nuestra América" (1891), in which he articulates a Bolivarian vision of the lands from the Río Bravo to Tierra del Fuego united in common cultural and political cause in order to counter their neighbor to the north.

Yet it should be remembered that one of Martí's main concerns in this essay is the cultural understanding between the two Americas. He warns that the "disdain of the formidable neighbor who does not know her is our America's greatest danger, and it is urgent . . . that her neighbor come to know her, and quickly."[20] This kind of exchange of knowledge is rooted in acquaintance rather than the control of information. (Indeed in the original Spanish, Martí's use of the verb *conocer* makes clear the distinction between this kind of knowing and Pan Americanism's accumulation and control of knowledge.) Martí therefore charges Latin

American intellectuals with the task of making the United States understand their region as a place of art and culture rather than a source of
material goods and exoticism. Already Martí is identifying the key tension within Pan Americanism, which set about to accumulate knowledge
about Latin American but not *from* Latin America. In the years that followed Martí's essay, the Pan American Union hastened the coming of
the United States to know its southern neighbors, though not perhaps in
the manner that Martí would have wished. Rather than a relationship in
which Latin America's cultural ambassadors controlled that knowledge,
the regions south of the United States became objects of study.

South American Subjects and North American Knowledge Production

In the early twentieth century there was a publishing surge in all topics
concerning Latin America and the Caribbean. North American readers,
it seemed, could not be sated since each year the number of books on
Mexico, Central and South America, and the Caribbean increased. Of
course U.S. artists' interest in the lands "south of the border" is well
established.[21] Fiction writers and poets often set their works in Mexico,
Cuba, or points farther south, sometimes inspired by the exotic, sometimes by politics, as in the case of the Mexican Revolution. From John
Dos Passos's portrait of the Mexican Revolution in *The 42nd Parallel*
(1930) to the Mexican epic Hart Crane was composing at the time of his
death, Wallace Stevens's Havana-inspired poems, and the Prohibition-
era smuggling of Ernest Hemingway's *To Have and Have Not* (1937),
the southern neighbors of the United States often provided a setting for
political turmoil, exoticism, and intrigue.

However, the texts that were explicitly Pan American (the kind that
appeared in the exhaustive bibliographies issued regularly by the PAU)
were far more concerned with making the region legible to scholars,
statesman, and investors, as well as the general public. This industry
of knowledge production was at once academic and popular, highlight-
ing the way the disciplinary specializations of U.S. universities could
be redeployed for the textual conquest of the hemisphere. We can look,
for instance, to the work of U.S. archaeologists of the time. While John
L. Stephens's 1843 travel book and archaeological study of the Yucatán went decades without a successor, books on archaeology became
a cottage industry in the early twentieth century with such best sellers
as Hiram Bingham's *Inca Land: Explorations in the Highlands of Peru*
(1922). Travel writing attained an even greater popularity, offering U.S.

readers a taste of an exotic, often primitive land, as was the case with William Seabrook's portrait of occupied Haiti, *The Magic Island* (1929). Published concurrently with so many U.S. military invasions in Central America and the Caribbean, these books seemed to make clear that these lands were ripe for the taking, or at least for the influencing. There were, as Richard Halliburton put it in the title of his 1929 travelogue, "new worlds to conquer."

Rather than celebrating or vilifying Pan Americanism writ large, this book explores the way Pan Americanism employed academic study and textual representation as a means of controlling the hemisphere. More than battlefields or diplomatic conferences, it was the knowledge about the hemisphere that the United States produced and organized during this period that shaped its relationship with Latin America and the Caribbean. Pan Americanism called for wide-ranging cultural exchange, and therefore the knowledge that U.S. scholars collected was freely distributed throughout the hemisphere. However, this knowledge first had to pass through the lens of U.S.-defined modernity.[22]

By interpolating Latin America into the narratives of U.S. history, scholars thus inscribed the kind of progress and mercantile modernity that was prized in early twentieth-century North America. When the peoples of Latin America appeared in the pages of *Pan American Magazine* or the *Bulletin of the Pan American Union* it was in celebration of their country's advance in agricultural technology, in transportation infrastructure, in shipping, or in industry. Certainly Latin American readers of these publications would recognize themselves and their native lands, but these were representations that had been filtered through the logic of Pan Americanism, presenting the region with an image of itself defined by the goals of U.S. modernity.

The historian Ricardo Salvatore's writings on Pan Americanism have illuminated its efforts to construct what he calls an "enterprise of knowledge." While the rise of Spanish American studies (and later Latin American studies) in the United States did indeed create interest in transnational cooperation, the accumulation and organization of knowledge about Latin America served the larger role of supporting U.S. hegemony. Salvatore defines his idea of the U.S. "enterprise of knowledge" as "an endeavor to concentrate and circulate representations and interpretations that could make the region more 'legible' to U.S. readers and producers."[23] We might start with a concrete example of this legibility by returning to the PAU's Columbus Memorial Library. It certainly had lofty goals of inter-American cultural exchange, but one of the PAU's annual reports makes clear the role of the library in facilitating economic expansion. The value of the library was made evident by numerous letters of inquiry it received from "exporters and importers, manufacturers and shippers, bankers and investors, industrial and trade agents." However, the list of those requesting information also included "editors and special correspondents of newspapers and magazines, writers of books and pamphlets, travelers and tourists, [and] professors in universities and colleges."[24] The PAU's library thus had two intertwined missions: to promote the academic study of Latin America and the Caribbean and to facilitate the growth of U.S. investment in the regions.

But such libraries are only the most literal examples of the apparatus of Pan American knowledge production. Beyond these physical spaces there was a network of disciplinary knowledge reaching from universities to academic conferences, to specialized and popular publications. As Foucault has described his understanding of the archive, it is not the sum of all texts and institutions but rather "the law of what can be said" and the reason why all things said are grouped together in a particular order.[25] And so, rather than a straightforward colonial model, in which the metropolis collects data about the periphery, the Pan American project worked to naturalize the power dynamics of the hemisphere by draping them in the logic of international cooperation.

Another useful way of understanding this aspect of Pan Americanism is by thinking about it as an extension of the logic of coloniality, which Walter Mignolo has explored in his trilogy. This logic is based on divisions, principally the binary of *humanitas/anthropos,* which separates the world's population into two groups: "civilizations" that observe the world and write their knowledge down and those who are observed and written about. But, Mignolo points out, this logic persists in the world defined by Western modernity. Any effort to resist these power structures, strategies that he presents as "decolonial thinking," require "a relentless analytic effort to understand, in order to overcome, the logic of coloniality underneath the rhetoric of modernity."[26] Similarly we might think of Pan Americanism as one enunciation of Western modernity, and beneath its rhetoric of progress and hemispheric cooperation, the logic of coloniality, with its particular insistence on the control of knowledge, is central to the achievement of U.S. domination *through* the rhetoric of Pan Americanism.

As the language of cooperation circulated throughout an obviously unequal hemisphere, the open contradiction of Pan Americanism made interpreting its true aims a crucial site of contestation, as the example of Martí makes clear. Therefore the texts I examine are deeply engaged with the body of knowledge produced during the Pan American era. Each is in dialogue with a particular disciplinary understanding, with a way of representing the Americas, from archaeological and eugenicist studies to documentary and travel writing. Each of the authors and artists I discuss must negotiate the contradictions embedded in a particular way of understanding the hemisphere and try to formulate their definition of transnational identity outside the hegemonic structures of Pan Americanism.

The Limits of Pan American Studies and the Scope of This Book

If there is a nascent field of Pan American studies, there is certainly not a singular idea of what Pan Americanism was. On the one hand, scholars such as Ricardo Salvatore have treated Pan Americanism as merely a euphemism for the continued expansion of U.S. political and economic dominance in the early twentieth century. This era was, according to Salvatore, "a moment of commercial and investment expansionism of U.S. business firms in South America."[27] David Luis-Brown's definition is closer to my own since for him Pan Americanism is "an institutional and ideological project defined by U.S. efforts to gain economic and political control over Latin America."[28] On the other hand, the architecture historian Robert Alexander González has argued that, while Pan Americanism may have been an Anglo-centric idea promoted by the PAU and the North American culture industry, it was reappropriated by U.S. Latinos, particularly in the Southwest, as a way of articulating a multinational identity.[29]

Such different understandings of Pan Americanism have consequently yielded different periodizations. The end date for the Pan American era is contestable, just as the end of modernism is still much contested and depends on one's definition of modernism. As an example of the variety of end points, Salvatore suggests that Pan Americanism ceased to be viable around the time of World War I, when U.S. interests shifted from being hemispheric to global. González, on the other hand, extends his study of Pan Americanism into the late 1960s, considering inter-American cultural exchanges such as San Antonio's 1968 HemisFair.

Another conceptual endpoint for Pan Americanism that must be considered is the Cuban Revolution since after 1959 the relationship of the United States with the rest of the Americas was clearly altered. Revolutionary Cuba was suspended from the Organization of American States in 1962 (and was readmitted only in 2009), and the subsequent block-ade of the island nation by the United States and its efforts to stifle left-ist movements elsewhere in Latin America came to dominate its foreign policy and dampen any discussion of a unified hemisphere. But even before the Cuban Revolution the United States was already moving away from hemispheric preoccupations and engaging in its cold war–era cam-paign to leverage artistic and cultural exchanges for political gains.

In the late 1930s and early 1940s the attention of the U.S. state was increasingly drawn away from its relations with the rest of the Ameri-can nations as the Eastern Hemisphere became ever more mired in war. With the bombing of Pearl Harbor and the U.S. entry into World War II in 1941, the nation's foreign policy as well as its cultural front were preoccupied with Europe and the Pacific. Relations with the rest of the Americas were soon motivated by the U.S. need to adapt to these new global conditions. The kind of study and organization of knowledge that I explore was really not seen after the war. This is not to say that the region was no longer studied by the United States—indeed the rise of Latin American studies coincides with the cold war—but those studies would be far more concerned with ideological differences (particularly the containment of leftist movements) than with the similarities that Pan American scholarship emphasized as it set out to enfold all of the Ameri-cas under the wing of U.S. modernity.[30]

Beyond limiting the historical period, other limits to the present study need to be imposed if it is to delve much below the surface of an idea that encompassed the entire Western Hemisphere. Therefore the chap-ters of this book focus largely on relations among the United States, Mexico, Cuba, and Haiti. Because of their geographic proximity, there was more frequent cultural exchange among these nations, and it was far more likely that U.S. writers would travel to these neighboring countries and vice versa. Furthermore the social and political upheavals during this time—the Mexican Revolution and its aftermath, U.S. involvement in Cuba and the 1933 revolution, the U.S. Occupation of Haiti—make these relationships fertile ground for thinking about transnational rela-tions in the Pan American era. Cuba plays a central role in this study since, as Luis A. Pérez points out, it "has served as something of a lab-oratory for the development methods by which the United States has pursued the creation of a global empire."[31] But Cuba is also a central site for the resistance to that empire, and the writings of Martí serve throughout this study as a touchstone for counterhegemonic versions of Pan Americanism.

Beyond geographic limits I have focused each chapter on how a single author or artist responded to a particular form of knowledge production. Chapter 1, for instance, explores the role that archaeology played in shaping perceptions of Mexico and Central America and the way conflations of Aztec and Mayan culture with present-day Mexico and Central America worked to "archaeologize" the region. This issue alone raises larger concerns than I can address in the course of a single chapter, and indeed each of these chapters could sustain its own book-length study. By moving on to different forms of disciplinary knowledge, I hope that the result is not a hodgepodge or sampling of the time period but rather a richer understanding of the way Latin America and the Caribbean were represented. The connection between archaeology and eugenics, for instance, may initially seem incoherent, but it has been the division of these disciplinary boundaries which has obscured the reach of Pan American knowledge production.

Growing out of their opposition to the disciplinary knowledge of the Pan American Era, each of the works I discuss also challenges the formal boundaries of artistic expression. These are all hybrid texts that are difficult to categorize. William Carlos Williams's prose works, for example, are notoriously genre defying. In *Spring and All* (1923) he intersperses among his collection of poems discursive prose sections on poetics and culture. And the prose works I discuss, *The Great American Novel* (1923) and *In the American Grain* (1925), blur distinctions between history and creative nonfiction. José Clemente Orozco's mural *The Epic of American Civilization* (1932–34) makes use of the two-dimensional elements of painting but also uses the architecture of Dartmouth's Baker Library to create meaningful associations across three-dimensional space. Alejo Carpentier's novel presents its own challenges since it responds to other avant-garde fiction of its day but also engages the discourse of scientific writing, particularly that of anthropology and eugenics. The collaboration of Carleton Beals and Walker Evans, which I argue is one of the first examples of the documentary book, merges text and image, but it is also a hybrid text in that it conflates exotic travel writing with political reportage. Ana Castillo's work is consciously experimental, merging the styles of avant-garde writers such as Julio Cortázar with the epistolary form in order to reflect on the history of the novel. However, Castillo's novel also engages travel writing and anthropological studies from earlier in the century, which allows her to rethinking the structures of knowledge inherited from the Pan American era. Finally, Katherine Dunham's career was a decades-long merger of her identities as anthropologist and dancer so that, as she was fond of saying, determining where the scientist ended and the performer began was a difficult task. As we shall see, this formal hybridity is a fundamental characteristic of these Pan American modernists who, by breaking down categories of artistic expression, are better able to challenge the disciplinary barriers that have constructed Latin America and the Caribbean as objects of study.

I have paired the chapters of this book in ways that suggest transregional connections but also, I hope, approach a related set of issues. In the first section, "Hemispheric Identity and the Uses of Indigenous Culture," the first two chapters consider the appropriations of pre-Columbian cultures, primarily in the works of Williams and Orozco. The second section, "Cuba, Race, and Modernity," explores the historical contexts that lay behind two books, both published in 1933: Alejo Carpentier's *¡Écue-Yamba-Ó!* and Carleton Beals and Walker Evans's *The Crime of Cuba*. These chapters consider how U.S. constructions of racial identity circulated as part of the Pan American ideal—both at the Pan American Conference on Eugenics held in Havana and through U.S. travel writing—and suggest ways these artists imagined alternative hemispheric communities outside of these racial hierarchies. Finally, I reappraise the idea of Pan Americanism from later in the twentieth century in order to understand why the term has been abandoned as a way to think about transnational relations in the Americas. This section, "Women, Migration, and Memories of Pan Americanism," considers the writing of women in the early twentieth century alongside later reconsiderations of this period by Castillo and Dunham.

By exploring the contradictions inherent in the Pan American project and reflecting on the hemispheric turn in American studies, I demonstrate how similar hemispheric rhetoric has been used to reinforce U.S. dominance. The hegemonic narrative of Pan Americanism was an entrenched part of U.S. knowledge production in the early twentieth century. Despite the often benevolent aims of universities and state institutions that set out to study Latin America and the Caribbean, the work done there helped to solidify the position of the United States as the archival center of the Americas, the place where all knowledge about the hemisphere would be stored, organized, and redeployed. In many ways the work of these intellectuals from a century ago serves as a cautionary tale for present-day scholars engaged in Hemispheric American studies. Alongside these institutions, however, I explore the work of a few Pan American modernists who variously incorporated and challenged the body of knowledge being produced about Latin America and the Caribbean. As an alternative to the unified understanding of the Hemisphere presented by the PAU, these writers and artists reorganized knowledge about the Americas in ways that crossed the disciplinary boundaries of academia as well as the formal boundaries of artistic expression. Through these pluralistic, hybrid visions they offer an alternative vision of what a place called Pan America might look like.

Hemispheric Identity and the Uses of Indigenous Culture

1 Mesoamerican Modernism

William Carlos Williams and the Archaeological Imagination

The land! don't you feel it? Doesn't it make you want to go out and lift dead Indians tenderly from their graves to steal from them—as if it must be clinging even to their corpses—some authenticity.

—William Carlos Williams, *In the American Grain*

To revive indigenous history and culture as archeology is to revive them *as dead*.

—Mary Louise Pratt, *Imperial Eyes*

AS A MAGAZINE DEVOTED to the avant-garde on both sides of the Atlantic, *Broom* had always insisted on bringing its readers what was new. At the back of its December 1922 issues, though, *Broom* promised even more for its readers in the upcoming number. The ad proclaimed that "the oldest and newest art of America" would be coming to them and that it would take the form of "Mayan sculpture and architecture" as well as "contemporary American prose and poetry." The magazine did indeed offer some of the best contemporary authors for the January issue since Marianne Moore, Gertrude Stein, Jean Toomer, and William Carlos Williams were listed among the contributors. But above all of these names, dominating the full-page ad, the editors placed a photograph of a Mayan statue, a thoroughly "all-American" figure who displayed all the markers of pre-Columbian civilization and yet somehow, to the glee of the editors, appeared to be holding a baseball bat (fig. 1). Next to this figure they issued a challenge to their readers: "Which prominent American does this portrait-statue represent? Prizes for best answers!"[1] The idea behind this contest, with its insistence on the common American qualities between old and new, opens up a host of issues about how avant-garde artists in the United States defined themselves in relationship to Europe and to the rest of the Americas.

The subsequent "all-American number" of *Broom*, which appeared in January 1923, is but one manifestation of the Mayan Revival that swept through the United States in the early part of the twentieth century. The obsession with Mesoamerican civilizations could be seen in

Figure 1. Advertisement from *Broom: An International Magazine of the Arts* 4, no. 1 (1922): n.p.

the architecture of the time. It could be seen in films that re-created the fall of the Aztec Empire and in similar romances of the Conquest that appeared in opera houses, in vaudeville halls, and on Broadway. These artists had various reasons for appropriating Mayan and Aztec sources, but much of their fascination revolved around the desire for an "indigenous" American art that was independent of European influence. In almost all of these cases the contemporary U.S. artist was framed as the immediate heir to the "dead" and "ruined" civilizations of Mesoamerica. Just as Mary Louise Pratt concluded of the nine-teenth-century interest in American archaeology, the Mayan Revival prefigured the indigenous culture as always already dead. In many of the works I explore in this chapter there is a necrophilic fascination with the "dead" cultures of Central America on which the suppos-edly young and vigorous culture of North America is predicated. This is the very sentiment that William Carlos Williams mocks in the epi-graph to this chapter, as he identifies the fascination with dead Indians running through the texts of American history. However, Williams's own work recapitulates these efforts to "revive" indigenous cultures for the benefit of the vigorous nation to the north. While his writ-ing is in many ways exemplary of the Mayan Revival, Williams was far more pessimistic, and this chapter explores his relationship with Mesoamerican cultures and the way he formulated the indigenous civ-ilizations of the Americas as an alternative position from which to cri-tique modern U.S. culture.

By locating Williams within the context of the Mayan Revival, I intend to reveal the sustained interest in archaeology that runs through his work. As early as 1918 he discouraged U.S. artists from pursuing European traditions (as T. S. Eliot had), declaring instead that "the New World is Montezuma."[2] Pre-Columbian civilizations were everywhere in Williams's work of the 1920s, appearing in *The Great American Novel* (1923), *Spring and All* (1923), and the "Rome" journal he kept on his travels through Europe in 1924. And of course *In the American Grain* (1925), especially "The Destruction of Tenochtitlan," presents Wil-liams's most sustained meditation on Mesoamerica. I argue that Wil-liams's appearance in the Maya-themed issue of *Broom* was more than mere happenstance and that his work during this period reflected the influence of the larger U.S. cultural obsession with Mayan and Aztec archaeology as well as the larger Pan American project of archaeolo-gizing Latin America. He frequently echoed much of the popular cul-ture's fascination with "reviving" these native civilizations even as he denounced what he deemed shallow efforts at appropriation, making his quest for an "indigenous" American art a deeply contradictory project.

The Vogue of Things Pre-Columbian: William Carlos Williams and the "American Background"

In the late nineteenth and early twentieth century the U.S. public was increasingly inundated with images of American archaeology. In the pages of *National Geographic* readers could learn about Hiram Bingham's discovery of Machu Picchu in 1913 and about the excavation of Mayan ruins in the early 1920s. They could read about Charles Lindbergh's aerial survey of the Yucatán peninsula in search of undiscovered Mayan ruins in 1929. In addition the World's Columbia Exposition of 1893 brought to Chicago full-scale plaster replicas of the temples at Uxmal and other Mayan sites, many of which remained in the Field Museum for years afterward. New York also had a new archaeological presence since the American Natural History Museum saw important additions to its holdings and the creation of its Hall of Mexico and Central America, featuring full-scale reproductions of much of the important stonework at Chichen Itza.

In the world of the arts the Maya-themed issue of *Broom* was not alone but rather one of many appropriations of Maya and Aztec civilizations that occurred in the United States during this period. In the fall of 1917 Cecil B. DeMille's silent film *The Woman God Forgot* brought Cortez's conquest of Tenochtitlan to the screen. From the film's opening scene depicting human sacrifice to the final combat on a back-lot Templo Mayor, DeMille re-created an exotic Aztec world that was decadent and ripe for self-immolation. The film was nevertheless an escapist romance, as was Henry Hadley's opera *Azora: The Daughter of Montezuma* (1919), which appeared in Chicago and New York. Soon afterward the dancers Ted Shawn and Martha Graham toured the country with a repertoire that included their Aztec ballet, *Xochitl* (1921).[3] However, U.S. architects were the leading appropriators of pre-Columbian cultures, and it was in the context of this architectural movement that the term *Mayan Revival* was coined. The most significant examples of this movement might be Frank Lloyd Wright's Hollyhock House (1918–21) or Robert Stacy-Judd's Aztec Hotel (1924–25), both of which I discuss in detail below.

There was, of course, a contemporary fascination with ancient civilizations from all areas of the globe. Along with DeMille's Tenochtitlan we find D. W. Griffith's re-creation of Babylon in *Intolerance* (1916), and for every Mayan-themed movie theater there was also an Egyptian theater. However, what set the Mayan Revival apart was its quest for a thoroughly "American" art form. It was a turn away from Europe, one that made modern North American artists the heirs to Mesoamerican cultures in an act of appropriation much more complicated than using Babylonian or Egyptian designs. In addition to being a gesture of independence, though, this movement also reformulated the indigenous peoples of the Americas as a central component of the avant-garde. Aztecs, Maya, and North American Indians were forged together as part of a Pan-Indian identity that would serve as an alternative heritage to that of Europe. In many ways this appropriation of indigenous cultures through archaeology was a product of Creole nationalism, whereby the descendents of European cultures had to assert their independence from Europe by aligning themselves with what was truly American.

Among Williams scholars there has been a recent move to situate him within a broader understanding of the Americas. However, these readings have typically focused on his biography rather than the contemporary U.S. fascination with the rest of the Americas. Julio Marzán's landmark study, *The Spanish American Roots of William Carlos Williams* (1994), opened up this line of inquiry, stressing the multicultural, multilingual nature of the Williams household and the effect that had on the literary work. Williams's father, though a British citizen, had grown up in Santo Domingo, while his mother, though from a complex background that included French and Jewish ancestry, was born and raised in Puerto Rico. As a result Spanish was the household language of Williams's childhood in New Jersey, and later in life he collaborated with each of his parents in translation projects.[4] While Marzán's book enriched the field of Williams studies by tracing the influence of Spanish poetry on the work, many of his conclusions oversimplified these issues, arguing that Williams's identity was divided between the Anglophone "Bill" and the Hispanophone "Carlos."[5] To be sure, this family background shaped Williams's sense of his own hemispheric American identity, and it left him vulnerable to Pound's accusation that he was a foreigner, but it seems unlikely that he would have thought of himself as a Spanish American poet. However, Latin America may have influenced Williams's childhood in quite another way. As Paul Mariani points out, his father, William George Williams, worked for a New York–based cologne manufacturer and, no doubt because of his fluent Spanish, was often sent on extended business trips in Central and South America, bringing back numerous goods for his children.[6] These early encounters through his father's travels may have piqued Williams's interest in the region while at the same time suggesting the U.S. view that relations between North and South were, at their essence, mercantile.

More recently Lisa Sánchez González has argued for an understanding of Williams as a "Boricua modernist," emphasizing that his family's own diaspora connects him with the common experience of the Puerto Rican community in the early twentieth century.[7] Sánchez González's work, particularly *Boricua Literature* (2001), offers an important new frame for understanding American modernism and for understanding Williams's poetry within the genealogy of U.S. Latino literature, but the Boricua reading of Williams does not explain his turn to Mayan and Aztec themes in his quest for an American identity. More than any one biographical detail, this larger Pan American attitude, which dominated late nineteenth- and early twentieth-century hemispheric relations, is crucial in understanding Williams's American experience. It is this cultural moment, I contend, that informs his prose work of the 1920s and shapes the way he approaches Mesoamerican cultures.

In her important cultural history of this period, *The Enormous Vogue of Things Mexican*, Helen Delpar explores the multifaceted way in which Latin American cultures, especially indigenous cultures, were appropriated. There was, she contends, an element of anti-industrialism in this movement: "To those who sought to foster the development of authentically American arts, the Indian—both north and south of the border—was of significance both as a creator and as a source of aesthetic inspiration to others. At the same time, neoromantics who rejected industrialism and urbanism could look at the Indian in New Mexico and other parts of the United States as well as in Old Mexico as an example of a more primitive yet more satisfying civilization, one based on the community rather than the individual."[8] This formulation of the Indian as an antidote to modernity is something we will see articulated most clearly in the writing of Williams. As much as his obsession with indigenous figures like Montezuma rescripts American history, it also critiques the crass consumerism of his day.

Although his use of indigenous tropes diverged in several important ways from the popular culture, Williams could not have missed the abundance of archaeological images surrounding him. Whether he ever saw DeMille's *The Woman God Forgot* at the Rialto on one of his Friday-night trips into the city, or caught a production of *Azora*, or read about the Maya in *National Geographic* (a publication with which he was certainly familiar) remains speculation.[9] It is far more important that we understand the cultural milieu in which Williams lived and realize how ubiquitous Mesoamerican themes were during this era. The frequent appearance of Montezuma in Williams's writing of the period reflects this larger cultural fascination with indigenous American identity.

In this context we should take more seriously Williams's fascination with Mesoamerican civilization as a sustaining force in his conception of a hemispheric American art. For instance, when Williams was in Paris in the spring of 1924 he met the French writer Valery Larbaud, an encounter he incorporated into the "Père Sebastian Rasles" section of *In the American Grain*. Overwhelmed by Larbaud's erudition and his deep understanding of American history, Williams was at a loss. He confessed later to Marianne Moore that, in his response to Larbaud's eloquent conversation, "perhaps I stammered a word about admiring something of the Maya culture."[10] Williams was also fond of comparing the well-honed verse of other poets to Inca masonry. Moore's work reminded him of "primitive masonry, the units unglued and as in the greatest early constructions unstandardized" (*Imaginations* 319), and later he wrote that the quality of Robert Lowell's rhyme was "like Inca stonework."[11] In Williams's own work he too aspired to the qualities of stonework, as he stated in his *Autobiography* and reiterated in *I Wanted to Write a Poem*: "The Destruction of Tenochtitlan" was "written in big, square paragraphs like Inca masonry."[12]

Williams's real obsession, though, was Aztec culture. He was thinking about Montezuma as early as 1918, as he demonstrates in the prologue to *Kora in Hell*, and he was still thinking about the Aztecs in 1934 when he lamented the loss of Tenochtitlan in his essay "The American Background": "One is at liberty to guess what the pure American addition to world culture might have been if it had gone forward singly. But that is merely an academicism. Perhaps Tenochtitlan which Cortez destroyed held the key. That also is beside the point, except that Tenochtitlan with its curious brilliance may still legitimately be kept alive in thought not as something which *could* have been preserved but as something which was actual and was destroyed."[13] Williams does not invoke Tenochtitlan for the purpose of reviving it, of forcing it into the twentieth century. All that is "beside the point." Tenochtitlan cannot be separated from its moment of destruction, and it is this vision of indigenous America that Williams wants to keep "alive in thought." His invocation of Mesoamerican civilization reflects a system of thought, an archaeological imagination. This is an atemporal way of thinking that operates by juxtaposing past and present and creating something new from the

undeniable and irreversible fact of the past's destruction. It is an archaeology that is less concerned with study than with provocation, a method
less interested in championing the "virile" culture of the North than in
shining a light on its decay. In order to appreciate this artistic archaeology, it will first be necessary to understand the central role that the discipline of archaeology played in framing the U.S. idea of Central America
and how the cultural phenomenon of the Mayan Revival participated in
this archaeologizing of the region.

Mesoamerican Archaeology and the Information Empire

Despite the attention that the Mayan Revival style would receive in the
early 1920s when well-known architects were employing it, the first
example of a Revival-style building in the United States was the Pan
American Union's House of the Americas, completed in 1910.[14] The
design by Albert Kelsey and Paul Cret presents a straightforward exterior of Georgian marble that was fitting of its location adjacent to the
Washington Monument (fig. 2). Inside, however, wall friezes and sculp-
tures were designed to represent the Union's twenty-one member nations
in architectural form. The result was a hybrid of Beaux Arts, Spanish
colonial, and "primitive" designs from Latin America. The patio at the
building's center included designs and "hieroglyphs" from indigenous
cultures of the Americas (fig. 3).[15] As the *Bulletin of the Pan American
Union* described it, the patio was "semibarbarous in design, [reproduc-
ing] well-known archaeological fragments from Mexico, Guatemala,
and Peru."[16] At the rear of the House of the Americas was its Aztec Garden, which included alongside its reflecting pool a statue of Xochipili,
the Aztec God of Flowers. Illustrating the close alliance of architecture
and archaeology, the statue was a concrete replica of an original Aztec
sculpture housed just down the street at the Smithsonian Institution.

However, the House of the Americas' central fountain made the most
significant comment on the status of Mesoamerican civilizations within
the hemisphere. The *Bulletin* referred to this fountain as the building's
"climax of aboriginal thought." Three figures surrounded the basin,
"each representing a period in the aboriginal civilization of the country south of the Rio Grande": the Maya, the Aztec, and the Zapotec.[17]
A closer look at these three figures, though, reveals two of them with
their eyes closed and the Mayan with his arms folded as though he were
part of an Egyptian sarcophagus. That this fountain presented a tomb
for Mesoamerican civilizations was perhaps fitting of the historical fate
each had suffered centuries before, but what makes this "dead" posture

Figure 2. Exterior of the House of the Americas, Washington, D.C. (1908–10; Albert Kelsey and Paul Cret, architects; photograph by the author)

more troubling is that these statues were also meant to symbolize the place of contemporary Latin American countries within the Pan American Union. After describing the Aztec Garden and the way its "archaic figures" recalled "the strange twilight time of American history," the *Bulletin*'s writer concluded by contrasting this "exotic" and "tropical" garden with the more practical designs on the surrounding walls: "Above there is a more modern and elaborate scheme of decoration symbolizing the young and vigorous Pan-American union of to-day and making the miniature jungle below appear to be but a picturesque background for the grouping of national arms and the great names of Pan-American history."[18] This formulation of a "young and vigorous" union in contrast to the dead or slumbering world of Latin America was to be a recurrent theme.[19] Among artists and architects of the Mayan Revival, it was crucial that the "vigorous" arts of the United States revive what had been neglected and slumbering in Latin America.

In the House of the Americas we see a convergence of the architectural and the political, both of which rely on an archaeologized vision of the land

Figure 3. Mayan tiles from the Tropical Patio of the House of Americas. (Photograph by the author)

south of the Río Grande. In his extensive analysis of the building, the architectural scholar Robert González argues that it projected the U.S. view of the hemisphere. The predominantly "Latin" themes were explicitly intended to welcome foreign delegates to the PAU, to make Washington a more familiar place, but these features also impressed upon them a particular vision of the Americas. "There was," González writes, "an implicit effort to get Latin Americans to identify with the Pan-American construct, as the U.S.-dominated organization defined it."[20] Visitors to Washington would have noted the displays of national power coded into the Mall's architecture, but the implied message of the House of the Americas divided the hemisphere along temporal line: the North was site of the Pan American future, while the lands of the South belonged to a quaint, even mythic past.

Rather than mere multicultural decorations, the architectural details of the House of the Americas reflect the view of Central American cultures as dead or vanished, lying in ruins in the jungles of Yucatán or preserved in U.S. museums. That act of preservation, or "revival," as the architects would term it, positioned the United States as the sole arbiter of cultural value in the twentieth century. Thus the elision of modern

Central American cultures from the hemisphere made those nations more likely receptacles for the U.S. brand of modernity that the Pan American Union promoted. Throughout the 1910s and 1920s the PAU funded archaeological expeditions to Latin America and published their findings to great acclaim in their *Bulletin*. Therefore the House of the Americas served as the locus of several important cultural and political forces in the early twentieth century. It was the home of the PAU (and continues to serve as the ceremonial home of the Organization of American States), and it was the first example of the Mayan Revival style of architecture in the United States. In addition, though, the House of the Americas was to take a central role in the PAU's project of knowledge production since it housed the Columbus Memorial Library, then the largest archive of Latin Americana in the United States.

Ricardo Salvatore has written about the formation of Latin American collections during this period in connection with the growth of U.S. business and diplomatic interests in the hemisphere.[21] Certain research agendas, such as that of the PAU, were instrumental in shaping these early collections and, Salvatore argues, in constructing Latin America as an object of study. While institutions such as the Columbus Memorial Library, Berkeley's Bancroft Library, and the Hispanic Society in New York included contemporary studies of Latin America, they were heavily weighted toward the periods of conquest and colonization. Salvatore suggests that the era of U.S. hegemony at the beginning of the twentieth century occasioned this curiosity about the Spanish Empire and its history of dominance in the region.[22] In producing a body of knowledge about Latin America and in producing an all-American form from indigenous roots, the strong connection between the newest and the oldest cultures of the Americas was central to each project. The Columbus Memorial Library and the archaeological studies of the time were part of the same desire to know Latin America and construct a usable archive in the United States.

The research and publications of the PAU during this period were all conducted in the name of hemispheric unity and cooperation, but there was also an obvious effort to promote U.S. business interests. It may come as no surprise that U.S. diplomacy supported U.S. business, but what is more interesting is the odd confluence of business and archaeology that manifested itself in the pages of the PAU's *Bulletin*. The *Bulletin* published numerous archaeological studies, from Bingham's early discoveries of Incan ruins, beginning in 1913, to work of important Mayanists like Sylvanus G. Morley in the 1920s and 1930s. These academic

studies usually appeared alongside reports on the material development
of the hemisphere, which was the *Bulletin*'s central concern. While many
of these reports were laden with quantitative data, keeping their readers
abreast of how many tons of sugar Cuba produced or how many miles of
rail had just been laid in Guatemala, the recurring series on the history
of single commodities revealed more explicitly the archaeologized view
of the region. For instance, "Maize or Indian Corn: The Great Native
Food Supply of America" is indicative of the rich blend that made up
the *Bulletin*'s vision of the hemisphere. Simultaneously invoking Central
America in terms of its ancient peoples and its material development, the
article explicitly links that material development with cultural achievement, combining history with business.

The author frames our understanding of corn in terms of the oldest
and newest civilizations of the Americas, beginning, as many of these
commodity histories do, with its pre-Columbian origin. The reader is
provided an account of the role corn played in lifting the native peoples
out of "savagery," and this link between material progress and cultural
progress is sustained throughout the article. The link is so strong, in
fact, that Mayan civilization can be used to pinpoint the date of agricultural development: "The Mayas did not emerge from savagery until
after the beginning of the Christian era, so the cultivation and use of
Indian corn can not antedate two thousand years."[23] As with many contemporary accounts of Mesoamerican culture in the United States, here
the Maya emerge as the beacons of civilization—and a model for transnational trade. The Maya were "the foremost agriculturists of America, who long preceded the Peruvians in this art and whose material
impress on their country is ineradicable."[24] From this initial cultivation,
the author recounts, corn spread north to the Aztecs, to the Pueblo Indians, all the way up to the Iroquois. However, this Pan American history culminates in the present-day domination of the corn market by
the United States, both in terms of production quantity and symbolism.
The centrality of corn to U.S. culture could hardly be denied after reading the article's account of the Corn Palace in Mitchell, South Dakota,
in 1908 and seeing the accompanying photo. By analogy we are to conclude that the United States, just like Mayan civilization, has simultaneously achieved commercial and cultural dominance. This would be a
claim made time and again in the *Bulletin*'s commodity histories, that
the history of the hemisphere began in Mesoamerica and culminated in
the United States. Therefore, at the same moment that the modern inhabitants of Central America are erased, its ancient civilizations smile down

on the commercial enterprises of U.S. business. As these commodity histories make clear, the archaeological work being done in Central America was interwoven with the desires of U.S. capital and played a very real role in shaping the way the United States conceived of Latin America. It was a land of ruins and vanished peoples, where vast resources lay sleeping, waiting for the right visionary, be he artist or venture capitalist, to awaken them.

If the Pan American view of commodities was archaeologized during this period, it was due in no small part to the expansion of U.S. trade in the region that had made the original archaeological expeditions possible. In addition to funding by Carnegie and other captains of industry, archaeologists often relied on adjacent corporate expeditions that sought the region's natural resources. In the 1922 *National Geographic* article that introduced the Maya to a wide public audience in the United States, the prominent archaeologist and Mayanist Sylvanus G. Morley made clear his debt to the burgeoning gum industry. After directly thanking the foreign companies for providing some of the transportation, shelter, and other resources that made the Petén expedition possible, Morley thanked U.S. consumerism writ large. Besides archaeology, he writes, the "only other business which brings man [that is, North American men] into these tropical forests of northern Guatemala is one of our most important American industries, which might be termed, perhaps, our national sport—chewing gum."[25] Thus the masticating jaws of young North Americans have created the demand for exploring Central America, and they have unwittingly strengthened the symbiotic relationship between U.S. capital and knowledge production. The archaeologists came to rely on the industry not only for material support but also for their very discoveries. Morley notes that the local *chicleros* were indispensable to the archaeologist since, as they searched for new trees to harvest, they frequently came upon new Mayan cities. So complete was his reliance on these workers that Morley had a "standing reward offered to all *chicleros* for 'information leading to the capture, dead or alive,' of any new group of ruins."[26] Just as ruins could easily be viewed as commodities to be "captured" and exported, so too did the control of Latin America's natural resources depend on exploring and discovering, mapping, and even, as the *Bulletin* demonstrated, rooting those commercial industries in pre-Columbian history.

What we might term the "archeology industry" yielded very real material gains for U.S. corporations. In addition the archaeologists would occasionally prove themselves valuable to U.S. intelligence, as can be seen from the revelation that Morley's archeological work provided him adequate cover to work as a spy during World War I.[27] However, aside from these tangential political and material gains, the appropriation of archaeological material itself played a significant role in the U.S. desire to lead the hemisphere. Since the middle of the nineteenth century John Lloyd Stephens and other archaeologist had steadily exported Mesoamerican artifacts back to the United States both for "safekeeping" and to strengthen the position of the United States as heir to the cultural patrimony of the hemisphere.[28] One Mexican historian dubbed this appropriation "archaeological Monroism," referring to U.S. efforts both to lead in this academic field and to control its partners in the Americas.[29]

However, the work of archaeologists in the early twentieth century is more complicated than simple imperialism since there was always a utopian element at play. Many of the archaeologists and artists who sustained the cultural obsession with the Maya were on a spiritual quest as well. Morley was not alone in referring to them as "the Greeks of the New World." These Mayan fantasies presented a version of the hemispheric utopia that was central to Pan Americanism, and the way U.S. Mayanists promoted this myth also furthered the ideological work that positioned the United States as the cultural and economic leader of this union.

The Construction of American Indigeneity: Frank Lloyd Wright, Robert Stacy-Judd, and *Broom*

Following the completion of the House of the Americas in 1910, Mayan-themed building projects began to appear more frequently in the 1910s and reached a crescendo in the 1920s. The popularity of this Mayan Revival style prompted the British architect George Oakley Totten to publish a guidebook in 1925. More than simply a how-to manual, *Maya Architecture* was intended as a gospel to inspire potential Mayanists to take up the mantle of this ancient culture. Totten's preface, after providing an account of the rise and fall of Mayan civilization, becomes a clarion call to young "Revivalists":

> Then death again did claim its toll, and once more Maya art was dead.
>
> Not dead, but only slumbering, to be awakened by a young and vigorous people of the North; their privilege it shall be to take up the work where Maya left it off, and carry on.
>
> The Second Renaissance has just begun.

O! Great Kukulcan, make clear to them their heritage sublime and inspire them to nobler ideals than Maya ever dreamed.[30]

This idea of a "Second Renaissance" resonates through the work of the Mayan Revival. Whatever was of value in Mesoamerican civilizations, it had to be rescued from the neglect of modern Latin American nations by "young and vigorous people of the North." This archaeological view had a two-pronged effect. On the one hand, it reinforced a cultural division in the hemisphere, in which Latin America was always the "slumbering" counterpart to the "vigorous" and industrious North. On the other, this idea of "carrying on" the Maya's work simultaneously bridged that gap to create a transnational American identity, though it was one from which modern Latin Americans were excluded. The architects of the Mayan Revival could hardly have had hemispheric politics in mind, but the work of two architects in particular—Frank Lloyd Wright and Robert Stacy-Judd—illustrates the extent to which this vision of Latin America was internalized within U.S. culture as part of the quest for a hemispheric American art.

Wright, the proud defender of his own genius, frequently denied that Mayan sources influenced his work. Mayan architecture merely affirmed, he claimed, the universal truths that he had found within himself. Nevertheless the influence on his work is undeniable, and in his less guarded moments Wright revealed that he too was caught up in the U.S. fascination with pre-Columbian civilizations. In his autobiography he recalls an early archeological attraction: "I remember how as a boy, primitive American architecture—Toltec, Aztec, Mayan, Inca—stirred my wonder, excited my wishful admiration, I wished I might someday have money enough to go to Mexico, Guatemala and Peru to join in excavating those long slumbering remains of lost cultures; mighty, primitive abstractions of man's nature."[31] Wright never made it to these locations, but they did come to him. The Columbia World's Exposition of 1983 brought to Chicago plaster replicas of entire Mayan buildings, and these models remained in the Field Museum for years afterward, allowing Wright to refer to them at his leisure.[32] In these designs he found a model for the utopian vision of human living he would try to articulate in the 1920s and in the decades after. It was again a case of linking the oldest American art forms with the newest, this time with Wright as the vigorous northern heir. As he explained in 1930, the civilizations of the "red man" were the key to an indigenous American architecture: "Lost in backward stretch of

time, almost beyond our horizon—the Maya, the Indian, we may learn
from them."[33]

While the buildings of Stacy-Judd are not as well known as those of
Wright, his obsessive and flamboyant use of Mayan tropes allows us
to see more clearly the archaeological desire that ran through all projects of the Mayan Revival more generally. Rather than a mere phase in
his development, Mayan civilization was a lifelong obsession for Stacy-
Judd, as Jesse Lerner has demonstrated in *The Maya of Modernism*.[34]
The British-born architect made his way to California in the 1920s and
attained notoriety in 1925 for his Aztec Hotel in Monrovia. Although
the House of the Americas and several of Wright's structures predated
the hotel, Stacy-Judd, ever the self-promoter, claimed that his was the
first modern building to make use of Mayan architectural ideas. (It was,
however, named the Aztec Hotel since it was assumed that the U.S. public was unfamiliar with the Maya.) Aside from the roof's allusion to
Palenque, the hotel's connection to Mayan civilization had largely to
do with the ornate patterns sculpted into the building's exterior. Inside,
the lobby was dripping with Mesoamerican ephemera, from the murals
at the hotel's entrance to the adjacent Toltec Café. Just as significant as
the design of the building was the promotional campaign that Stacy-
Judd launched on behalf of his work. Critics from across the nation were
invited to visit the hotel and view the new style that he was promoting
for a new generation of U.S. architects. So significant was the novelty of
this work it led one reviewer to conclude that the Aztec Hotel was "the
only building in the United States that is 100% American."[35]

But for Stacy-Judd the Maya were not merely the key to a new style
of hemispheric American architecture. This noble civilization, which
he believed had descended from the lost continent of Atlantis, would
shed light on the moral and spiritual shortcomings of his own day, all
of which Stacy-Judd dismissively referred to as "modernism." He clung
to this theory for decades, finally developing it into a book, *Atlantis:
Mother of Empires* (1939). Although the connection between Atlantean and Mayan civilizations suggests a utopian desire on his part, it
is important to note the fundamentally lost or destroyed elements that
define such civilizations. Stacy-Judd demonstrated the modern relevance
of this "lost" civilization in his architectural designs, but the best record
of his thoughts on the subject can be found in his travel narrative, *The
Ancient Mayas* (1934), which recounts his travels through Yucatán and
his encounters with indigenous peoples, both living and dead. There
he writes, "Yucatan may be a land of the dead, its people vanished,

forgotten, their temples and palaces in ruins, buried; but the incomparable spirit of the people lives on, a spirit whose light may prove a beacon to guide the young but virile nation of the north, beyond the Gulf of Mexico."[36] It is in this belief, that North America was the rightful heir to the Mayas, that Stacy-Judd most clearly expresses the core belief of the Mayan Revival, the idea that links architects like Totten and literary endeavors like *Broom*'s Maya-themed issue.

Although Stacy-Judd's attitude toward indigenous peoples echoes the idea of the vanishing Indian common in North America, his fixation on the ghost-like presence of the ancient Maya distinguishes him and other Mayan Revivalists. The living Maya are very much present in Stacy-Judd's account of his travels through Yucatán in 1932, but he continually ignores them, or looks past them, in his search for their "noble forefathers." Accompanied by at least two Mayan guides at all times, he nevertheless refers to himself as being "alone" in the jungle. For Stacy-Judd, the ancient buildings often have more life and more character than twentieth-century Yucatecans, since these ruins are the constructions of the "noble forefathers." In Uxmal, for instance, he describes his thrilling, spiritual encounter as he stands "in the presence of a by-gone race; in the midst of a ghost-like city of the spirit world."[37] As he engages in repopulating Uxmal with his mind, he imagines that the city is equally thrilled by his arrival there. He anthropomorphizes its buildings as slumbering giants who have been waiting for him: "In the diaphanous haze of the jungle screen this half-buried structure looked forlorn, yet relieved, as one whose long night of vigil is over, whose pent-up feelings are relaxed through the knowledge that the crisis is passed."[38] Similar to Uxmal, Chichen Itza, this "Rip-Van-Winkle of cities," as he calls it, has been asleep, merely waiting for him to arrive.

Stacy-Judd's writing exemplifies the history of "archaeologized America" that Pratt has discussed. With regard to European travel writing about America, particularly that of Alexander von Humboldt in the early nineteenth century, she observes, "The European imagination produces archeological subjects by splitting contemporary non-European peoples off from their precolonial, and even their colonial, pasts."[39] Stacy-Judd certainly evinces this attitude in both his architecture and his travel writing as he looks past the modern indigenous peoples toward the "vanished" civilizations of the Americas. We might, however, complicate Pratt's understanding of archaeology with the example of Williams. Certainly the colonial framework applies to Williams since, like the U.S. archaeologists and like Wright and Stacy-Judd, we see a North

American appropriating pre-Columbian culture. However, Williams makes this archaeological link in order to warn a potentially doomed U.S. culture about where its crass consumerism will lead. In many of the texts I discuss in this chapter, he presents a direct correspondence between the ancient cultures of the Americas and twentieth-century U.S. consumerism, emphasizing that both share a potential for creation and an inherent drive toward destruction. This will become evident in the critique of the twentieth century imbedded in "The Destruction of Tenochtitlan." Like the magazine in which it appeared, Williams's essay is concerned with linking the present U.S. culture with an indigenous past, but the conclusions that he draws from that juxtaposition are far more foreboding that those of *Broom*'s editors.

While Stacy-Judd sought the Maya as part of a spiritual quest that would revive the arts in America, the editors of *Broom* incorporated the Maya into the fast-paced world of the modern United States. This literary Mayanism strove to construct the same lineage from ancient Mesoamerican civilizations to the twentieth-century United States, but while Stacy-Judd envisioned this as a means of putting the brakes on modernism, *Broom* placed the Maya in a continuum that led to "baseball / the jazz band / the cinema / and the dizzy skyscraper."[40] These were the indigenous art forms that distinguished the national culture and kept it from being the wholly European derivative that U.S. artists feared it still was.

Throughout its five-year history *Broom* placed a premium on publishing the new and, as its name suggested, sweeping away the old. Its aim, especially in the early numbers, was to publish a wide array of European works in translation alongside avant-garde texts from the United States. By October 1922, though, the magazine had switched gears from international to national, from educating the North American reader to what the editor Matthew Josephson called a "militant modernism," which would promote what was new and daring in U.S. art.[41] This nationalist turn, and the resulting all-American number, may have been partly the result of a letter Williams wrote to the editor Harold Loeb earlier in the year: "What in hell it can mean to anyone that a magazine shall be International is more than I can say. A piece of work is international when it is good but a magazine that attempts to be international must be mediocre—the least common denominator. . . . The good work you might just as well be instigating in some actual locality where you would be IN IT—up to the ass hole."[42] The subsequent all-American number, in which Williams's "The Destruction of Tenochtitlan" appeared, was

O, I have known metallic paradises
Where cuckoos clucked to finches
Above the deft catastrophes of drums;
While titters hailed the groans of death
Beneath gyrating awnings I have seen
The incunabula of the divine grotesque.
This music has a reassuring way.

The siren of the springs of guilty song —
Let us take her on the incandescent wax
Striated with nuances, nervosities
That we are heir to: she is still so young,
We cannot frown upon her as she smiles,
Dipping here in this cultivated storm
Among slim skaters of the gardened skies.

HART CRANE

Smoke is on the hills. Rise up.
Smoke is on the hills, O rise
And take my soul away.

Karintha is a woman. Men do not know that the soul of her
was a growing thing ripened too soon. They will bring their
money; they will die not having found it out . . . Karintha at
twenty, carrying beauty, perfect as dusk when the sun goes down.
Karintha . . .

Her skin is like dusk on the eastern horizon,
O can't you see it, O can't you see it,
Her skin is like dusk on the eastern horizon
. . . When the sun goes down.

Goes down . . .

JEAN TOOMER

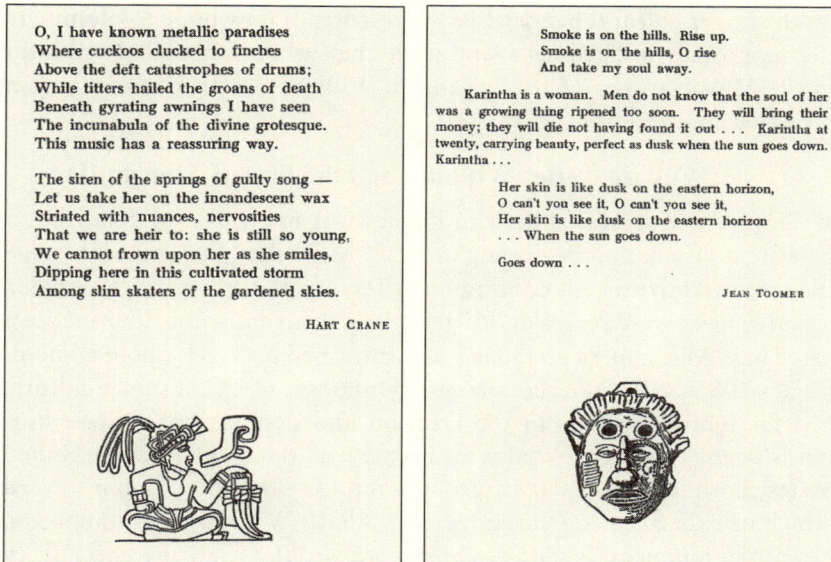

Figure 4. Mayan decorations from *Broom* 4, no. 2 (1923), the final page of Hart Crane's "The Springs of Guilt Song" and the final page of Jean Toomer's "Karintha."

certainly "in it." Every writer included in the issue was a North American, and, though their texts covered a broad range, from the U.S. South of Jean Toomer's "Karintha" to the strange transatlantic voyage of Charles Galway's "Fugitives," they were linked together by the Mayan drawings that concluded each piece (fig. 4). In addition there were photos of Mayan ruins and an essay by the U.S. artist George Sacken on "Maya art." In his best Revival tone, Sacken suggests the familiar idea of Maya-U.S. lineage: "All Maya works display this creative intelligence, and conscious use of definite aesthetic principles. Today, when a new order of artists is trying to rescue art from the morass of misused realism and to bring direction to an inchoate aesthetic Maya art particularly recommends itself."[43]

From the "morass of misused realism" this issue of *Broom* would rescue contemporary art. Its editors juxtaposed the "oldest and the newest art of America," but they were not quite sure what the two would have to say to one another. Because the Mesoamerican themes of *Broom* have not been considered in the context of the contemporary Mayan Revival in the United States, they have been largely ignored or dismissed. Based on the larger cultural history I have presented, I now hope to illuminate the supposedly indigenous avant-garde that was being articulated both in the Mayan tropes of *Broom* and in Williams's extended meditation on Aztec civilization.

William Carlos Williams and the Idea of Tenochtitlan

Williams's use of Mesoamerican themes was not a passing fancy but a persistent fascination beginning in 1918. More than just part of his history of the Americas, his conception of Tenochtitlan and the broader idea of indigeneity were central to his genealogy of an authentically American art. These Mesoamerican themes also informed his views about contemporary U.S. society and the corrupting influence of its consumer culture. His fascination with both the creation and destruction of Tenochtitlan is deeply interconnected with his view of the contemporary United States, both its fertile artistic ground and the impending doom toward which its excess leads. During the early 1920s Williams was composing almost simultaneously *The Great American Novel*, *Spring and All*, *In the American Grain*, and his "Rome" journal. I will trace the recurrence of Mesoamerican imagery through these works in order to arrive at a larger sense of Williams's thinking during this period. Tenochtitlan was for Williams a foundation from which to challenge the tradition of American history, and it ultimately served as an alternate site of knowledge production, an alternative archive to counter the "common sense" of U.S. consumerism.

Just after completing both *The Great American Novel* and *Spring and All*, Williams took a long-anticipated leave from his medical practice. Finally he would have one year to focus on his writing without distractions. Williams had already begun writing the historical essays that would make up *In the American Grain*, and he spent the fall of 1923 in New York conducting research in the Public Library and working on his book in earnest. The spring, though, presented new promise. After years of putting it off (and after years of chiding from Pound), Williams was going to Europe. For a writer so insistent about the importance of native soil to the U.S. avant-garde, it is ironic that many of the crucial sections of *In the American Grain* would be composed abroad.

Williams spent considerable time in Paris reuniting with expatriate friends and making French acquaintances (like the important meeting with Larbaud). He spent time in Austria studying pediatrics, and in Rome, where he had visited his brother in 1910. Throughout these travels he kept a journal of his thoughts, which he tentatively titled "Rome" and which he initially considered publishing as another instance of the improvisational writing he modeled in *Kora in Hell*.[44] Deciding that it would take too much work to revise (and too much time away from his other projects, like *In the American Grain*), Williams kept the "Rome" manuscript unpublished, and it did not surface until its posthumous appearance in 1978. While the text is rough and disjointed, fifty-odd pages of hurried notes and free associations, it offers an unexpurgated record of Williams's thoughts at the time. Composed when all his important works of the early 1920s were still on his mind, the journal presents a convergence of many ideas that preoccupied him. It reveals his fascination with creation and destruction, a theme that Williams saw linking the ruins of Rome and the ruins of the Americas. "Rome" also makes clear the symmetry Williams finds between the ancient and the modern, explicitly articulating the connection between old and new that he expressed more subtly in *The Great American Novel* and *In the American Grain*.

The journal focuses, if it could be said to focus, on Roman architecture and Williams's musings on this crumbling but still extant city. He reflects on the city's decadence and decline, often juxtaposing these historical reflections with his criticism of U.S. capital, including the new "emperors" like J. P. Morgan. It is a tangled and loosely associated argument that Williams puts forward in these notes, but his juxtapositions are extremely suggestive. Along with Rome's architectural beauty, Williams sees at every turn the destructive, cannibalizing impulse of the civilization that created it: "Rome is the smile of Rome and when the masters begin to collect—to drive and murder and tear our flesh."[45] This image resonates with a passage of "The Discovery of the Indies," which Williams was simultaneously revising: "With its archaic smile, America found Columbus its first victim" (*American Grain* 10). The promise and decay that he describes repeatedly link Rome with two cities of the Americas: Tenochtitlan and New York. Centuries apart, they both face destructive ends brought on by the logic of European greed.

It is the church, in Williams's view, that has destroyed the New World. In the version of the fall of Tenochtitlan that he presents in "Rome," he locates the cause of its doom less with Cortez and "the awkward names men give their emptiness" (27) than with the coming of the church and Western knowledge. The waves that crash against the shore at Veracruz bring with them this destructive force from Rome:

and churches, and churches, one destroying the other, rolling away to
Tenochtitlan—in a beastly wave

and now a new tide creeping—up, up toward the churches——forget that
one cannot wrong another man—only himself— ("Rome" 51)

One temple in Rome destroys another in Tenochtitlan with all the inevitability of a tidal wave. However, beyond these ancient civilizations, Williams also extends his wave of destruction to the present, to the same
corrupting traditions that frame his apocalyptic vision of twentieth-century U.S. culture. In contrast to Rome, which has been torn apart but
still offers its ruins for display, Williams presents New York. It shares
the qualities of the ancient economic and cultural center, "but New York
is different / Without money N.Y. doesn't exist. to think of the horror of
N.Y. without cash is the end" (46). The hostility toward Wall Street and
the foreboding sense of New York's doom are feelings that Williams also
transposes onto the markets of Tenochtitlan in *In the American Grain*.
This is the key for all of Williams's writings on Tenochtitlan and on
Rome—the apocalyptic warnings they hold for the United States. Unlike
the architects of the Mayan Revival, who viewed Mesoamerican civilization as lying dormant, waiting to be "revived" by white North Americans,
Williams's view is more complicated. These ancient sources fuel the cre-
ativity of modern America, but, as always with Williams, they also signal
the destructive potential inherent in the American background.

What threatens the bedrock of the U.S. rise, according to Williams,
is its emphasis on accumulation. It is a culture bent on amassing material wealth and piling up knowledge in a similarly acquisitive fashion.
We see in the pages of "Rome" the seeds of what would become *The
Embodiment of Knowledge* (1928–30), his indictment of the increased
disciplinarity and fragmentation of learning that offered no synthesis.
Already in 1924 Williams lamented "the fractures of the whole, breaking down in all branches" ("Rome" 32). He saw in individuals and in the
larger culture an interest in compiling knowledge rather than applying
it; so too does his critique of U.S. consumer culture lie with its organization, or rather disorganization, of knowledge. The nation has amassed
an information empire but lacks the poetic genius that would link that
information in a clear manner.

Where his countrymen have chosen to apply knowledge, it has been
only in a linear manner, not making the richer connections that Williams argued for. This linearity, he finds, is the logic of capitalism, which
applies information to increase profit and thinks only in direct lines of

trade. The men of value are the J. P. Morgans and Andrew Carnegies, the men who "organize," as Williams puts it:

> So we have a class of witty men who are able to drill the lesser gluttons, men who "organize," great rulers of natural aptitude who are able to bring bananas in quantity from Central America, nectarines from Cape Town and pearls, sables etc., coffee, rubber, tea, ivory, anything from the various hot and cold and temperate and deep and difficult places of the earth
>
> This is the natural history of America. The plain solution is to let this natural and beneficial tendency go free. ("Rome" 40)

This is not knowledge but "wit." It is the cleverness of U.S. consumerism that holds up for veneration any man who can bring in bananas for the Yankee breakfast table or *chicle* for his gum-chewing countrymen. Pan Americanism, with its vast body of information about the hemisphere, enables these "men who 'organize'" to more easily reap the material goods of the region, but it is also a system of knowledge intended to valorize these "great rulers" as intelligent. Thus the Pan American systems of trade and system of knowledge production run in unison, each validating the other. In targeting the "men who 'organize'" as the objects of his scorn, Williams mockingly contrasts these "great rulers" with the Roman emperors and with the great ruler who always preoccupied him: Montezuma.

This indictment of trade, especially with its abundance of Central American products, recalls Williams's vivid re-creation of the markets in "The Destruction of Tenochtitlan." The Aztecs had created their own empire, after all, which drew material resources from across the region. If, as Williams would later muse, Tenochtitlan "held the key," then his depiction of that city in the pages of *In the American Grain* may indeed hold the key to understanding the symmetry between old and new that runs through his work of the 1920s. However, the moment of the Conquest resonates through several of his texts because it serves as an apocalyptic vision of European consumption and demonstrates the violence inherent in an imperial society. I want to read the essays of *In the American Grain* alongside *The Great American Novel* since it too suggests that indigenous thought may indeed be a counter to the "witty men" of U.S. industry.

The Great American Novel

As with *Broom*'s desire to link the oldest art of America with the newest, in *The Great American Novel* Williams constructs an alternative lineage extending from the indigenous civilizations of the Americas directly to their North American heirs. This means that, in addition to turning away from the European path that Eliot had taken, the writer must also renounce many forbearers from the nineteenth-century U.S. canon. Williams dismisses the "complacent Concordites," insisting, "We can look at that imitative phase with its erudite Holmeses, Thoreaus, and Emersons. With one word we can damn it: England" (*Imaginations* 211). However, in the next sentence Williams takes an abrupt turn toward the indigenous counterpoint: "In Patagonia they kick up the skulls of the river men out of the dust after a flood. In Peru, in Machu Picchu the cyclopean wall on the top of the Andes remains to rival the pyramids which after all may have been built of blocks of some plaster stuff of which we have lost the combination" (211). In his invocation of Machu Picchu, Williams returns to the image of verse as "Inca masonry" that he was so fond of. Rather than being "imitative," the idea of masonry involves refunctioning material, piling up old stones to construct a new building. This was Williams's own technique in the *Novel* and *In the American Grain* as he built pyramids out of found texts.

In this same passage Williams enacts the recovery and recontextualization that would dominate his work of the early 1920s. The image of "the skulls of the river men" comes from William Henry Hudson's classic *Idle Days in Patagonia* (1893), which Williams owned.[46] Hudson's account of his travels in South America is consonant with much of the travel writing of the period, looking past the contemporary inhabitants of the land and fixing a romantic gaze on the dead civilizations. In *Idle Days in Patagonia* Hudson presents the bleached skulls that he finds as windows for understanding some ancient consciousness: "And here I would sit and walk about on the hot barren yellow sand—the faithless sand to which the bitter secret had so long ago been vainly entrusted; careful in walking not to touch an exposed skull with my foot, although the hoof of the next wild thing that passed would shatter it to pieces like a vessel of fragile glass."[47] Though Hudson is careful not to kick them himself, the skulls are destroyed with the same carelessness that Williams captures in *The Great American Novel*. Williams invokes the skulls as an image of fragility to stand against the durability of Machu Picchu and its timeless stones. By alluding to Hudson's *Idle Days*, though, Williams also introduces the necrophilic fantasies of archaeologists and travel writers into the *Novel*. For long passages the Patagonian skulls inspire Hudson's musings on indigenous civilizations, a moment so central to the text that he even reproduced an illustration of himself at the burial ground (fig. 5). These moments reflect the same revivalist fantasy that we see in Stacy-Judd's writing on

Figure 5. "An Indian Burial-Place," in William Henry Hudson, *Idle Days in Patagonia* (1883; New York: E. P. Dutton, 1917), 41.

the ancient Maya, and Hudson's admiration for the "vanished" indigenous peoples is as evident: "When on this quest I sometimes attempted to picture to myself something of the outer and inner life of the long-vanished inhabitants. . . . If by looking into the empty cavity of one of those broken unburied skulls I had been able to see, as in a magic glass, an image of the world as it once existed in the living brain, what should I have seen?"[48] By alluding to Hudson's *Idle Days in Patagonia*, Williams incorporates the figure of the North American digging through the soil of the Americas for his inspiration. Hudson's is a literal archaeological act, but Williams's act of textual digging in *The Great American Novel* performs its own kind of archaeology.

This offers an early glimpse of Williams's archaeological imagination. His manifestos of the period call on the avant-garde U.S. artist to embrace a native land and indigenous forms of knowledge, yet the work of excavation (and "digging") that he calls for in the *Novel* and elsewhere exhibits the truly modernist act of archaeology. Williams was not alone in this particular method of making things new. Sasha Colby has traced the way poets from the late nineteenth and early twentieth century appropriated the tools of archaeology into their poetics. Since "archaeology was able to both create coherent narratives about the distant past as well as destabilize pre-established historical assumptions," it became a natural accomplice to the modernist project.[49] In the 2004 special issue of *Modernism/Modernity* devoted to archaeology, the editors explain that archaeology is predicated on a break with traditional ways of understanding the past—a thoroughly modernist gesture. Rather than understanding history vis-à-vis the formulation of one's ancestors, this archaeology insists on "moments of decontextualization and recontextualization" by which the old is made to signify in an entirely new way.[50] This is a positivist approach to understanding the world since "archaeology shows us, not the course of civilization, but the force of the object—modern and ancient are equal."[51]

This way of thinking seems well suited to Williams's writing in general, and the dictum he would later issue in *Paterson* that there were "no ideas but in things" can be seen already in his early work, where stones and greasy blankets are the springboards to new insights. The insistence on "things" is not a denial that abstraction exists but rather a warning against the dangers of ideas that are unmoored from the veracity of objects. The project of both *The Great American Novel* and *In the American Grain* is to call into question all the traditional accounts of American history and to start anew at the origin, at the documents, to forge a new, recontextualized understanding of the past. Thus Williams enacts a *different* kind of archaeology, one that is concerned not with resurrecting dead civilization but rather with an archaeology that works as a system of thought to create meaning through insistently presentist recontextualizations of those civilizations. In these two prose works he makes meaning by juxtaposing the past and present in new ways, always less concerned with reviving the past than he is with using that ancient past to critique the modern consumerism around him.

In the American Grain

Williams's endeavor in writing *In the American Grain* was to escape the stale, Puritan vision of U.S. history that had been handed down by tradition. As Bryce Conrad observes, *In the American Grain* was for Williams "a way of knowing history outside the practices of the institution."[52] He wanted to take those schoolchildren of *The Great American Novel* and "release" them from the classroom into an understanding of the world that made them "discoverers." When *In the American Grain* was finally reissued in 1938, Williams reflected on his initial project: "Nothing in the school histories interested me, so I decided as far as possible to go to whatever source material I could get at and start my own valuations there: to establish myself from my own reading, in my own way, in the locality which by birthright had become my own."[53] This is the same "locality" Williams had insisted Harold Loeb should embrace. In his quest for a way of understanding history outside the disciplinary knowledge of the academy, Williams championed the role of indigenous knowledge. But from the "dark earth" that he locates in Tenochtitlan to the dead Indians that he exhumes "gently" from the soil, *In the American Grain* offers conflicting ideas of indigeneity.

As much as Williams sought a native art, one that insisted on "contact" with the land and its native peoples, his representations of indigeneity in *The Great American Novel* and *In the American Grain* are far more complicated than his earlier invocations. The Indian has become, for Williams, a way of thinking. An alternative to the logic of the "witty men" of U.S. industry and the logic of traditional American history, co-opting indigeneity becomes a way for him to think outside those structures of knowledge and formulate his own recontextualized understanding of America. This epistemological project of the *Novel* extends into *In the American Grain*, in which Williams sets out not just to tell the story of indigenous people but to think in an indigenous context. This "rhetorical project," as José María Rodríguez García calls it, is part of the larger project of textual archaeology I have been exploring in Williams's work.[54] It is a project that challenges not only the tradition of American history but also the very boundaries of America. Rodríguez García's observation comes out of the "Père Sebastian Rasles" section of *In the American Grain*, in which Williams reconstructs his 1924 conversation with Larbaud and, just as he did in the *Novel*, juxtaposes this twentieth-century moment with Rasles's encounter with the Abenaki Indians. It is a historical moment that predates the United States as a nation and offers two potential paths down which Europeans might go with their relations with the indigenous peoples of the Americas. This chapter is the key to understanding the symmetrical relationship between past and present that runs through the book. The "Rasles" essay is traditionally read as Williams's reflection on the North American Indian; however, he forges a common indigeneity in the hemisphere, placing himself in the role of both North American Indian and Aztec in a transnational appropriation of Indian identity.

This "love and theft" on Williams's part is based on a reaction to European learning, symbolized by Larbaud's heavy books. Upon his introduction to the European intellectual, Williams bristles, "Who was this man Larbaud who has so little pride that he wishes to talk with me? The lump in my breast became like the Aztec calendar stone which the priests buried because they couldn't smash it easily, but it was dug up intact later. . . . He is a student, I am a block. . . . But he is a student while I am—the brutal thing itself" (*American Grain* 107). By other accounts Williams was at a loss in the face of Larbaud's erudition, stammering a word about Maya culture, as he told Moore. However, in his re-creation of the event in *In the American Grain*, Williams turns his shortcomings into heroic qualities, the "lump" of anxiety is transformed into a sturdy "Aztec calendar stone," impervious to the threat of European orthodoxy embodied by "the priests" and Larbaud. This passage flirts with self-effacement but even redeems Williams's status as a "block." At first glance the dichotomy of student/block places Larbaud in the superior position to Williams, the blockhead who cannot absorb the scholar's knowledge. But this block has the resilience of stone. It is a part of the "Inca masonry" of Williams's prose, his "pyramid of words," the enduring symbol of creation and destruction that makes Williams "the brutal thing itself."

Williams's fictionalized dialogue with Larbaud is set up to reveal the connections between old and new, indigenous and industrial, that Williams was trying to articulate during this period. As his logic and reasoning get him nowhere ("A herd of proofs moved through my mind like stumbling buffalo"), the knowledge of the Indian simply "*is*" without linear force and illusion of progress. "Who are we?" Williams asks. "Degraded whites riding our fears to market where everything is by accident and only one thing sure: the fatter we get the duller we grow" (*American Grain* 108). The "market" is where all Western thought leads. In "Rome" it is the reason men "organize" and the reason they ship their bananas from Central America, their nectarines from Cape Town. Here, in the "Rasles" chapter, Williams repeats the same mercantile vision of the United States, in which "we are nothing but an unconscious pork-yard and oilhole" for the rest of the world (109). The logic of industrialization has become so ingrained, Williams suggests, that there are really no other options. Facetiously he considers the alternatives that lie before the United States, only to find none: "There are—so many things, there's Edison, there's—Must I make a choice between to scream like a locomotive or to speak not at all?" (108). In the face of this Hobson's choice Williams suggests that a new understanding of American history can provide another way. His answer, though, is not a simple turning away from U.S. modernity and toward indigeneity. Instead he layers together old and new so that by excavating a lost past he simultaneously reveals a new way of understanding the present. And so it is the vast market of Tenochtitlan that will provide a comment on the market that drives the "degraded whites" of the twentieth century.

Despite its title, "The Destruction of Tenochtitlan" is far more invested in the creation of that Aztec city. Only the last two pages of the essay recount Tenochtitlan's fall at the hands of Cortez, the rest being devoted to a meticulous catalogue of the splendor that was Montezuma's capital. Cortez is a predictable conquistador, Montezuma an avatar of native dignity, but they both recede into the background to make Tenochtitlan the true protagonist of Williams's narrative. The city represents "the orchidean beauty of the new world" (*American Grain* 27), the product of the fertile cultural soil of America. Williams's essay, then, is a tale of missed aesthetic appreciation as "the old [world] rushed inevitably to revenge itself" after the return of Columbus and destroyed this local culture without ever venturing to be "in it." As Williams portrays it, the fall of Aztec civilization was an inevitable result of European civilization encountering a culture it could not comprehend. "And bitter as the thought may be," Williams reflects, "Tenochtitlan, the barbaric city, its people, its genius wherever found [was] crushed out because of the awkward names men give their emptiness, yet it was no man's fault. It was the force of the pack whom the dead drive" (27). This is an image of two incompatible knowledge systems colliding. Again, as Williams puts it in "Rome," we see two "churches, one destroying the other, rolling away to Tenochtitlan—in a beastly wave." What these descriptions offer is a parable of European culture meeting the American soil.

The essay is also, like much of *The Great American Novel*, an act of pastiche since it takes substantial portions from Cortez's original letters to the king of Spain. When Williams later wrote that the text of "Tenochtitlan" was composed of "big, square paragraphs like Inca masonry," he referred to the process whereby the stones of Cortez's text were picked up and refunctioned to create another edifice. He further explained the metaphor of stonework: "I admired the massive walls of fitted masonry—no plaster—just fitted boulders. I took that to be a wonderful example of what I wanted to do with my prose; no patchwork."[55] He cuts huge pieces of Cortez's text, sometimes crediting the original, sometimes not, and alongside these "boulders" places his own. The meaning of the essay derives from this construction that removes Cortez's text from its original context and places it within Williams's view of contemporary America. It is this act of textual archaeology that makes the idea of Tenochtitlan so significant to understanding Williams's work.

Williams's source for *In the American Grain* was the *Old South Leaflets*, which reprinted famous original documents in American history, including George Folsom's 1843 translation of *The Despatches of Hernando Cortés*.[56] Cortez himself devoted a good deal of space to describing the city and its markets, but the manner in which Williams borrows from and adds to this original text makes the foreboding suggestion that, just below the text's surface, this is also about the destructive drive inherent in U.S. culture. Rather than the romance of Aztec exoticism and Spanish heroics that could be found on stage and screen, Williams chose among the numerous records of battles and adventures chronicled by Cortez and Bernal Díaz and decided to write about the markets. In its splendor and its decadence Williams offers Tenochtitlan as a mirror held up to Western civilization.

Williams prefaces the physical description of Tenochtitlan by emphasizing its rootedness in the soil of America. Its "orchidean beauty" grows out of the soil, and we can feel Williams digging through the layers of colonial history to excavate this understanding of Tenochtitlan:

> Streets, public squares, markets, temples, palaces, the city spread its dark life upon the earth of a new world, rooted there, sensitive to its richest beauty, but so completely removed from those foreign contacts which harden and protect, that at the very breath of conquest it vanished. The whole world of its unique associations sank back into the ground to be reënkindled, never, Never, at least, save in spirit; a spirit mysterious, constructive, independent, puissant with natural wealth; light, if it may be, as feathers; a spirit lost in that soil. (*American Grain* 32)

The city is still removed from the coming wave of destruction that the Spaniards bring with them. Its architecture pushes up from the "dark earth of a new world" like plants growing from the native soil until the arrival of Europeans, those "foreign contacts," causes the vitality of Tenochtitlan to "harden and protect" itself from the coming destruction. Williams anticipates his own later claim in "The American Background" but insisting here that the city will "never" return. However, he equivocates from that position by allowing that Tenochtitlan might be rekindled "in spirit," one that is "constructive, independent, puissant with natural wealth." The significance of this "natural wealth" becomes clear as Cortez's description of the city zooms in to catalogue "everything which the world affords," and the salivating Spaniard begins to transform the Aztecs' natural wealth into material wealth with his very gaze.

This gaze reverses the scene of Columbus landing in *The Great American Novel*; now it is the Spaniards who are in awe at the site of Aztec "trifles." However, instead of responding with a mute silence, Cortez presents his lush description of the objects. Cortez finds everything from "precious metals" and "gems" to elegant clothing and textiles and "many beautiful and curious artifices 'of so costly and unusual workmanship that considering their novelty and wonderful beauty no price could be set on them'" (*American Grain* 31). In the very act of writing his letter to the king, though, Cortez is in fact setting a price on these goods by cataloguing them among the Crown's new possessions and thereby introducing them into the European economy. By describing Tenochtitlan in such detail, he has, in Conrad's words, presented "an aesthetic rather than military" conquest.[57]

While Tenochtitlan lies in ruins, incapable of being materially reconstructed, Williams focuses on resurrecting that "earthward" logic since, for him, "only art advances" (*American Grain* 34). The city is destroyed, but there is the sense that that violence adds to the fertility of the land and that the archaeological poet has once again benefited from the burial of indigenous culture. As much as Williams attempts to honor what he frames as the spiritual character of Aztec society, he repeats the necrophilic impulse of the broader Mayan Revival by depicting that society as always already dead. The image of Tenochtitlan's fall is far more solemn—but no less exploitative—than that of the necrophilic historian whom Williams mocks in *In the American Grain*: "The land! don't you feel it? Doesn't it make you want to go out and lift dead Indians tenderly from their graves to steal from them—as if it must be clinging even to their corpses—some authenticity" (74). This enthusiastic exhumation of a native corpse comes at the end of "The Founding of Quebec," and the context of this speech and the way

Williams positions himself in relation to it serve to further elucidate his textual archaeology.

The essay is structured around a conversation between two speakers debating the role of the French, particularly Samuel de Champlain, in American history. Conrad has argued that this chapter anticipates the conversation between Williams and Larbaud in "Père Sebastian Rasles" and that the primary speaker in "Quebec" is a proxy for Williams. On this point my reading differs from Conrad's since the naïve tone of this speaker clearly marks him as the fool of Williams's text. When a man is strangled and his head placed on a pike, he exclaims, "To me the whole thing's marvelous—all through" (*American Grain* 73), and he becomes absolutely frenzied over the dead Indian who has been brought back above ground. This speaker is the white travel writer who digs up indigenous culture but takes pleasure in its ruin. He exhibits the same joy as Stacy-Judd among the ghosts of Yucatán or Hudson examining skulls in Patagonia. This is the understanding of the hemisphere that insists on the *revival* of indigenous civilization and simultaneously asserts that that civilization is fundamentally nonvital without some northern intervention.

It is in the remarks of the interlocutor that we find Williams, who, speaking from Larbaud's Paris apartment, insists that such fantasies are appropriate for France but not the New World, "here not there" (*American Grain* 74). Thus the history of Champlain, with its "marvelous" decapitated heads and Indian corpses dripping with "authenticity," is the academic's history, a story told at one remove without the vital contact that Williams was looking for. If we put the dialogue of "The Founding of Quebec" alongside that of "Père Sebastian Rasles" there is indeed a symmetry in which the primary speaker is, like Larbaud, "a student," and the interlocutor is, like Williams, "the brutal thing itself" (107). This scene anticipates the scorn for the "academicism" that Williams would write of in "The American Background." The primary speaker of "Quebec" and his fantasies are, as Williams says, "beside the point" and worthy of reproach. Instead the later essay offers Williams's own brand of archaeology, an alternative to this mode of "revival": "Tenochtitlan with its curious brilliance may still legitimately be kept alive in thought not as something which *could* have been preserved but as something which was actual and was destroyed." For Williams, the indigenous culture remains a foundation, a root, meant to remain in the "American soil" but not one to be revived. While he shared many of the necrophilic elements of the larger Mayan Revival, there was in his view nothing to be gained by merely imitating these cultures. Building new ruins in Southern California did not advance the cause of hemispheric American art, and neither did Williams believe such appropriations would renew American culture. Instead Tenochtitlan offered Williams a harbinger of a coming American apocalypse brought on by U.S. greed and consumption.

Finding Relics in Puerto Rico and New Jersey

No understanding of Williams's vision of the Americas would be complete without a look at his journey to Puerto Rico in 1941 to attend the First Inter-American Writers' Conference. It was a trip of many "firsts" for Williams, his first time on an airplane as well as his first setting foot in his mother's native Puerto Rico. At the age of fifty-seven he had a renewed interest in this heritage and, as Jonathan Cohen suggests, this was in many ways a meaningful trip for the poet.[58] The trip also deepened his engagement with the poetry of the Americas, leading to a number of significant translations in the 1940s and 1950s, which Cohen reprinted in *By Word of Mouth*. This was also an opportunity for Williams to engage more formally in a project he had pursued for most of his career, namely to articulate a shared hemispheric American identity, which was part of the conference's aim.

However, the talk Williams gave at the conference, "An Informal Discussion of Poetic Form," reveals a very mixed engagement with this project. It covers the very broad terrain of poetry and metaphysics, yet it is interspersed with selections from Williams's own poetry, which seem to be chosen solely for their mention of Puerto Rico.[59] Each of these poems, including "Adam," "Eve," and "To Elsie," is rich, and there's a good deal to be said about them, but instead the talk continues to turn back centuries, to Lope de Vega and the continuing relevance of Spanish verse. After his reading of "To Elsie," for instance, Williams poses a fairly important question: "If, in a work of art, it is by the nascent form that the fullest . . . and most timely significance is expressed—what function might not Latin America exercise toward the United States and Canada in this respect?" This question gets to the core of what an Inter-American Writers' Conference might mean, but his answer is not so ambitious. Latin American poetry serves to "introduce us to Spanish and Portugese [*sic*] literature—pure and simple."[60] Given the context of this talk, Williams's answer is more than a little disappointing. Where is the poet who strives to capture the "American idiom," the writer who retells the continent's history throughout *In the American Grain*?

It seems that for Williams the Spanish language was not the path to the American idiom since in his mind it always signified Quevedo, Lope de Vega, and a Golden Age of Spanish literature. It was instead the pre-Columbian civilizations of Central America that served repeatedly as his touchstones for a hemispheric American identity. Even here, in Puerto Rico, Williams brought these ruins with him. At the conclusion of his talk he qualifies his remarks about poetry by once again invoking these Mesoamerican cultures as a uniting, American bond: "And if everything else that I have said is wrong-headed, destructive to that precious soul of things which the true poet should cherish! If I have been mechanical and crass in my concepts, relying for my argument on mere techniques and materials—Well, in that case, from the old and alien soul of America itself, may the reliques [*sic*] of its ancient, its pre-Columbian cultures still kindle something in me that will be elevated, profound and common to us all, Americans. There is that path still open to us."[61] In 1941 Williams found himself among American poets who clearly shared his artistic vision. There was the Puerto Rican poet Luis Palés Matos, for instance, whose "Prelude in Boricua" engaged vernacular language and which Williams would later translate.[62] And yet this is not the common quality he identifies. Williams looks past these living poets and toward "the old and alien soul of America itself" to the "reliques" of an ancient civilization. This image reveals the two central aspects of Williams's conception of Latin America. First, he echoes the popular perception of the region as dead, a land of past glories and lost civilizations. But his emphasis on common American relics is a fixation all his own. This is part of his poetics of materiality, which always looks to the thing itself as the starting point for poetry. Any relic is invested with meaning and with a cultural significance that is understood by all members of that culture. By returning to such "ancient objects," Williams still has in mind the poet's role as archaeologist, unearthing the past and drawing out new meaning for the present.

While he rejected the contemporary tendency to revive indigenous culture "as dead," Williams continually made use of the episteme of archaeology, removing the "thing" from tradition in order to understand it in a new context. The textual archaeology that we see at work in both *The Great American Novel* and *In the American Grain* is fundamentally a break from the larger systems of knowledge production in the United States and the destruction toward which they lead. We might think of this distinction, as Vera Kutzinski has, as the difference between the Library and the Archive. The idea of European tradition, she suggests, is embodied by the Library, "a homogenous representational space that would promote textual unity through semantic stability." Against this Kutzinski suggests the alternate organization of the Archive, claiming that "Williams's texts, unlike Eliot's and later Hart Crane's, are characterized by a conceptual disorder that evolves into a literary method."[63] As we have already seen in "Rome," Williams is hostile to the traditional organizations of knowledge. One must, as he would later put it, "embody" knowledge, be the "brute thing itself." For Williams, Kutzinski suggests, this "break," this move from intellectual unity to disorder, is "equivalent to the burning of the Library."[64]

With this image Kutzinski of course invokes the burning Library that Williams depicted over two decades later, in Book III of *Paterson*. Before the fire the kind of stale knowledge that the building contains is ripe for destruction: "The Library is desolation, it has a smell of its own / of stagnation and death."[65] Again, for Williams, destruction and creation are part of the same gesture, and even the act of reading itself is an exercise in exhuming the dead.

> We read: not the flames
> but the ruin left
> by the conflagration
>
> Not the enormous burning
> but the dead.   (*Paterson* 123–24)

In the burning library of Paterson, the embers of Tenochtitlan still smolder. It is the moment of destruction to which Williams wishes to return since it eliminates the distortions of history, which offers "not the flames / but the ruin." Williams's evocation of Tenochtitlan at the moment just before it is destroyed attempts to recover it from the province of the dead, to which contemporary archaeology had resigned the Aztecs and so many other indigenous civilizations. Tenochtitlan, then, is an alternative to the traditional structures of academic archaeology and an alternative to the logic of the "men who 'organize.'" In an era when the hemisphere was increasingly "organized" by U.S. academics and businessmen, Williams breaks Mesoamerican culture out of the museum, out of the library, and out of the sarcophagus of Pan American knowledge production. Rather than the archaeology that reproduces indigenous peoples as always already dead, Williams's textual archaeology forces past and present together in a way that recasts our understanding of history. At the end of *Paterson* III Williams articulates this desire to evade the melancholy of the dead past and to create instead new meaning:

> I cannot stay here
> to spend my life looking into the past:
>
> the future's no answer. I must
> find my meaning and lay it, white,
> beside the sliding water. (145)

2 Hemispheric Mythologies

Rethinking the History of the Americas through Simón Bolívar and Quetzalcoatl

Can you imagine the effect it would produce if an individual should appear among them manifesting the signs of Quetzalcoatl, this Buddha of the rainforest, or Mercury, who has been the object of so much discussion in other countries? Don't you imagine that this would affect each of the states? Is not unity the only thing needed to encourage them to expel the Spaniards, their brigades, and every partisan of corrupt Spain, so that they could then establish a powerful empire with a free government and benevolent laws?
—Henry Cullen, quoted by Simón Bolívar, "The Jamaica Letter"

The American continental races are now becoming aware of their own personality as it emerges from the two cultural currents, the indigenous and the European. The great American myth of Quetzalcoatl is a living one, embracing both elements and pointing clearly by its prophetic nature, to the responsibility shared equally by the two Americas of creating here an authentic American civilization.
—José Clemente Orozco, "A Note from the Artist"

THE ARTIFACTS AND MYTHOLOGIES of pre-Columbian cultures were not only repurposed by U.S. artists, but they also became the foundation for many forms of nationalism in the former Spanish colonies. Mexico in particular placed Aztec imagery at the center of its state-defined national identity, both after Independence in 1821 and after the Revolution. For instance, the work of the Mexican anthropologist Manuel Gamio to excavate the ruins of Teotihuacán and reconstruct the lives of its inhabitants was deeply intertwined with the project of creating a new Mexican national identity. His book *Forjando patria* (1916), or *Forging the Fatherland*, is a clear illustration of the way science and the state were mutually supportive of one another's aims.[1] After the Revolution cultural institutions were also central to the subject formation of the Mexican state. Mary Coffey has traced the function of state-sponsored museums, particularly the Palace of Fine Arts, the National History

Museum, and in the 1960s the National Anthropology Museum, as techniques of government power.[2] By dominating the narratives of history, anthropology, and ultimately mural painting, the state was able to project a unifying mythology about Mexican identity, and a good deal of this mythology was rooted in the use of pre-Columbian cultures.

In this chapter, however, I explore the transnational potential of pre-Columbian cultures and how they have been redeployed to articulate a vision of the hemispheric unity outside the dominant narrative of Pan Americanism. The idea of hemispheric unity is a very old one; in the epigraph above Simón Bolívar recounts the suggestion by Henry Cullen, the British "gentleman" to whom his "Jamaica Letter" was addressed, that pre-Columbian ideas be revived as part of a new revolutionary mythology. Cullen clearly imaged this as a hemispheric mythology, which would unite the colonies in opposition to Spanish rule. He invokes the return of Quetzalcoatl, the Toltec ruler and deity whose reappearance would mark a rebirth of the indigenous civilizations in Mexico and whose mythology became entwined in the story of the Spanish Conquest, when Cortez was supposedly mistaken for the returning god. While Cullen's suggestion regarding a unifying messianic figure may have been intended to flatter El Libertador, he is also appealing to the ideological work that mythology can perform in unifying a national, or in this case multinational, community. For his part, Bolívar was much more skeptical of this tactic. He writes:

> I believe as you do that individual actions can produce general effects, especially during revolutions. But it isn't the hero, Quetzalcoatl, great prophet or god of Anáhuac, who would be capable of bestowing the prodigious benefits you propose. This figure is hardly known at all by the Mexican people, nor highly regarded, for such is the lot of the defeated, even if they are gods. Only historians and literary scholars have dedicated themselves to carefully investigating his origins, his mission, whether true or false, his prophecies, and the termination of his cult.[3]

That such a myth was not known in all parts of the Americas made it difficult for Bolívar to accept its unifying potential. He did, however, note that revolutionary leaders in Mexico had had success deploying a more familiar symbol, "proclaiming the famous Virgin of Guadalupe as queen of the patriots and invoking her name at every critical moment and raising her image on their flags," suggesting that such strategies could work on a national level.[4] Bolívar's responses here, and his attitudes about Spanish American unity in general, were always practical ones. He believed that unity among the newly formed nations of South America would arise out of necessity, out of their shared opposition to Spanish oppression, and that no such mythology would be required.

This exchange between Cullen and Bolívar, however, reveals a debate over hemispheric unity that has spanned centuries and, with surprising frequency, has involved Quetzalcoatl. Cullen was not merely an out-of-touch Brit for suggesting that a pre-Columbian myth be refashioned into a modern symbol of unity. It may have been an object of interest for "historians and literary scholars" rather than a popular myth, as Bolívar noted, yet Quetzalcoatl has been redeployed in various retellings of the history of the Americas, usually with the purpose of breaking with the established order and establishing a new, hemispheric American future. It is precisely this refashioning by scholars and later by artists that makes the modern mythology of Quetzalcoatl so compelling since these retellings offer an alternative vision to the more popular version of Pan Americanism.

My argument in this book centers on the modes of representation and knowledge production that the United States deployed as a means of controlling the hemisphere, and there is perhaps no more thorough means of doing this than through the control of myth and history. It is well established that national myths are essential tools used by states to inculcate their dominant ideologies, and within the field of American studies the Myth-and-Symbol School—as well as later critiques of this methodology—has demonstrated the way such myths have worked to reinforce the domestic ideologies within the United States. Similarly the logic of Pan Americanism depended on controlling the history and mythology of the hemisphere, all of which was used to create a larger narrative of a shared struggle against European colonialism and a postrevolutionary cooperation that would inevitably lead to U.S.-defined modernity. This particular avenue of knowledge production entailed the appropriation of mythologies from Mesoamerican peoples and even the appropriation of Bolívar himself as the symbol par excellence of Pan Americanism and a favorite icon of the PAU. However, during the height of U.S.-led Pan Americanism, from the late nineteenth to the mid-twentieth century, there were also efforts to tell a different story of the Americas and to imagine what an alternative version of hemispheric cooperation might look like. The example of Bolívar alone illustrates the mutability of hemispheric mythology since he was celebrated in the United States and also held up as the forefather of united opposition to the United States by José Martí, José Vasconcelos, Augusto Sandino, and Hugo Chávez, all of whom advanced their own particular version of Bolivarism. With regard to the pre-Columbian past, though, some of the most significant and most revolutionary reimaginings of the history of the Americas were produced by Mexican muralists in their effort to position pre-Columbian myths as the grounds for a new revolutionary Mexico as well as a unified Western Hemisphere.

Writing over a hundred years after Bolívar's "Jamaica Letter," José Clemente Orozco also thought beyond the limits of nationalism as he framed Quetzalcoatl as a "great American myth" and a "living one."[5] This statement was made upon the completion of his mural at Dartmouth, *The Epic of American Civilization* (1932–34), which included Quetzalcoatl in a prominent role and, I will argue, reimagined this figure as a founding symbol of hemispheric unity. While Orozco's mural critiques the violence and neocolonialism of U.S.-style modernity and industrialization of the early twentieth century, it also imagines a cooperative future in which Quetzalcoatl returns to enact an era of transnational solidarity led by the mestizo worker. With Orozco articulating his vision of the hemisphere from within the United States—and from within one of its oldest institutions of knowledge production—this analysis inverts the cultural exchange I explored in chapter 1. Mexican muralism is typically understood as a nationalist movement, yet many works, the Dartmouth murals chief among them, need to be considered within the framework of the Pan American imagination.

I focus on Quetzalcoatl for several reasons. First, the sheer frequency with which the ancient god appears in texts and works of art causes us to ask why this particular myth was so fascinating to so many hemispheric thinkers. From the Spanish scholar Fray Bernardino de Sahagún's sixteenth-century account of the myth in his *General History of the Things of New Spain* to its twentieth-century apparitions in the writing of D. H. Lawrence and the painting of Diego Rivera and Orozco, Quetzalcoatl has had a unique appeal across centuries and across the colonial divide. My second reason for dealing with Quetzalcoatl is the changeability of the myth, which partly explains its broad appeal. Modern historians have unearthed a multitude of different versions of Quetzalcoatl—in some he is a god, in others a prophet-king, sometimes cruel, sometimes the model of self-sacrifice—and somehow these versions all coexist.[6] Thus Quetzalcoatl is an especially hybrid figure, which makes him easier to appropriate and also makes him a productive space from which to think about the very hybrid status of the Americas. It is, after all, the *use* of Quetzalcoatl I am interested in, not the original figure, whether historical or mythic. These are not the myths that may have been part of a Toltec or Mexica culture; rather these are colonial and Pan American myths that have attempted to naturalize various visions of hemispheric unity. Tracing the incarnations of this figure through the more recent hemispheric mythologies reveals just how contentious the idea of Pan Americanism can be, especially when its narratives seek to unify the history of the Americas.

Myths and Symbols in a Hemispheric Context

Over the past two decades the transnational turn in America studies has had several goals, but chief among them has been the move away from idea of U.S. exceptionalism that informed so much of mid-twentieth-century scholarship. As Shelley Fisher Fishkin remarked in her 2004 presidential address to American Studies Association, "In many of its earliest incarnations American studies aspired to overarching generalities about the United States . . . and a fixation on American innocence blinded many scholars to the country's ambitious quest for empire."[7] As Fishkin sees it, moving American studies beyond the geographical borders of the United States is a way for scholars to challenge U.S. exceptionalism so that, as a methodology, transnational American studies by its very nature undermines nationalist ideologies. While we have a thorough understanding of the way myths (about the frontier, the "City upon a Hill," and so on) have informed nationalist ideologies, it remains unclear how we might respond to myths that themselves operate in a transnational context. The figures of Quetzalcoatl and Simón Bolívar both gained the status of hemispheric myths and were deployed in a variety of contexts, which provokes several questions: Is it possible to construct salient hemispheric mythologies, and if so, what ideological work have they done? Who has authored these myths, and at whom have they been aimed? How might the tools of Hemispheric American studies be applied to mythologies that are also hemispheric?

Before answering these questions, it will be helpful to revisit the nationalist ideologies in earlier scholarship, particularly in the Myth-and-Symbol School of American studies. Some of the most insightful critiques of this mode of criticism have come from these same scholars later in their career, such as Henry Nash Smith's own reevaluation of his Myth-and-Symbol classic, *Virgin Land: The American West as Symbol and Myth* (1950). The original volume presents the concept of the untouched frontier as the controlling metaphor for understanding the American expansion west. Reflecting on the book in 1986, Smith observed that alongside *myth* and *symbol*, the word *ideology* was conspicuously absent.[8] He therefore proceeded to reanalyze his work in terms of a Marxist understanding of ideology in order to rescue *Virgin Land* from being one more example of "consensus history." As he begins the process of recontextualization, Smith stresses that "the distinction between myth and ideology is less important than that between both myth and ideology on one hand and what I call 'empirical fact' on the other."[9] There is, however, some distinction between myth and ideology, as Richard Slotkin points out in the same volume: *myth* is often our term for other people's religion and *ideology* the marker for other people's politics, and both terms are pejorative.[10] It is important to think of myth, as Smith does looking back on his own work, not as a denial of the ideology at work within a culture but rather as the historical evidence of that ideology, authored, as Slotkin suggests, for no other purpose than to sustain the dominance of the myth maker.

Looking back on the work of the Myth-and-Symbol School, John Carlos Rowe has pointed out that "none of these influential scholars fully believed such national symbology; all understood its ideological purposes." Despite their awareness of these ideologies and their liberal critique of U.S. failures, "many of the scholars in this mode were captivated by American idealism and optimistic that social problems eventually would be overcome. The intellectual focus on organizing symbols and unifying national myths tended to reinforce consensus-based history and assimilationist ideals in the settler society of the US."[11] It is precisely this mode of "consensus-based history" that we can also trace in hemispheric myths. More recently, as American studies scholars have moved toward a hemispheric model, the beginnings of a such a mythology have aggregated around José Martí.

Since the early 1990s scholars in the United States have increasingly invoked the Cuban writer and revolutionary as a foundational figure for critiquing U.S. imperialism. We can see this in several works, most notably Jeffrey Belnap and Raúl Fernández's *José Martí's "Our America": From National to Hemispheric Cultural Studies* (1998). The editors write that their objective is "to explore the tension in Martí's work between national and transnational perspectives, a tension that makes his analysis of the Western Hemisphere's different national formations and their intrahemispheric relations extremely significant for reconfiguring the way we think about 'America.'"[12] Martí has provided U.S.-based scholars with an important alternative to a legacy of American studies that is intertwined with U.S. exceptionalism, and yet this shift might just be substituting one mythology for another. Hemispheric American studies runs the risk of mythologizing Martí himself by holding him up as the progenitor of a mode of transnational scholarship that is located almost solely in U.S. and Northern European universities. Laura Lomas points out that some studies have glossed over Martí's more subversive writing in their efforts to frame a new, positive approach to studying the Americas. "Martí," she writes, "is still claimed by scholars and politicians . . . as an authorizing figure for pan-American economic, cultural, and political programs," including the project of Hemispheric American studies.[13] Lomas stresses instead the oppositional nature of Martí's writings, but she has also returned to the complexities of his anti-imperial critique, which cannot be reduced to anything like a consensus history. It is for this reason that Martí the icon is less useful than the texts themselves since they offer "the thinking process by which a modernist disruption begins."[14] The key distinction between Lomas's understanding of Martí and what we might think of as a latent Myth-and-Symbol reading of Martí is that she offers not a totalizing narrative but rather a *process*. His writings, she claims, will "enable us to remap American Studies," but this is an ongoing project that resists neat conclusions and the sense of telos that are the telltale signs of myth.[15]

The Pan American Union and Simón Bolívar

While the field of American studies continues to wrestle with totalizing histories of the Americas, such grand narratives were central to the project of Pan Americanism. If the United States was to present itself as the "natural" and inevitable center of the Western Hemisphere, it needed foundational myths that stressed a common American cultural history. Simón Bolívar was and continues to be invoked frequently as the forefather of Pan Americanism, and it is for this reason that he is key to an understanding of hemispheric mythology. Just as Quetzalcoatl was proposed to him as a unifying idea, so too has he been invoked for an array of political ends since his death in 1830. Christopher Conway points out a very useful reflection from one of Bolívar's letters: "In my name both good and evil is sought in Columbia, and many invoke it as the text of their madness."[16] Indeed the invocation of Bolívar—his words, his actions, his image—were central to the internal conflicts of the newly independent American republics in the 1830s and 1840s. Since then he has been deployed as part of the nationalist mythology of Venezuela, from the nineteenth century to Hugo Chávez's declaration of a "Bolivarian Republic." In his study of the "cult of Bolívar" in Latin America, Conway explores the various ideals he has come to represent, among them the image of progress: "In modern Latin America, the symbol of Bolívar has been charged with the defense of the promise of tomorrow. History is plotted through continuities and Bolívar is a powerful wellspring of myth capable of joining the past to the present and to a providential future."[17] This method of plotting history is central to all sorts of politically motivated mythologies. By laying claim to a revered figure like Bolívar and placing him as the origin point for one's own present—whether that present is the U.S.-centered Pan American Union of the 1930s or the Bolivarian Republic of Chávez's Venezuela—this obviously legitimates that narrative and constructs the condition of the present as provident and even inevitable. This phenomenon of mythologizing Bolívar in Latin America has a long history and a large body of scholarship devoted to it. Less familiar, though, is the way the image of Bolívar has been deployed in North America. In the late nineteenth and early twentieth century he was appropriated by the Pan American Union as part of a hemispheric mythology in which they could root their own vision of U.S.-led modernity as the "natural" mode of partnership in the Americas.

The use of Bolívar was but one part of a larger Pan American culture industry. Beginning in 1930 the PAU in conjunction with the White House encouraged the celebration of Pan American Day on April 14 of each year, marking the anniversary of the founding in 1890 of the organization that would one day become the PAU. U.S. schoolchildren were made to study the history and geography of the other member nations, and anthologies such as *Pan-American Day* (1943) provided poems, plays, speeches, and historical documents to help study for and celebrate the day. At the heart of the Pan American tradition was, of course, the legacy of Bolívar; students could read about the Congress of Panama, join a seventeen-year-old Bolívar on an "exciting ride" one night in Spain, and grieve with John Greenleaf Whittier in his elegy for the Liberator, feeling, even in their northern schoolhouse, "a sob that shakes like her earthquakes the startled continent!"[18] Young boys and girls could even act out a play written especially for the volume, which includes a fictitious dialogue in which Bolívar's tutor, Simón Rodríguez, advises him to visit the United States and study government and leaders:

> Bolívar: I shall follow your advice, Rodriguez. I shall take a ship to Boston. I shall study the American system. Perhaps I may be able eventually to weld all the American states into a union to promote brotherhood, liberty, and peace!

Rodriguez: That's the idea, my boy! (*Loudly.*) A Pan American Union! God
bless you, my son! You have the qualities of a great leader![19]

To be sure, there were benefits to the Good Neighbor curriculum of
the 1930s and 1940s and it was far better to supplement the standard
mythologies surrounding George Washington and Abraham Lincoln
than to leave students ignorant of the other American revolutions. However, representations of Bolívar such as this exchange remove any sense
of his complex attitudes toward the United States and his concerns about
its growing hegemony. Such fictionalized history lessons begin the ideological work of legitimizing the Pan American Union and associating it
clearly with a legacy of anticolonial struggle.

For its adult audience, the main vehicle for proliferating these Pan
American values throughout the Americas was the PAU's monthly publication, the *Bulletin of the Pan American Union.* We saw in chapter 1
that the *Bulletin* participated in archaeologizing Latin America and in
cataloguing the region's material resources, ripe for development. Yet
these were narratives aimed at its U.S. readership. For part of its history
the *Bulletin* was published simultaneously in four languages—English,
Spanish, French, and Portuguese—with the goal of finding readers in all
twenty-one member nations. The magazine included articles in its regular series, "Pan American Progress," which held nations like Haiti and
Cuba up to the bar of economic and material development defined by the
United States, but these articles often celebrated the work of local leaders in moving their nation down the road of progress. Such modern-day
developments, though, were part of a longer narrative of Pan American
cooperation that the PAU liked to tell, a narrative rooted in the shared
legacy of Simón Bolívar.

In 1930, when nations throughout the Americas were observing the
centenary of Bolívar's death, the *Bulletin of the Pan American Union*
put out an entire issue devoted to his legacy in the hemisphere. The issue
began with an introduction by Leo S. Rowe, the longtime director general of the PAU, who emphasized the clear lineage between Bolívar's
version of Pan Americanism and his own: "Although the time was not
ripe for the international organization which Bolívar visualized more
than a century ago, the great purposes which he had in view are slowly
but surely moving toward fulfillment. The International Conference of
American States, which met in Washington in 1889, was the logical successor to the Congress of Panama which Bolívar assembled in 1826."[20]
Bolívar was not inclined to even invite U.S. representatives to Panama,[21]

but by stressing the "logical" connection between these moments—the Congress of 1826, the Conference of 1889, and the Pan American Union of 1930—Rowe legitimizes the PAU as a potentially "liberating" institution and presents Bolívar as the South American face of the Washington-based institution. It was for this reason that Bolívar was continually evoked in PAU publications and in the speeches at its conferences. As Rowe phrased it, "Bolívar will always occupy a high place as the spiritual father of Pan Americanism."[22]

However, the "spiritual" role extended beyond the halls of the Pan American Union itself. The Liberator's importance could also be seen in U.S. statuary, which, though not as plentiful as in Latin America, was no less significant. Following the first Inter-American Conference, in 1889, a statue of Bolívar was installed in New York's Central Park in 1891 at a site that came to be known as "Bolívar Hill."[23] This representation of Bolívar was derided by art critics and ultimately removed, but a new statue, sponsored by the Venezuelan state, was made and dedicated in 1921. At the dedication ceremony, President Warren G. Harding suggested that Bolívar's significance extended beyond the PAU and was indeed part of the national political agenda. He noted that the day chosen for the ceremony, April 19, was an important one for both North and South American freedom, marking anniversaries of the Battle of Lexington in 1775 and the liberation of Caracas in 1810. Harding hoped that April 19 "might have an added significance from this day," and he proposed a new era of hemispheric partnership. Less than two years after the end of World War I, Harding's motives are clearly mercantile, having everything to do with securing stable trade relationships in the event of future disruptions of trade with Europe. That the hemisphere would be a storehouse for U.S.-defined progress was, as Harding envisioned it, preordained by the divine: "The Western continent afforded a favorable soil for a marvelous development. God had bestowed with limitless bounty and nature was prodigal with her offerings. The Americans hold virgin riches conserved against the day when science and intellect and spiritual ambition should impel man to seek new fields for new enterprises. Trade was calling, learning encouraged the adventuring navigators, and wherever they touched they opened gateways and marveled, never dreaming of the reality."[24] One wonders what Bolívar, enshrined in bronze above Harding, would have thought of this dream. This is clearly a U.S.-centered vision of hemispheric solidarity, in which the people of Latin America and the Caribbean unite to provide their "virgin riches" to the northern land of "science and intellect and spiritual ambition."

Bolivarism and Monroism:
Two Visions of the Hemisphere

Although Harding articulated this view of the Americas while dedicating a statue to Bolívar, his words more accurately reflect an ideology that intellectuals in Latin America frequently labeled "Monroism." Looking back to the idealistic rhetoric of the Monroe Doctrine and the imperialist reality it enabled, twentieth-century critics of the United States applied this term to any Pan American policies they found duplicitous. José Vasconcelos, the Mexican philosopher and education minister who was also an important supporter of the muralist movement, articulated these two opposing views of the hemisphere in his book *Bolivarismo y monroísmo* (1934): "We shall call Bolivarism the Hispano-American ideal of creating a federation with all the peoples of Spanish culture. We shall call Monroism the Anglo-Saxon ideal of incorporating the twenty Hispanic nations into the Nordic Empire, through the politics of Pan Americanism."[25] Thus in 1934 Vasconcelos is extending the critique of Pan Americanism that began with Martí, namely that it was a means by which the United States could incorporate the rest of the Americas into its informal empire. Vasconcelos has traditionally been thought of as an intellectual closely engaged with nationalism, and so too has the muralist movement he supported become closely linked with Mexican national identity. By invoking Bolívar, though, Vasconcelos reveals the transnational vision that underpins much of his work.

There is a longer history of the "Bolivarism" Vasconcelos identifies, which places Bolívar at the center of an oppositional pantheon for rethinking U.S. hegemony. Anthea McCarthy-Jones and Alistair Greig have traced this intellectual tradition, which they refer to as "radical pan-Americanism," and the way that various political movements in Latin America have invoked "key 'heroes and martyrs' in order to present their struggle as part of a continuous line of hemispheric solidarity."[26] They mention Martí's use of Bolivarian solidarity in constructing his notion of "Nuestra América," and they also discuss Sandino's aspirations for transnational opposition to the United States as well as his repurposing of Bolívar. McCarthy-Jones and Greig single out Sandino's "Plan for the Realization of Bolívar's Ultimate Dream" as the Nicaraguan leader's clearest expression of the link between the past and the future he saw for the Americas. This document called for a new path of economic and material development for the region (including a Nicaragua Canal) and insisted that its resources not be exploited solely for the profit of U.S. companies. In calling for a united "nationality" that would extend from the Río Bravo to the Strait of Magellan, Sandino's plan was motivated by necessity as much as Bolívar's was.[27]

Bolívar has, of course, been mythologized in his native Venezuela, where nationalist debates over his legacy began soon after his death and have continued into the twenty-first century. The best analysis of this phenomenon is still that of the Venezuelan historian Germán Carrera Damas, *El culto a Bolívar*, which explores how the Liberator inhabits the nation's political discourse and haunts its everyday life. The cult of Bolívar, he writes elsewhere, has been "set up to legitimate the national state in historically specific circumstances"; what's more "it has come to constitute the spinal column, and in not a few occasions the universe, of Venezuelan thought."[28] The most recent Venezuelan promoter of the Bolívar cult was the late Hugo Chávez, who continually branded his presidency as part of a "Bolivarian Revolution." In many ways Chávez's rhetoric was not unlike that of nationalist politicians from across the globe who frequently align themselves with the "fathers" of their nation in order to legitimize their own programs. However, his fascination with Bolívar extended beyond the predictable speeches and into the realm of worship, perhaps best illustrated by his decision to exhume the body of Bolívar. Late on the night of July 24, 2012, Chávez oversaw a team of forensic pathologists and soldiers as they opened the tomb of Bolívar and ceremonially removed his remains for further inspection, all of which was broadcast live on state-run television. The ostensible reason for this was to investigate the "true" cause of Bolívar's death, which Chávez suspected was assassination. But exhuming the material remains of Bolívar was also an occasion for Chávez to pay homage to El Libertador and celebrate his own Bolivarian Revolution. Throughout the night and into the next day Chávez posted updates on his Twitter feed, frequently quoting lines from Pablo Neruda's "Un canto para Bolívar." At one point Chávez actually contacts the poet in person and tells his followers, "Digo con Neruda. . . . Bolívar despierta cada cien años cuando despiertan los pueblos. Viva Bolívar!! He aquí su rostro!!" (I'm talking with Neruda. . . . Bolívar awakens every hundred years when the people awake. Long live Bolívar!! I have his face here before me!!)[29] This bizarre moment of national theater was part of a personal obsession, and it also reveals how much political significance has been foisted onto the idea, and in this case the body, of Bolívar.

As much as Chávez redeployed Bolívar as an icon of Venezuelan nationalism, it should be remembered that his Bolivarian vision was also a transnational one. Throughout most of his presidency Chávez culti-vated an image of himself as the leader of a coalition of left-leaning nations in Latin America that opposed the neo-imperial policies of the United States. This vision was formalized in 2004 with the formation of ALBA, the Alianza Bolivariana para los Pueblos de Nuestra América. This multinational alliance was a direct response to the U.S.-led free trade agreements of the 1990s and early 2000s. Beginning with an agree-ment between Cuba and Venezuela, ALBA expanded to include six other nations, including Bolivia, Ecuador, and Nicaragua. This trade organi-zation was a response to contemporary conditions, a chance for Chávez and Fidel Castro to foster trade conditions in the Americas that did not center on the U.S. economy. However, by invoking Martí's "Nuestra América" in the very title of the organization, ALBA clearly locates itself in a longer history of solidarity against U.S. interests. On ALBA's own website it expands this connection even further, drawing forth an array of nineteenth-century revolutionaries as its forbearers:

> If we look back to the past, we can find the roots of this project in documents such as the "Letter from Jamaica," when for the first time Simón Bolívar established the doctrine of unity and sovereignty of the countries that became free from the colonial power. We can analyze other historical documents that are evident background to ALBA and it is clear that this idea was upheld by Bolivar, Martí, Sucre, O'Higgins, St Martin, Hidalgo, Pétion, Morazán, Sandino and so many other national heroes, without selfish nationalism or restrictive national policies that reject the objective of constructing a Big Homeland in the Latin America, according to the dreams of the heroes of our emancipating fights.[30]

A key part of Chávez's Bolivarian Revolution was therefore predicated upon the notion of a hemispheric Bolívar, the one who proposed the Congress of Panama. As idiosyncratic as Chávez's understanding of *Bolivarian* may seem, and as much as he used it to support his own national ambitions, he is part of a longer tradition of thinkers who have positioned Bolívar as the mythological origin figure of a unified Latin America. This is the same concept that Vasconcelos articulated in *Bolivarismo y monroísmo* since ALBA is clearly a project aimed at opposing modern-day Monroism, which Chávez identified in NAFTA and other free trade agreements.

However, Bolívar is only one unifying myth for the hemisphere. What's more, the notion of Bolivarism versus Monroism splits this intel-lectual history into a simple dichotomy that does not adequately capture all the complexities of inter-American relations. The appropriations of

Quetzalcoatl, on the other hand, have been far more varied. From the colonial encounters of the sixteenth century to the Creole independence movements of the nineteenth century and even in the Pan American era of the early twentieth century, versions of the Quetzalcoatl myth have reappeared as strategies for explaining the hybrid nature of the Americas. Though the political goals of these mythologies have varied, they all present a narrative in which racial and cultural differences merge into some shared modernity, so that, as I will argue, Quetzalcoatl serves as the foundation for a transnational *mestizaje*.

Sahagún and the Colonial Reorganization of Mythology

Just as the work of Manuel Gamio retrieved pre-Columbian civilizations for the purpose of forging a new nation, so too has the appropriation of Quetzalcoatl always required disciplinary knowledge to identify and categorize elements of pre-Columbian culture, and this has typically worked through the nexus of anthropology, history, and archaeology.[31] Gamio himself saw his anthropological work as part of a tradition beginning with the so-called first Mexican anthropologist, Bernardino de Sahagún, and so it is worth revisiting this colonial appropriation of Quetzalcoatl in order to understand how dominant narratives can be constructed out of the mythologies of the colonized.[32]

As important as Spanish military victories were, the Conquest was equally dependent on their efforts to either destroy or repurpose what was left of indigenous culture. Bernardino de Sahagún (ca. 1499–1590) presents a particularly interesting case since his work with Mexica informants is largely the reason why many Aztec histories and myths are preserved. Yet the way Sahagún catalogued this indigenous knowledge made it legible to European modes of understanding by resolving these Mexica stories within the master narratives of Christianity. This control of indigenous knowledge made such work a central pillar in the project of conquest and colonization.

Sahagún's principal work was the *General History of New Spain*, also known as the *Florentine Codex*. Working with neophytes who had learned Spanish and Latin in addition to their native Nahuatl, Sahagún and his assistants transcribed stories about Mexica history, religion, and government which their informants reported to them. The resulting codex presented this information in both Spanish and Romanized Nahuatl texts and also included Mexica-style drawings. Thus the *Florentine Codex* is a transculturated text, merging the colonizing language with native visual practices. Of course in this hybrid form the power relations are not equal. By looking at Sahagún's organization of the codex, and his depiction of Quetzalcoatl in particular, the imposition of European ideologies onto Mexica culture becomes clear. In *The Darker Side of the Renaissance*, Walter Mignolo explores how Mexica modes of thinking and recording events were recast by Sahagún within the strict, logical concept of history inherited from the Greco-Roman tradition. Therefore, as Mignolo puts it, "Sahagún's *Florentine Codex* helped to save the known in Mexica culture from oblivion, at the same time that it repressed (although not suppressed) Mexica ways of knowing."[33]

While Mignolo has done extensive work on the repressive systems of organization in Sahagún's work and the way they privilege the Western mind, I want to examine what may be even more readily apparent in the *Florentine Codex*: the repression of native mythologies. The repression grows out of the same scholarly origins Mignolo identifies; it is a means of conquest by categorization, in which Sahagún records in detail the indigenous myths only to denounce them as pagan and heretical. In his account Quetzalcoatl is regarded as a "demon" and a "liar" along with the rest of the pantheon, but Sahagún salvages the values in the myth that are useful in disciplining the colonial subject, such as self-sacrifice and martyrdom. While we take for granted Sahagún's religious motives for doing this, his scholarship is also attuned to the politics of colonial government. We must remember that political ideology and mythology are always interlaced, so that mythological and historical events are part of the same project. Even when he is writing about Quetzalcoatl, Sahagún is simultaneously inscribing the Mexica into a history of colonial domination.

Book 3 of Sahagún's *General History* is devoted to "the origin of the gods," and Quetzalcoatl figures prominently. However, the prologue explains that these are "lying gods" whose stories will be retold to the Mexica in order to show them the error of their former beliefs and more easily convert them.[34] Following the main text, Sahagún adds an appendix "in which the idolatry described above is refuted by means of sacred scriptural texts."[35] Sahagún's appendices always follow this pattern of methodically refuting the main text, a kind of catechism in which Fray Bernardino clearly has the final word. But why catalogue these native myths so thoroughly if they are only to be refuted? Certainly numerous gods in the pantheon are identified, categorized briefly, and dismissed, but Quetzalcoatl commands several chapters of the book. There must therefore be something in the myth of Quetzalcoatl that Sahagún found instructive and ideologically useful. His is one of the first attempts to appropriate the mythic past of the Americas in order to forge a new, politically stable future.

Sahagún's first account is of the historical Quetzalcoatl, the Toltec prophet-king, whom Sahagún refers to as the "great wizard." He is described as a monstrous, ungodly figure with a hideous long beard, but Sahagún also portrays him as a benevolent ruler. In this account the Toltecs flourish under his rule, beginning a Golden Age in early Mexico. His vassals are rich and learned, which Sahagún stresses proceeded from Quetzalcoatl's influence. The chapter concludes, however, by depicting the ruler's role as the creator of autosacrifice, since he bled his own leg as a form of penance. It is this principle of sacrifice and martyrdom that, in Sahagún's account, becomes the cornerstone of the cult of Quetzalcoatl and by extension the culture of Mexico. Representations of the autosacrifice do exist in the archaeological evidence, but the image does not play the central role that it does in Sahagún's narrative.[36] We can readily imagine why a Catholic priest would emphasize this part of the story. Quetzalcoatl cutting into his own calf represents on a smaller scale the values of self-sacrifice represented in the crucifixion of Jesus. Sahagún, like most colonial missionaries, was eager to point out the similarities between indigenous deities and values and the stories in scripture. In the process of reshaping Quetzalcoatl he was converting the Mexica to a Catholic worldview. The same type of "conversion" could be said to take place in twentieth-century mythology, whereby peoples throughout the Americas were asked to embrace the narratives of modern progress set forth by the United States.

The messianic version of the Quetzalcoatl myth had very evident ideological aims of repression, yet this is not the only use to which the myth of Quetzalcoatl has been put. Beyond its function during the Spanish colonization, an anticolonial mythology was also created around this figure during the nineteenth and twentieth century. While these myths worked at cross-purposes, they provided legitimizing narratives by grounding their cause within an indigenous story. The deep ambivalence of the Quetzalcoatl myth, which represented both colonization and the coming of modernity, made it an important touchstone in the wake of the Mexican Revolution, which itself struggled to resolve the nation's colonial and modern identities.

Modern Myths of Quetzalcoatl

With the independence movements of the nineteenth century, pre-Columbian cultures were put to new uses. Rather than being repressed in favor of Spanish master narratives, indigenous cultures were redeployed by the Creole elite as a means of solidifying a new nationalist identity. In Mexico, for instance, the struggle between Indigenism and Hispanism has a long history, and in the nineteenth century this played out in part through the growth of a national mythology surrounding Quetzalcoatl. In his study of both Quetzalcoatl and the Virgin of Guadalupe, Jacques Lafaye suggests that we think about Quetzalcoatl as a specifically "Creole myth."[37] It is a Creole myth in two senses: as Lafaye explains, the myth was taken up by the nineteenth-century Creole elite in their struggle for independence, but it is also a Creole myth in that it blends elements from multiple cultures. Quetzalcoatl is a hybrid deity in his original form, serving as the god of the wind and of water, symbolizing the earth and air united in the winged serpent, and his conflation with Christ places him in a unique position between the two cultures. These overlapping stories supposedly helped both sides of the colonial divide to orient themselves in relation to the "New World." As Lafaye writes, "By a type of tacit agreement, the wills of one side and the other reclaimed the legend of Quetzalcoatl, as a way to escape a situation intolerable to their religious consciousnesses: to live in a moment, not foreseen by their respective prophets, a history in which they all had a share."[38] The messianic elements of the myth also provided an explanation of the Conquest for both sides. This is because the return of Quetzalcoatl has a bivalent interpretation: for the European it represents a new, modern era in which the heathen race will be saved from their excesses; for the Mexica it is a return to a past era of enlightenment. This conflict within the myth, suggesting revolution as a simultaneous looking forward and looking back but feeling bound to neither, makes it a perfect fit for Creole ideology. To create a new world while maintaining the traditions of the old (particularly the hegemonic traditions) was a central problem for nineteenth-century Creole revolutionaries as they forged a new concept of national identity.

As a new generation of cultural revolutionaries worked to redefine Mexican national identity in the early twentieth century, Quetzalcoatl would once again be part of that its iconography. However, the myth's significance was up for debate. While this figure would appear in the paintings of Rivera and Orozco, for foreign artists, such as D. H. Lawrence, Quetzalcoatl became a very different sort of touchstone for Mexican identity. These diverse interpretations of the myth reflect a central tension in the way Mexican history has been imagined and where the indigenous past fits into that larger historical narrative. As Orozco observed in his *Autobiography*, "In Mexico history seems to have been written throughout from the racial point of view alone. Discussion apparently reduces to proclaiming and imposing the superiority of one or the other of the two races, and the worst of it is that this is no merely domestic argument, for foreign pens have intervened and go on intervening in the composition, with mischievous intent. The efforts of our historians might be a prize fight between an Indianist and a Hispanist, with a foreigner for referee."[39] In chapter 1 I traced the work of several "foreigners" who appropriated Mesoamerican cultures for their own ends. In the thinking of the Mayan Revival, indigeneity had an entirely different meaning than it did for Mexican historians since it was an abstraction that could be put on and taken off as easily as Robert Stacy-Judd's costume. And in reimagining the history of Mexico, such "foreign pens" also turned to the trappings of Quetzalcoatl as the symbol of an ancient past that, they believed, held the key to understanding modern Mexican identity.

Anita Brenner, an expatriate living in Mexico, opens her book *Idols behind Alters* (1929) with a chapter on Quetzalcoatl, the "Mexican Messiah," as she terms him. She begins, of course, with the fulfillment of prophecy: "An old prophecy current in Mexico announces that 'when the chief temple of the Aztecs shall appear in the principal plaza of the city of Tenochtitlan, bearing upon it the sun, then shall the ancient people possess their ancient rights.' In August, 1926, during the course of restoration and repair of the National Palace, in the main plaza of the capital, once Tenochtitlan, a monolith was brought to light. It is a model of the chief temple of the Aztecs, with a stone symbolic of the sun carved on its surface."[40] The scene is the discovery of the Piedra del Sol, which now stands as the centerpiece of the National Museum of Anthropology. What is interesting here is that Brenner sees this event as revealing the "ancient" culture hidden but ever-present within modern Mexico. The title of her book reflects the sentiments of many foreign writers of the time who were fascinated with Mexican culture. The assumption is that behind the modern face of the nation and its entrenched Catholicism, the old idols were still worshipped in secret.

The messianic idea that the "ancient people" will once again possess their "ancient rights" is also what drives Lawrence's *The Plumed Serpent (Quetzalcoatl)* (1926). Two years before he ever visited the Americas, Lawrence wrote enthusiastically about the promise of reclaiming the indigenous past and suggested that the inhabitants of these lands should "catch the pulse of life which Cortés and Columbus murdered."[41] In the novel the cult of Quetzalcoatl returns quite literally as a growing sect in Mexico, made up of characters who reenact the old rituals.

The "dark" and indigenous character Don Ramón takes on the role of Quetzalcoatl (other characters assume the names of other gods, such as Huixtlipochtli), and he even attempts to ritually sacrifice another character, perhaps forgetting that Quetzalcoatl opposed such sacrifices. The rituals of this mythology excite Lawrence's imagination in a way that the Mexican Revolution did not, and he indulges in all sorts of racial generalizations about the "spirit of the Mexican." His race theories center on the rupture within the mestizo, which he explores as a site of metaphoric possibility. Like Brenner, Lawrence saw in the mestizo a latent Aztec past, as he theorized elsewhere: "The Aztec lives unappeased and destructive within the Mexican, waiting to emerge as a 'new race.'"[42] This seems a provocative and inclusive gesture, and yet a "new race" formed only when "the soul of the dead red man will be at one with the soul of the living white man."[43] The trouble with this unity, of course, is that it is predicated upon a "dead red man." While it may seem as though this view of indigeneity as dead and relegated to the past was only that of foreigners—British writers or perhaps U.S. archaeologists—the Mexican state has had its own fraught relationship with its indigenous population. Vasconcelos's notion of *mestizaje*, on which much of the state's postrevolutionary cultural production was based, saw indigeneity and modernity as mutually exclusive conditions. If Vasconcelos was the organizing force behind the muralist movement of the 1920s, then his thoughts about race and history are extremely relevant to any understanding of those murals.

Mexican Muralism and Transnational *Mestizaje*

During the early 1920s Vasconcelos was the main proponent of state-sponsored muralism in Mexico, funding the works of *los tres grandes*—Rivera, David Alfaro Siqueiros, and Orozco—by commissioning them to adorn government buildings with murals deeply invested in the subject of Mexican national identity. Around the same time that Vasconcelos was promoting the muralists, he was also formulating his ideas about Mexican racial identity in his book *La raza cósmica* (1925), a text that is in many ways the foundation of twentieth-century thought on *mestizaje*. His vision of the mestizo is very much a biological and, inseparably, nationalist utopia. Vasconcelos after all held a government office as education minister, and, in this post-Revolution era, he was interested in establishing a Mexican identity that was rooted in something other than European imitation. Just as his contemporary Gamio was excavating ancient ruins with the goal of "forging a fatherland," so too did Vasconcelos look to forge a link between past and future cultures of Mexico. Both of these cultural visions were structured around two goals: identifying an ancient location from which to understand ethnic identity and assimilating the indigenous peoples of Mexico. Both of these proved problematic over the course of the twentieth century.

If Gamio's vision was rooted in the material ruins of Teotihuacán, Vasconcelos's vision was based in mythology, even making metaphoric use of the lost civilization of Atlantis. This is a frequently forgotten part of Vasconcelos's argument in *La raza cósmica* but one that is important for understanding his thoughts on indigeneity and its place in the narrative of modern Latin America. He begins the section of his book titled "Mestizaje" by discussing various theories of Atlantis and ultimately claims that "traces of [a lost civilization] are still visible in Chichén Itzá and Palenque, and in all the sites where the Atlantean mystery prevails."[44] This genealogy is the basis for advancing his idea of a rich and continuous American culture. "If we are, then, geologically ancient," he writes, "how can we still continue to accept the fiction, invented by our European fathers," of the novelty of the American continent? Here Vasconcelos rewrites European mythology for his own ideological purposes. Linking the modern Americas to this ancient past makes it the cultural equal to Europe rather than its colonial "discovery," but, significantly, Vasconcelos links his own culture to a *lost* indigenous past. As much as *La raza cósmica*, and a good deal of post-Revolution Mexican ideology, looked back in order to move forward, the indigenous peoples whom he evoked in all their Atlantean grandeur had no place in the cosmic future. "The Indian," he wrote, "has no other door to the future but the door of modern culture, nor any other road but the road already cleared by Latin civilization."[45] Thus with his *raza cósmica* Vasconcelos articulated a hemispheric cultural identity, but his racial model mirrored other eugenicist discourse of the early twentieth century.[46] *Mestizaje* involved mixing, but it also demanded assimilation and biological conformity. As Vasconcelos himself writes, "The fifth race does not exclude but [instead] accumulates life."[47] This is the most troubling aspect of Vasconcelos's work. If *mestizaje* has been an intellectually and politically productive idea within Latino identity, the extent to which the term has recently been viewed as problematic can perhaps be traced back to Vasconcelos's biological emphasis.

Looking at the work of the muralist movement, and the work of *los tres grandes* in particular, it is evident that Mayan and Aztec cultures were extremely influential in the formulation of their post-Revolution aesthetic. However, while Mayan and Aztec elements were ubiquitous, there was much debate over how these cultures should be incorporated or what they signified in the twentieth century, reflecting the larger debate between Hispanism and Indigenism that Orozco identified. Siqueiros, for his part, wrote in 1921, "We must adopt [the] synthetic energy [of the Mayan and Aztec painters and sculptors], but avoid the lamentable archaeological reconstructions (*Indianism, Primitivism, Americanism*) which are so fashionable today and which are leading us into ephemeral stylizations."[48] Siqueiros could just as easily have been denouncing someone like Robert Stacy-Judd with this phrase about "lamentable archaeological reconstructions," but what he has in mind here is the work of Mexican painters who, he believed, simplified the indigenous past either out of a kind of patriotism or as a marketing strategy for tourists.

The accusation of "playing Indian" to please the tourists was frequently leveled against Diego Rivera. The art historian Alejandro Anreus recalls a rare and telling moment in 1947 when, late in their careers, *los tres grandes* met and posed for a photo, and even then the old argument about how to represent the Mexican past to a foreign audience resurfaced. As Siqueiros remembered the encounter in his memoir, Rivera proposed that the three present to the president of the Republic a plan for a "City of Art" in Mexico City, which Rivera had already sketched out. Orozco told him candidly, "Not a single Mexican will come to this; there, English will be spoken and you are always imagining things for tourists." To which Rivera supposedly replied, "I am tired of the tourist thing being blamed on me. And what do you live off, you old *hija de la chingada*, if not from the tourists?"[49] This exchange reveals the anxiety about making art for U.S. patrons, but it also suggests the complicated problem of how to represent indigeneity, both within Mexico and abroad. This issue cannot be reduced to a Rivera/Orozco dichotomy since both struggled with the way the indigenous past should be represented. As their careers continued, however, their representations were enriched by this struggle to intertwine the past with the present as they used pre-Columbian culture to comment on modernity.

I want to trace this tension in their work, and the implications for our understanding of a hemispheric mythology, by considering versions of Quetzalcoatl done by these two leading muralists: Rivera's *Ancient Mexico* from his National Palace mural (1929) and Orozco's *Coming of Quetzalcoatl* from *The Epic of American Civilization* in Dartmouth's Baker Memorial Library. Rivera's depiction of Quetzalcoatl presents an exotic version of Mexico's past. In the foreground lies the carnage of war, which was associated with the time before Quetzalcoatl's arrival, but the apex of the fresco presents the seated prophet with all of the Buddha-like calm that Henry Cullen ascribed to him. As with many of Rivera's other murals, *Ancient Mexico* presents a nostalgic view of the indigenous past. To be sure, Rivera reclaims this cultural knowledge as part of a shared national identity, but this pre-Columbian prophet and his followers have no connection with the present day.

In *The Epic of American Civilization*, Orozco presents several versions of this figure, but it is in *The Coming of Quetzalcoatl* that he depicts the same historical period that Rivera has in mind (fig. 6). We see the same Mesoamerican Golden Age in which Quetzalcoatl's arrival ends the violence associated with the god of war, Huixtlipochtli, and ushers in a new era of enlightenment. While this mythological scene is located in the past, in Orozco's version there is a conceptual bridge between Quetzalcoatl and the modern world. The figures reclining in the foreground mirror the posture of Orozco's *Modern Industrial Man*, which occupies a facing wall of the Baker Library (fig. 7). The meaning of this association between the pre-Columbian Golden Age and the modern mestizo worker is not at all straightforward, and I explore them more fully in a moment. For now, though, it is important to note that it is through these spatial associations that Orozco suggests a continuing value for mythologizing Quetzalcoatl in modern America.

This sort of association across multiple walls is part of Orozco's artistic method, and it also reflects his way of rethinking history. When the *Epic of American Civilization* was finally completed in 1934, Orozco issued "A Note from the Artist," in which he declares, "In every painting, as in any other work of art, there is always an IDEA, never a STORY." He goes on to explain that "stories and other literary associations exist only in the mind of the spectator, the painting acting as the stimulus."[50] So while Orozco does not provide a narrative link between Quetzalcoatl and *Modern Industrial Man*, there is an idea behind this association, and it is up to the viewer to reconcile these images and to make meaning from them. The association between these particular panels will not tell us the history of the Americas from beginning to end, but perhaps that is not Orozco's intent.

In his reflections on Orozco's work, Octavio Paz has suggested that the painter's use of history resists the linear narrative of progress that most Western history entails: "His real subject is not the history of Mexico but what lies behind or underneath, what the historical event conceals. The past, the present, and the future are a temporal current that flows past and then flows back in the other direction, a deceptive and enigmatic

Figure 6. José Clemente Orozco, *The Coming of Quetzalcoatl*, from *The Epic of American Civilization,* 1932–34, at the Baker Library, Dartmouth College. (Courtesy of the Hood Museum of Art, Dartmouth College; Commissioned by the Trustees of Dartmouth College; © 2014 Artists Rights Society [ARS] New York / SOMAAP, Mexico City)

succession that the eye of the artist or the prophet penetrates: another reality appears therein. . . . Orozco neither recounts nor relates; nor does he interpret: he confronts the facts, questions them, searches for a revelation in them."[51] Paz's observations help to explain Orozco's treatment of indigenous cultures since, unlike Rivera's murals, his Quetzalcoatl is not resigned wholly to the past but is free to become part of a new hemispheric mythology for the future. But with the description of a "temporal current" that flows back and forth, Paz also helps us understand Orozco's methodology and the way that he creates meaning across multiple images and multiple historical contexts. In *The Epic of American Civilization* in particular, Orozco suggests associations across the space of the Baker Library and across the past, present, and future of the Americas.

Orozco follows the same "currents" in a short essay he wrote just a few years before going to Dartmouth. In "New World, New Races, and New Art," written and published in New York in 1929, he pulls together disparate moments in the history of the Americas and disparate cultures in order to imagine a shared hemispheric modernity with *mestizaje* at its core. He declares, "If *new* races have appeared upon the lands of the *New* World, such races have the unavoidable duty to produce a *New Art* in a

new spiritual and physical medium."[52] This "new art," however, proves to be located in the skyscrapers of Manhattan. In celebrating the architecture of New York and positioning it as the foundation of a New World art, Orozco avoids the divisions of nationalism and a reductive anti-U.S. politics. Instead he stresses the common, American qualities of this towering cityscape. He goes on to explain that in creating an art for the New World, "the architecture of Manhattan is the first step. Painting and sculpture must certainly follow as inevitable second steps."[53] We see the realization of these "steps" only a few years later in the Dartmouth murals, in which this industrial landscape undergirds the "IDEA" of the mural.

As much as Orozco insists on the "new," though, the images he has painted are very much a blend of new and old. This "next step" in his art at Dartmouth College also argues for a hemispheric American identity based on the unique condition of "new races" and "new arts" since the Conquest. In his "Note from the Artist," he explains that the central idea behind the Dartmouth murals is part of this shared hemispheric identity, that "it is an AMERICAN idea developed into American forms, American feelings, and, as a consequence, into American style."[54] Though this American style is open to all, Orozco's vision of a common American future grows out of the mestizo worker reclining in *Modern Industrial Man*. In her essay "An 'AMERICAN Idea,'" the mural scholar Mary K. Coffey explains that *mestizaje* informs Orozco's use of indigenous cultures as well as his sense of history: "Within the logic of *Mestizaje*, indigeneity is not confined to a prehistorical past but is rather an essential component of modern life and the national experience of each citizen within the Americas. Orozco rejected the anachronistic idealization of the past that one often sees in the work of his peer Diego Rivera. Rather than seeking a return to Quetzalcoatl's 'golden age,' Orozco suggests that a new, perhaps better age may arise from the ashes of the modern world."[55] Orozco's fusion of the indigenous past and

Figure 7. José Clemente Orozco, *Modern Industrial Man II*, from *The Epic of American Civilization,* 1932–34, at the Baker Library, Dartmouth College. (Courtesy of the Hood Museum of Art, Dartmouth College; Commissioned by the Trustees of Dartmouth College; © 2014 Artists Rights Society [ARS] New York / SOMAAP, Mexico City)

modern present, his "logic of *Mestizaje,*" as Coffey terms it, helps us better understand the relationship between race and historiography in his work. Of particular interest is Orozco's realization of these ideas within a physical space in the Anglo North. That he articulates his hemispheric vision of Quetzalcoatl in one of the centers of U.S knowledge—the Baker Memorial Library at Dartmouth College—allows him to reformulate the history of the Americas as it had been written by the "foreign pens" of North America.

Orozco's *Epic of American Civilization*: An "AMERICAN Idea"

The *Epic of American Civilization* encircles the Reserve Room of Dartmouth's Baker Library, which, as Orozco remembered it in his autobiography, was "the pride of the College, with a collection of books in Spanish which by itself is greater than many very important libraries in Spanish America."[56] By traveling to New England and working in the material archive of North American knowledge about the South, Orozco had an opportunity to subvert the dominant structures of knowledge in the hemisphere. In Mexico in the 1920s *los tres grandes* routinely used their art to challenge the very institutions on whose walls they painted.[57] While Orozco clearly valued the institution of Dartmouth and its supportive environment, his mural still questions the hegemonic structures of the Western universities and the narrative they have been allowed to tell about the history of the Americas and the ideology of modern progress. To be sure, this is not a denunciation of the university or the library, but the mural is clearly in dialogue with its surroundings and critiques the linearity of Western history. It presents, as Orozco argues, "an IDEA, never a STORY."

Orozco was particularly interested in Dartmouth's historical relationship with indigenous peoples, and he felt that this made it a fitting place to articulate his *Epic of American Civilization*. When he visited

the campus in 1932 he gave the heads of the college a formal presentation of what he envisioned for the library's walls. In a letter Dartmouth's
president Ernest Hopkins recalled Orozco's particular focus on the college's link with indigenous culture:

> Moreover, he argued, and our authorities in archaeology, in anthropological
> sociology, and in art bore him out, that at Dartmouth more than anyplace in
> the country the theme was appropriate in view of our original relationship
> to the Indian culture of the country, despite the fact that our relationship
> was one of trying to overthrow it. Orozco's ultra-enthusiasm in regard to
> the whole project seemed to be based on a conviction that at Dartmouth
> more than anywhere else in the world the circumstances existed which would
> make his work of major appropriateness.[58]

Murals by their very nature respond to their surroundings, the architecture of the building and its imagined uses. As we take a closer look
at Orozco's Dartmouth mural I want to keep several aspects of this
location in mind. First, Orozco is working in New England, in the
heart of what he referred to as "Gringolandia."[59] Second, Dartmouth
as an institution had a fraught relationship with Native Americans,
to say the least,[60] and so Orozco's exploration of "new races" leading
to new art forms seems particularly suited to this setting. Third, it is
important to remember that Orozco is working in a North American
library, where so many of the "foreign pens" had already inscribed the
history of the Americas and where he now sets out to reimagine that
history through the spatial associations he creates across the library's
walls.

The mural's major panels present—and ultimately challenge—a chronological history of the Americas, from the migration of indigenous peoples
out of Aztlán to the arrival of Cortez and the wars and political corruption of the twentieth century. There is an apparent sequence to these panels,
which can be read left to right in chronological order, as a "STORY," and I
will go over this linear understanding of the mural first before complicating
this interpretation and exploring the "IDEA" at the center of Orozco's *Epic*.

The first sequence of panels recounts a history of pre-Cortesian civilization, which Orozco structures around the story of Quetzalcoatl's
arrival and departure (fig. 8). Indigenous peoples migrate from Aztlán to
central Mexico in order to found what will be Aztec civilization, complete with the practice of human sacrifice, which Orozco depicts on the
western wall. The next panel reveals *The Coming of Quetzalcoatl*, who

persuades the people to turn away from their pagan gods and who brings them an age of enlightenment and civilization (fig. 6). These Mesoamerican people, however, eventually abandon Quetzalcoatl, who spurns them and leaves across the ocean, vowing to return one day. This is a familiar story, but what is more significant is that Orozco draws an indexical correlation with the later sequence of panels. As he departs, Orozco's Quetzalcoatl points to the other half of the Reserve Room as if to suggest that everything it depicts of the history of colonialism and modernity is a direct result of the people's rejection of him.

The next sequence of panels depicts this history of the Americas since the Conquest, beginning with the arrival of Cortez (fig. 9). Of course upon his arrival the historical Cortez was supposedly mistaken for the returning Quetzalcoatl, according to the accounts of Bernal Díaz and others, and so Orozco has good reason to position the two figures in parallel positions in the Reserve Room. Yet Orozco's larger suggestion is that, in their own ways, both Quetzalcoatl and Cortez usher in new eras in American civilization. As Paz has suggested, in Orozco's mythology "Cuauhtémoc is not a hero. Nor is Cortés. They are not reformers or victims transfigured by their sacrifice: they are tools, instruments of cosmic justice."[61] Thus Cortez serves as a vehicle for bringing both coloniality and modernity to the Americas, with all of the violence and material progress they entail. At his feet Orozco places a pile of indigenous bodies, trampled under the forward movement of Spanish Conquest, but he also suggests that they are victims of the coming industrial era. The black and gray colors that dominate the Cortez panel clearly associate him with the next panel in the sequence, *The Machine*. Thus the post-Cortez era extends to the modern drive for progress, which can be understood as enacting violence on non-industrial peoples just as Cortez did himself. This historical progression leads to Orozco's division between *Anglo-America* and *Hispano-America* and finally to *Gods of the Modern World*, the panel that ultimately challenges the teleological progression depicted in the mural. Here skeletal university dons watch over the birth of yet another skeleton, complete with mortarboard. The logic of Western knowledge is stillborn and, according to Orozco, does not offer a "living" ideology in the same way that the myth of Quetzalcoatl does.

However, there are other associations that the viewer of the mural can make aside from this linear progression. Rather than just the forward-moving line of chronological history, *The Epic of American Civilization* makes use of the three-dimensional space of the Reserve Room to suggest geometric associations between various nonsequential panels and, ultimately, to make thematic links between its subjects. It is in this way that the Dartmouth mural offers the fulfillment of Orozco's insistence that painting offered an "IDEA" rather than a "STORY," and so it is worth tracing the ideas that do not have a clear beginning, middle, and end.

While in New York Orozco explored the ideas of Dynamic Symmetry put forward by Jay Hambridge. This aesthetic philosophy was particularly informed by geometry, and Orozco's most faithful use of this aesthetic can be seen in his New School mural, where diagonals are used to structure the composition of each panel. When Orozco first

Figures 8 and 9. Arrangement of the Dartmouth Panels, before Cortez (fig. 8, *top*) and after Cortez (fig. 9, *bottom*), from *The Epic of American Civilization*, José Clemente Orozco, 1932–34, at the Baker Library, Dartmouth College. (Courtesy of Hany Farid and the Hood Museum of Art, Dartmouth College; Commissioned by the Trustees of Dartmouth College; © 2014 Artists Rights Society (ARS] New York/SOMAAP, Mexico City)

arrived at Dartmouth in 1932 to paint his demonstration fresco, these compositional principles were still quite central to this thinking. However, as he continued to develop this method and adapt it to the panels inside the Reserve Room, he dispensed with some of the rigidity in favor of the conceptual associations he might make across panels. As he explained it, "After doing the pictures in the New School I abandoned the overrigorous and scientific methods of Dynamic symmetry, but I kept what was fundamental and inevitable in it and with this I shaped new ways of working. I had the explanation of many former errors and I saw new roads opening up."[62] We might understand these "new roads" as the potential for meaning making that Orozco found in three-dimensional geometric associations between the panels of the Dartmouth mural.

In some cases the titles of the panels themselves make clear that Orozco intended there to be a dialogue between the panels. For instance, the panels *Ancient Human Sacrifice* and *Modern Human Sacrifice* face each other and, though over ninety feet apart, work together to present

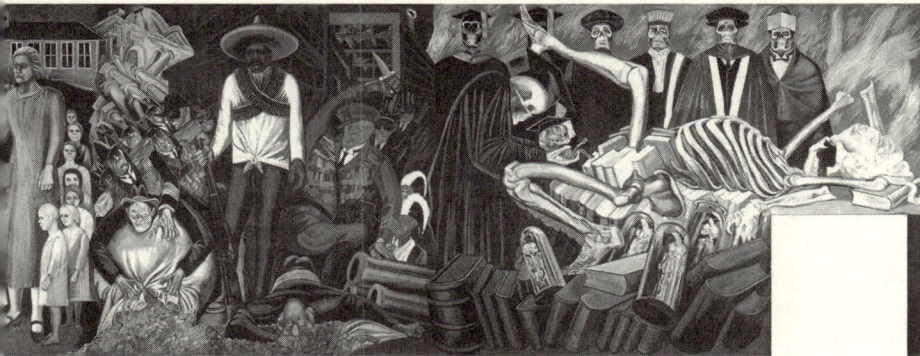

a unified idea. The latter panel depicts the body of a dead soldier buried under flags and wreaths, which Orozco suggests are the false idols of patriotism and the causes of a ritual sacrifice no less barbaric than that of the Aztecs. Similarly *Symbols of Nationalism* and *Chains of the Spirit* face one another at the east end of the room and are meant to be an obvious critique of the nationalism that led not only to the sacrifice of the modern soldier but also to the artistic and spiritual constraints placed on all of Western modernity. The most suggestive associations, though, are made with the frescos on the opposing wall, a group of panels collectively titled *Modern Industrial Man* (fig. 10). Here an anonymous group of workers erects an iron-red skyscraper whose harsh lines and simple elegance embody the Manhattan architecture Orozco had praised in "New World, New Races, and New Art." Above them another worker reclines and reads a book, resting from his work on the skyscraper (fig. 7). In many ways this panel is unconnected from the linear history of the other wall. The figures certainly exist in a contemporary moment, so they might be understood chronologically, but their relation to the linear narrative on the opposing wall is unclear. Is this an image of progress that we are to understand as the logical outcome of the arrival of Cortez and modernity? Is it a utopian fantasy, an escape from the violence of American history depicted on the facing wall?

In order to connect these modern workers with the rest of *The Epic of American Civilization* we need to consider the mural's use of diagonal associations. Orozco's use of Dynamic Symmetry led him to use diagonals in each panel to structure his composition, but in this case the diagonals play on the viewers' line of sight across the Reserve Room. Standing in front of *Modern Industrial Man* the viewer can turn around and take in most of the mural from that location. The viewer is free to "read" the mural from right to left and see the chronological parallels Orozco is suggesting (*The Coming of Quetzalcoatl* and *Cortez and the Cross*, for instance), but other nonlinear associations become apparent as well, which more meaningfully connect the modern workers with the rest of Orozco's epic. The figures in these panels are hard at work constructing the metropolis of tomorrow, losing their individuality as they extend themselves in the same direction, working toward the same goal. While this image of unity certainly is of an idealized utopian future, it echoes the figures of Orozco's most "ancient" panel, *Migration*, which the viewer can see by turning west (fig. 11). Here the indigenous figures merge into one another in just the same way. And just as the workers pull against the steel in a joint effort, these figures move as one gray mass across the wall.

Figure 10. José Clemente Orozco, *Modern Industrial Man I* from *The Epic of American Civilization,* 1932–34, at the Baker Library, Dartmouth College. (Courtesy of the Hood Museum of Art, Dartmouth College; Commissioned by the Trustees of Dartmouth College; © 2014 Artists Rights Society [ARS] New York / SOMAAP, Mexico City)

The similarities within Orozco's palette, the grays of the figures and the red tones of their surroundings, also link the two panels and suggest symmetry between the mythic origin and the equally mythic future. Further complicating the resolution of the *Industrial Man* panels with the rest of the mural is the only worker whose face we can see. Reclining over a bookcase, reading a book, this solitary worker is clearly mestizo. This is Orozco's new America, in which the old and the new meet in a new race.

But by associating this figure with those in *Migration*, has Orozco implied the old idea of a latent Aztec identity, the kind of Indigenism he rebuked Rivera for prizing? The answer to this lies in another panel in

Figure 11. José Clemente Orozco, *Migration*, from *The Epic of American Civilization*, 1932–34, at the Baker Library, Dartmouth College. (Courtesy of the Hood Museum of Art, Dartmouth College; Commissioned by the Trustees of Dartmouth College; © 2014 Artists Rights Society [ARS] New York / SOMAAP, Mexico City)

the library, *Modern Migration of the Spirit.* The dramatic figure stands out from the rest of the panels with its explosively bright colors and provocative iconography. This Christ figure stands firmly in the foreground, axe in hand, having chopped himself down from the cross. In the background Western Antiquity lies in ruin amid a pile of scrapped guns. This is not precisely Christ, but it is an American avatar who has freed himself from the cross brought over by Cortez. This cross represents the same messianic narrative to which Quetzalcoatl was nailed by Sahagún, and by breaking the cross in this panel Orozco has also freed his representation of Quetzalcoatl from the teleological story that ends in subjugation.

In this image we return to the true hybrid nature of the Quetzal-coatl myth with a look to the future and a look to the past. Orozco has painted this man's skin in unreal yellows and reds, suggesting mixed heritage and the raw palette of the mestizo. If we look to his calves and feet, however, we find both the gray tones and the sinuous muscles from the first *Migration*. Orozco has linked all of these figures together, but not in a linear way. The migration of the soul has no predetermined direction, just as the original myth of Quetzalcoatl contained no reso-lution. Orozco's *Epic of American Civilization* takes up the myth in a wholly new way by constructing meaning through spatial relations. This is Quetzalcoatl's true return to a pre-Cortesian way of thinking, to a version of the myth that has not passed through the annals of the colo-nizer. Quetzalcoatl takes on entirely different ideological implications in Orozco. Salvaged from his role as the quiet martyr in Sahagún and the just legislator in Bolívar, Quetzalcoatl no longer reeks of the nostalgia of the oppressor but instead offers a triumphant mythology to the colo-nized subject.

In tracing these associations across the Reserve Room of Baker Library, I hope to suggest the potential in Orozco's mural for a decolo-nial vision of the hemisphere as well as a decolonial method for articu-lating that vision. In adapting the trope of Quetzalcoatl for the modern era, Orozco endeavors to think outside the binary opposition of Indigen-ism and Hispanism that has haunted Mexican history. This is partly a function of his geographic location, as he uses this site of North Ameri-can learning to challenge the dominant history of the hemisphere that has constructed the division between "developed" and "underdevel-oped" nations. In addition to offering a different history, though, *The Epic of American Civilization* also offers an alternative historiography, and Orozco's nonlinear meaning making can be understood as a chal-lenge to literary structures of knowledge. As we have seen in the work of Sahagún, the work of colonizing Mexico involved the partial pres-ervation of pre-Columbian culture, but only once these cultures were transcribed as a form of textual knowledge that the Spanish both pro-duced and controlled. This was the ideological revision Sahagún made to the Quetzalcoatl myth in its pre-Conquest state, transforming it from a loose association of stories into a master narrative of messianic return. This literary historiography is part of what Orozco challenges in pre-senting his visual epic.

It is the imposition of precisely this kind of Western thinking upon the colonial subject that Mignolo traces throughout *The Darker Side of the Renaissance.* Whereas the pre-Conquest civilization often recorded events visually, the Spanish scholar colonized by means of his alphabet. Mignolo illustrates this opposition most clearly with regard to the work of a Franciscan friar, Juan de Torquemada, who catalogued Mexica narratives thirty years after Sahagún. As Torquemada transformed these oral expressions of knowledge into written texts, he brought them within the organization of Western epistemology, as Mignolo explains:

> Torquemada was certainly bothered by what he perceived as erratic narrative and unstable meaning as opposed to a steady control of meaning through an alphabetically written narrative under the rule of historical writing. He was unable to make a distinction between the human need to record the past and the variety of forms the fulfillment of that need might take. It was hard for him, as for any Spanish man of letters, to understand that narratives recording the past could function independently, outside speech and its control by alphabetic writing; and that a visual language and spatial relations are perfectly understandable to those familiar with the pictorial conventions.[63]

By using visual language to create a vision of the New America, Orozco has sidestepped the ideology inherent in the linear narrative and its alphabet and constructed a Quetzalcoatl independent from colonial myth. While his work does not try to re-create pre-Columbian art forms, as some of Rivera's murals do, his *Epic of American Civilization* can be understood to reclaim the "visual language and spatial relations" of pre-Columbian knowledge.

In arguing that Orozco's Dartmouth mural challenges the logic of alphabetic writing, I do not mean to suggest that his work dismisses the value of literary knowledge. After all, his mestizo worker, the *Modern Industrial Man*, is seen reading a book. Instead we might think about Orozco's mural as antiliterary in its methodology. By creating spatial connections within the mural, beyond the linear left-to-right "reading," he provides an alternative understanding of the history of the Americas. Certainly there is a "STORY" about the Americas that we might construct, but all too often, Orozco suggests, that story is part of a master narrative aimed at validating the dominant ideology, be it colonialism, nationalism, or modern industrialism. Instead Orozco's *Epic* presents an "IDEA" about the Americas, one that resists categorization within disciplinary structures of knowledge and instead resides at the level of myth. It is by resisting the organization of the archive—from within the library itself—that Orozco is able to articulate an alternative vision of the hemisphere based on an alternative mythology.

Cuba, Race, and Modernity

3 Academic Discourse at Havana

Pan American Eugenics and Transnational Capital in Alejo Carpentier's *¡Écue-Yamba-Ó!*

With the appropriate application of Eugenics laws, we shall try to avoid improper unions between sick or vicious persons, who may generate children with pathological defects and who cannot develop their life in a satisfactory manner. We will insist that marriage parties bear the "vital capital" necessary for the adequate development of their children, with the object of avoiding the procreation of human beings who are biologically unfit, and therefore unfit for the enjoyment of a healthy and strong life.

—J. A. López del Valle, Cuban delegate to the First Pan American Conference on Eugenics and Homiculture of the American Republics, January 1927

Longina's belly grew day in and day out. The marriage prospered. The memory of the Central San Lucio was being lost in veils of fog. . . . The *ingenio* remained mute.

—Alejo Carpentier, *¡Écue-Yamba-Ó!*

WHEN IT WAS FIRST PUBLISHED in Madrid in 1933, *¡Écue-Yamba-Ó!* must have been an object of curiosity. As Roberto González Echevarría has imagined it, the few readers who came across this book were most likely puzzled by its indecipherable title (which in Afro-Cuban vernacular would translate to *Praised Be the Lord!*) and by its virtually unknown author, who, until then, had authored only music reviews and a few poems.[1] The novel is devoted, as the subtitle promises, to an Afro-Cuban story about Menegildo Cué, who grows up in rural Cuba and, after committing a murder that lands him in a Havana jail, is initiated into the city's strange criminal underworld. The novel's main characters speak a mix of underworld cant and vernacular Spanish, the text exchanging *r*'s for *l*'s and eliding whole syllables. There is an accompanying glossary to guide the reader through this cant, and interspersed amid this strange text are illustrations of black dancers and photographs of orishas and animist deities. At first glance the book might have seemed to early readers a study in anthropology rather than a novel.

If it confounded readers of its time, the novel has met with a similar reception among critics. While much attention has been paid to Carpentier's later novels, most scholars have excluded *Écue* from the larger conversation surrounding his work.[2] Moreover nearly eighty years after its publication it has yet to be translated into English.[3] The few critics who have examined the novel in detail have read it very much in the context of its European publication in 1933 and argued for understanding it as a surrealist work.[4] In this reading, though, Carpentier's focus on Afro-Cuban and Haitian workers, their labor in Cuba's sugar plantations, and their incarceration is subsumed under a broad surrealist fascination with the "primitive," and the original context of the setting is largely lost.

The text of *¡Écue-Yamba-Ó!* ends with two sets of dates framing the composition: "*First version*: Havana Prison, August 1–9, 1927 / *Definitive Version*: Paris, January–August, 1933." In order to understand the novel's complexity, we need to attend not only to the context of 1933 Paris but also to that of 1927 Havana. Therefore I situate the novel within that historical framework, for several important reasons. First, it should be remembered that Carpentier composed the first draft of the novel while in Havana's Prado Jail serving time for signing a manifesto opposing the dictatorship of Gerardo Machado, whose close ties with the U.S. government and with U.S. business facilitated the labor conditions that Menegildo and the other characters of *Écue* face on the sugar plantations. Second, the Afro-Cuban prisoners with whom Carpentier shared his cell provided him with the source material for his novel, making his investment in the characters less abstract than the "primitivist" reading of the novel might suggest.[5] Third, I situate Carpentier's novel in 1927 because in that year Havana played host to the First Pan American Conference on Eugenics. This conference demonstrated the efforts of U.S. scientists to export biologically defined conceptions of race to Latin America and the Caribbean and to prevent supposedly undesirable individuals from reproducing. At key points in his novel Carpentier directly engages the eugenicist discourse and correctly identifies it as an extension of the U.S. Empire and the Pan American project to know and contain the Americas. Ultimately reproduction plays a crucial role in the novel since it simultaneously defies the eugenicist codes and, as the epigraph demonstrates, it is the only event that can mute the hum of the U.S.-owned sugar mill (the *ingenio*). While delegates from eighteen American nations met in Havana to parse the distinctions of racial "vitality" and "degeneracy," Carpentier was nearby, in the Prado Jail, alongside such supposed degenerates. Reading the novel within this context reveals how Carpentier reformulates the prison as an alternative archive from which to understand transnational relations.

The "Landscape" of Havana: Afro-Cubans, Sugar, and Transnational Capitalism

The plot of the novel is fairly simple, following the life of Menegildo Cué from birth to death. His childhood in the cane fields of rural Cuba is intended to show the "typical" life of black Cubans, defined by physical labor and traditional African culture. Along the way he passes through a series of initiations. In the "Infancy" section of the novel, Menegildo is introduced to his family's animist deities (which, significantly, he knocks over and breaks). "Adolescence" brings his sexual initiation when he meets Longina, a Haitian immigrant who labors at a nearby cane field. They eventually conceive a child, but things become complicated when Longina's common-law husband, Napolión, assaults Menegildo. In retaliation Menegildo murders him and is sent to Havana's Prado Jail, where his final initiation into the criminal underworld of the *ñáñingo* takes place. It is in this final section, titled "City," that Menegildo's story moves into decline, his criminal activities leading to his eventual death at the hands of a rival gang.

Rather than a conventional story of development *¡Écue-Yamba-Ó!* presents the story of Menegildo's underdevelopment. More precisely, the plot marks his path toward delinquency, a key term among criminologists of the time. While these scientists set out to identify the biological reasons that would explain why so many black Cubans were in prison, Carpentier's narrative offers an alternative explanation, one that looks to the social and political conditions of 1927 Cuba in order to understand Menegildo's "delinquency."

In his 1977 preface to the novel Carpentier describes how the characters grew out of his childhood acquaintances, who "learned to welcome me, the white boy whose father, to the scandal of our family friends, 'let him play with blacks.'" He claims to have found in "their misery in the *bohío* [shanty]" a "dignity" worthy of celebrating in his novel, but more important to his political purposes in *Écue*, the blacks of his childhood possessed "ancestral beliefs and practices that signified, in reality, a resistance against the dissipating powers of external factors."[6] Although Carpentier presents himself as a transgressor of Cuba's racial hierarchy and an advocate for Afro-Cuban culture, this preface also reveals his ethnographic approach to the island's black population. In these "ancestral beliefs" there was supposedly a more authentic version of humanity, an idea that has a long history in European thought and which Carpentier reencountered in the early 1930s through French surrealism. In *Los paso perdidos* (1953) he satirizes this fascination with the primitive even as the novel reinforces many of the same ideas about the "noble savage." Similarly *¡Écue-Yamba-Ó!* pulls in two directions, promoting the "dignity" of Afro-Cubans while presenting one-dimensional Afro-Cuban characters whose admirable qualities stem from their simplicity.

Of the complexities of representation in *Écue* and similar novels of the time, Paul Miller observes, "These ethnographic novels, with their frenetic activity of gathering information, 'mastering' it, ordering and organizing it to produce a final written account, tended to reproduce in microcosmic form the entire colonial enterprise the writers wished to decry."[7] Even though its portrayal of Afro-Cubans is conflicted, *Écue* is at its core a novel of "resistance," as Carpentier describes it in his preface. This is nominally the resistance of the black laboring class against the repression of Cuban law and medical science, but these characters are ultimately symbols for the larger anti-imperial argument Carpentier wants to make in the novel.

More than just an anthropological fascination, then, the novel's immersion in the details of Afro-Cuban religious practices reflects Carpentier's desire to offer an alternative reading of the transnational forces corrupting Cuba: the sugar industry, U.S. support of the Machado dictatorship, Pan American eugenics, and immigration policies. These "external factors" constructed the Afro-Cubans of Carpentier's childhood as degenerate and criminal, but they had also recolonized the Cuban economy. So in *¡Écue-Yamba-Ó!* he attempts to understand both issues as part of the same global system, and he assumes the Afro-Cuban subject position as the material evidence of this system's domination of Cuba. I explore the novel within this national context, particularly the pathologized and criminalized view the Cuban society had of its black population, but it is crucial also to understand the Pan American forces that shape the lives of Carpentier's Afro-Cuban culture. All of the external factors that he rails against are there from the beginning of the novel.

Carpentier makes clear at the outset that the machine of capitalism, symbolized by the rhythmic churnings of the local *ingenio*, is the dehumanizing force that dictates the rhythms of life and drives Menegildo, and the novel, into Havana's underworld. As the novel opens, the first image that Carpentier offers the reader is the *ingenio*, as Menegildo's father, Usebio Cué, watches it rise with a creeping force of inevitability to dominate the landscape: "Angular, with simple lines like the figure of a theorem, the block of the Central San Lucio rose in the center of a wide valley bordered by a crest of blue hills. Old Usebio Cué had seen the fungus of steel, plaster and concrete grow over the ruins of the ancient sugar mills, attending year after year, in the manner of an admiring ghost, to the conquest of space achieved by industry" (15). As part of one of the novel's several chapters titled "Landscape" ("Paisaje"), these first sentences do far more than establish a pastoral setting. Carpentier first uses the vocabulary of geometry to describe the sugar mill, as if it were an abstraction, as intangible as a "theorem." In the next sentence, though, the Central takes on the organic properties of a "fungus," feeding on dead tissue and growing rapidly and inevitably over the valley's decaying sugar mills. This brief chapter recounts the story of how Usebio, before Menegildo's birth, came to lose the land that had been in the Cué family for generations. Once the foreign-owned *ingenio*, the San Lucio, moved in, it began to buy up land from the local peasants for somewhat large sums, the result of the high value of sugar during World War I, when U.S. trade options were limited, a period known in Cuba as the "Dance of Millions." Usebio, however, waited too long to sell his land. The sugar market crashed and his land was worth half of what it had been, but by then the San Lucio had achieved a monopoly in the region and it was Usebio's only option. Ultimately the Cués end up working the same sugar fields they always have, but now they do so as tenant farmers on land owned by a foreign company. Thus, in a few pages, Carpentier conveys the "conquest achieved by industry" (15).[8]

Even though the novel will move away from the cane field, all of Carpentier's themes, from his celebration of local Afro-Cuban culture to his critique of the Cuban state and transnational capital, pass through the mill in this chapter. We see the conflation of all these issues within the *ingenio*, as the machine rips indigenous materials from the ground and whitens them for export: "The locomotive pulls out millions of sacks full of red crystals that still know the earth, hooves and bad words. The foreign refinery will return them pale, lifeless, after their journey over discolored seas. From the doctrine of the sun, to the doctrine of the manometer" (16). In this scene the land and its materials are the literal objects of conquest, but it is important to note the shift in knowledge formation that Carpentier implies. Along with the raw sugar, the "bad words" muttered by the workers as they bring in the harvest are also consumed by the *ingenio*, effectively silencing their complaints and extinguishing their language. By indicating a shift in "doctrine," from traditional agricultural life to the scientific pressure gauges of the Central's machines, Carpentier emphasizes the extent to which the growth of industry depends on a reorganization of knowledge and, as we shall see throughout the novel, an insistence on measurement.

Once the language of the workers has been processed, we are left with the "lifeless" language of capital. As Usebio and the other workers throw their crops into the refinery's oven, they encounter a burning bush of capitalism: "But the cut made, the fiber breaks under the arc of the steelyard. The fire speaks: 'For each hundred *arrobas* of cane that the sugar planter delivers to the Company, he will receive the equivalent in official money of X *arrobas* of refined sugar, polarization 96 degrees, according to the fortnightly average corresponding to the fortnight in which the cane for sale was milled'" (15–16). The language itself transforms the "doctrine of the sun" by which the Cués have lived into an economic system of weights and measures whereby the value of labor is calculated according to the market price of sugar. If the *ingenio* produces only what is "pale" and "lifeless," it is in black culture that the novel locates all that is vital. This vernacular culture is therefore the site of resistance to transnational capital. As Carpentier phrases it at one of the novel's anti-imperialist high points, "The bongo [is the] antidote to Wall Street!" (118). Carpentier's use of Afro-Cuban culture is at times problematic as he formulates his characters as *gente de la tierra* (people of the land) in a way that can make them one-dimensional. But behind the superficial white/black dichotomy there lies a much more complicated tension between the rise of "global" systems of thought and the more "local" kinds of knowledge that Carpentier locates in the Cué family.[9]

Perhaps the most obvious sign that Cuba's population was subject to transnational forces was the way U.S. business interests were protected by the dictatorship of Gerardo Machado. Having been elected to the presidency in 1925, Machado then altered the Constitution to extend his term, from four years to six, and then suspended the following election and appointed himself to a new term, which would have kept him in office until 1935.[10] His regime was eventually toppled by the revolution in 1933 (the same year that *¡Écue-Yamba-Ó!* was published in Madrid), but in 1927 Machado was at the height of his power. Any opposition to the government was quickly suppressed. So when Carpentier, along with other artists, signed the Minorista Manifesto, demanding, among other things, free elections, he was quickly arrested and imprisoned. The manifesto, released in May 1927, declared that the members were working

For the revision of false and tired values

For vernacular art and, in general, for new art in its diverse manifestations

For the introduction and popularization in Cuba of the latest artistic and scientific doctrines, theories, and practices

For reform in the public education system ... and autonomy for universities

For the economic independence of Cuba and against Yankee imperialism

Against political dictatorship in the world, America, and Cuba

Against the excesses of our pseudodemocracy, the falsity of our suffrage, and for the effective participation of the people in government.

For the betterment of the Cuban farmer and worker

For Latin American cordiality and union.[11]

The manifesto makes it quite clear that its members were engaged in a politicized vanguard, and in *¡Écue-Yamba-Ó!* there is little doubt that Carpentier's intentions are political. What the Minorista Manifesto also demonstrates, though, is the interconnection between "vernacular art," "artistic and scientific doctrines," and the forces of transnational capitalism driven by "Yankee imperialism." While those in power—Machado and his U.S. backers—manipulated this interconnection between science and capital to measure and contain the population, Carpentier co-opts this same system in order to critique it from below. One of his goals in the novel is to offer an alternative vision of how a hemispheric community might function, how immigrants of all nationalities might recognize their common cause. The recognition is as yet unattainable, however, since, as the Minorista Manifesto stresses, Cuban workers still live at the mercy of the world's oligarchs.

As Carpentier introduces the world of Cuban agriculture in the opening "Landscape" chapter, it is clear that the same political and economic forces that artists were protesting against in Havana also shape the daily lives of those workers in the countryside. Continuing the novel's anthropomorphism, he describes the sugar mill itself as imposing a "tyrannical dictatorship" on the local workers. Carpentier goes on to describe the power that the San Lucio held over workers: "The heartbeats of their pistons—breathless pistons, forged in lands smelling of Christmas trees—were able to change at a whim the rhythm of the lives of men, beasts and plants, imprinting on them frenetic trepidations or at times immobilizing them in cruel fashion" (16). Carpentier sees the obvious intersection of the sugar industry and Machado's power over the island as the *ingenio* metonymically stands in for the dictator himself. The "rhythms" of mechanized labor and the surveillance of Machado's police work in tandem to discipline the population within the confines of transnational capitalism. Indeed the sugar that the Cués produce sustains the very system that keeps them tied to land they no longer own. It is clear by the end of the chapter that "the *ingenio* is the law!" (21).

Along with the influx of capital to the island, the sugar industry also brought waves of new immigrants to Cuba in order to meet the demands of production. The population was consequently transformed by this importation of labor, and indeed Carpentier peoples his "landscape" with a variety of immigrant workers. He emphasizes the global nature of the phenomenon that leads workers, scientists, and investors to converge on Cuba and reap its sugar: "Then the invasion began. Throngs of workers. American foremen chewing tobacco. The French chemist who cursed the inn's cook every day. The Italian weigher, who ate chilis with bread and oil" (18). Throughout the novel there are similarly transnational scenes as Carpentier juxtaposes his exaltation of local folk culture with more global influences on Cuban culture. In this passage each immigrant is characterized by his country of origin, and the military language of "invasion" and "throngs" (*tropeles*) reinforces the status of the nation-state as the primary marker of identity. In actuality most immigrants to Cuba during this period were workers from nearby islands, and so the novel's streets are also filled with "asthmatic accordions" from Haiti and African rhythms of Kingston as more and more immigrants flow into the region in anticipation of the harvest (18). But in the novel, as in reality, these immigrants meet with resentment and racial hatred in their new homeland.

After the catalogue of immigrants from the United States and Europe, the tone shifts to the language of contagion to describe the Haitian and Jamaican immigrants. These workers are ordered in by "el Tiburón" (the Shark), the country's nickname for President José Miguel Gómez (1909–13), in order to meet the demand for labor: "And later, the new plague consented to by the Shark's decree two years before: squadrons of ragged Haitians, who surged over the distant horizon bringing a black mercenary captain with a palm leaf hat and a machete in his belt" (18). The image of troops invading from Haiti certainly strikes the revolutionary tone that we find in the Minorista Manifesto. But it also evokes the Haitian Revolution of the eighteenth century and hints at themes Carpentier would later develop in *El reino de este mundo* (1949), in which Haiti's Creole gentry flee to the safety of Cuba but anxiously look over their shoulders for the next revolt. These immigrants at once portend revolution and disease. It is tempting to read this "plague" as the sole result of Cuban racism and anti-immigrant sentiment. Indeed the Afro-Cuban characters in *Écue* freely refer to the Haitians as "inferior blacks," and much of the action revolves around Menegildo's forbidden union with a Haitian woman. But even in this opening chapter Carpentier wants to make clear the transnational forces at work. He locates the source of the perceived plague not in the immigrants but instead in the sugar industry that has made their migration necessary. The *ingenio* consumes both sugar and human labor despite the harm this does to the body politic. Carpentier suggests that the illness ultimately lies in transnational capitalism when, at the end of the long description of immigrants, he collectively refers to them as "those who will enter daily into the belly of the diabetic giant" (19). While Cuba had become entirely centered on sugar production, its "body" was incapable of metabolizing the consequences that came with that industry.

This language of plague and disease tapped into the global immigration debates of the 1920s, which were largely targeted at excluding immigrants from East Asian countries. Carpentier includes in his landscape an odd assortment of Chinese immigrants, including "Asian horticulturists" who "knelt in the garden making fortune teller's gestures" and "Chinese storekeepers" who made millions of dollars, only to send them to "Sung-Sing-Lung," the "alimentary cacique of the capital's yellow neighborhood" (18–19). These allusions to the criminal underworld reflect the way Chinese immigrants were perceived in the popular imagination. Such immigrants pose a threat to the economic system because they create networks of exchange outside the authorized channels. But this economic threat, as Carpentier makes clear, was framed as a genetic threat so that this imminent "yellow peril" was the driving force behind new immigration policies throughout the Americas.

In the United States eugenics research and nativist fears had led to the Immigration Act of 1924, which set quotas for immigration in an attempt to keep the balance of national origins equal to that of the 1890 Census. Although the act was aimed at Chinese and Eastern European immigrants, it was very much on the minds of intellectuals and policymakers in Latin America and the Caribbean. At the Pan American eugenics conference in 1927 they were under pressure from the United States to enforce similar restrictions or else have the migration of their own citizens into the United States similarly limited. Most countries needed little persuasion. Cuba, for instance, reacted with hostility to its Chinese immigrants, criminalizing and demonizing them almost to the extent it did its black population. In approaching Carpentier's novel it is important to understand the circulation of immigrants, and the circulation of these immigration laws, within the transnational framework of the Americas.

In the same way that Carpentier constructs the immigrants in his novel as a "plague" while demonstrating that they were necessary to the health of the Cuban state, the immigration codes adopted by the Cuban government as a result of U.S. influence simultaneously pathologized and criminalized the very workers who made the material wealth of both nations possible. This contradiction is evidence of the shift in transnational capitalism, whereby global systems allowed money and goods (such as Cuban sugar) to flow freely across borders while national identity was firmly inscribed upon individual workers in order to better police and contain them. Foucault has described this historical transition from a world in which states conquer and control territory to one in which states control populations, a formulation that is clearly applicable to the Americas in the early twentieth century. He describes

> the emergence of a completely different problem that is no longer that of fixing and demarcating the territory, but of allowing circulations to take place, of controlling them, sifting the good and the bad, ensuring that things are always in movement, constantly moving around, continually going from one point to another, but in such a way that the inherent dangers of this circulation are canceled out. No longer the safety (*sûreté*) of the Prince and his territory, but the security (*sécurité*) of the population and, consequently, of those who govern it.[12]

As this system took hold in the Americas, it was less crucial that the United States lay claim to territory than it was to control the terms by which capital and people were allowed to circulate. We might turn to several thinkers, such as Immanuel Wallerstein or Mignolo, to understand this global system, but Foucault's formulation is especially helpful because of his emphasis on control, on "sifting the good and the bad," since these were precisely the terms that were employed in the contemporary immigration debate. U.S. laws were increasingly informed by biological criteria, as made evident by the Immigration Act of 1924, and North American scientists were eager to proliferate these fundamentally eugenicist immigration polices throughout the Americas. The proposed code debated at the First Pan American Conference on Eugenics would have categorized the populations of all participating nations into groups of "good," "bad," and "doubtful" and barred all but the genetically fit from migrating throughout the hemisphere.

The eugenics movement is but one part of the larger Pan American effort to reorganize knowledge systems within Latin America. This is a vision of the hemisphere in which North American conceptions of race would proliferate, and the United States would regulate all borders, using complicit nations like Cuba to construct biological buffer zones against nonwhite immigration. But this plan was predicated on medical science and the notion that eugenicists across the Americas might cooperate to achieve this goal. Before turning to the proceedings of the eugenics conference and anthropometric calipers that would find their way into Carpentier's novel, it's necessary to first explore the other academic discourses at work in Havana in 1927. Just as the *ingenio* in *¡Écue-Yamba-Ó!* initiates the "doctrine of the monometer," so too did the discipline of anthropology insist on "measuring" the populations of the Americas.

Archives of Folklore: Knowledge Production in Machado's Cuba

In order to think about the multiple Pan American forces at work in the novel, let us consider two conferences of the Pan American Union held in Havana less than a month apart: the Sixth International Conference of American States, held from January 16 to February 20, 1928, and the eugenics conference, held from December 21 to 23, 1927. The Conference of American States was a grand affair, attended by heads of state, diplomats, and celebrities from twenty-one nations, including U.S. president Calvin Coolidge and Charles Lindbergh, who received the Order of Merit as well as the key to the city of Havana, both presented to him in person by President Machado himself.

Carpentier was certainly aware of and deeply influenced by the Conference of American States. The impending arrival of dignitaries and heads of state had, after all, been part of the reason that Machado cracked down on dissidents and arrested Carpentier and others. If he had been critical of Yankee imperialism before, as the Minorista Manifesto certainly shows, then his incarceration followed by the fawning welcome that the United States received at the conference would have done nothing but bolster Carpentier's resentment of Yankee influence. Thus *¡Écue-Yamba-Ó!* champions Afro-Cuban culture in large part as a counterpoint to the ever-encroaching U.S. culture on the island. In the chapter entitled "Política," Carpentier lays bare the symbolic weight that the novel's black characters are intended to carry. They, the "low-cost laborers," are lost in a world of Yankee cultural imperialism. Not only does the *ingenio* make the country's economy beholden to foreigners, but the Cués must also turn to import food for their sustenance. Rather than grow their own food (on land they no longer own) they are forced to "harvest" the grocery shelves: "They ate—when they ate—what could be harvested from the horizontal rows that spread within the walls of the bodega: sardines fished in Newfoundland, apricots locked in cans with the name of a romantic novel" (117–18). The tragedy of imperialism becomes, at the Cués' grocery store, a farce of consumer goods: "The Creole country folk still produced images of foreign fruit, now maturing in ads for soft drinks! *Orange Crush* was a tool of imperialism, like the memory of Roosevelt and the Lindbergh plane . . . ! Only the blacks, Menegildo, Longina, Salomé and their offspring jealously preserved an Antillean character and tradition. The bongo, antidote to Wall Street! The Holy Spirit, venerated by the Cués, did not allow Yankee sausages within their votive buns . . . ! None of these 'hot-dogs' with the saints of Mayeya!" (118). Exclamatory passages like this one, in which Afro-Cuban culture (the bongo) is to oppose the economic forces at work on the island (Wall Street), leave little doubt about Carpentier's attitude toward the Yankee. The passage also lashes out against Roosevelt, whose Rough Riders were still a "memory" in Cuba, and Lindbergh, who had just completed his tour of Latin America and the Caribbean in *The Spirit of St. Louis* (which he documented in reports to the *New York Times*) before arriving in Havana in time for the 1928 conference. Against these "tools of imperialism" Carpentier positions his black characters, who turn away from Yankee materialism and protect their own culture. It is interesting that Carpentier does not simply substitute indigenous products for imported ones, countering the hot dogs with more traditional foods, for instance. His answer is religious: the characters take a stand by refusing to offer the hot dogs to their gods. Therefore the function of Afro-Cuban religion in the novel is to offer an alternative, if compromised, way of life to the logic of capitalism. It provides the black characters with a way of understanding themselves in relation to the world and a means of being reborn into a life that has not consigned them exclusively to the role of laborers.

Rebirth, however, was also a policy of the Cuban state. Machado's campaign of national regeneration, as he called it, required Afro-Cuban laborers to complete numerous public works projects during his rule, including the seven-hundred-mile central highway that was Cuba's main thoroughfare and an exact replica of the U.S. Capitol in the middle of Havana, both of which were celebrated in the pages of the *Bulletin of the Pan American Union*.[13] The Machado administration also took a great interest in promoting scientific development in tandem with the island's material development. Alejandra Bronfman has explored in great detail the relationship between science and the Cuban state during this period. To demonstrate Machado's investment in intellectual projects, she quotes one of his speeches: "We must stimulate literary and scientific production. . . . Since we have received so much knowledge from the rest of the world, we must participate and reciprocate with our own contributions."[14] These contributions centered on the anthropological study of Afro-Cuban folk culture, which flourished during the 1920s, as an effort to "salvage" Cuba's heritage and bring it into the fold of modernity. However, Bronfman argues, the initial goal of incorporating black Cubans into the "regenerated" nation as full citizens was eventually replaced by the goal of controlling and containing this population through the social sciences, namely criminology and eugenics.[15]

Perhaps the work of Fernando Ortiz is the best illustration of how these social projects of salvage and control could work in tandem. In 1923 Ortiz founded the journal *Archivos del Folklore Cubano*, an intellectual enterprise approved by the state, which had the declared goal of becoming "an organ for the collaboration and exchange of new ideas between those in Cuba who like to scrutinize the past, to savor the fruits of popular knowledge and to survey the soul of our people."[16] *Archivos* was a complicated mix of academic research and literary work. It featured detailed anthropological studies of Afro-Cuban cultural practices, from music to ceremonial teeth filing, as well as philological studies of vernacular, the *r/l* distinction (which Carpentier's characters switch) being of particular interest. On the other hand, *Archivos* also reprinted Nicolás Guillén's important poem *Motivos del son*, though it added glosses by Ortiz in order to explain Guillén's use of the vernacular.[17] But it is Ortiz's own early work that demonstrates the slide toward criminalizing and pathologizing Afro-Cuban culture. In 1926 *Archivos* began the serial publication of Ortiz's *Los negros curros*, which was described as a "study in criminal ethnography" and which extended his investigation of black criminality that began in his 1906 book, *Hampa afrocubana: Los negros brujo*. This fascination with the "Afro-Cuban underworld" is an aspect of Ortiz's work that is often forgotten. In the context of U.S. American studies, he is best known for his later work introducing the concept of transculturation, which Mary Louise Pratt has extended.[18] In Cuban scholarship Ortiz's legacy is also centered on his later work, which celebrated Afro-Cuban culture and promoted the work of artists like Wifredo Lam. However, in the 1920s Ortiz was predominantly known for his work as a criminologist.

It is important to recall these early works if we hope to grasp fully the cultural setting of *¡Écue-Yamba-Ó!* and understand the complex intersection of science, prisons, and politics that Carpentier was engaging. The intense study of Afro-Cubans during this period, even when their culture was claimed as part of a regenerative nationalist project, was at base interested in correctly identifying and containing the variety of "delinquents" brought before the scientists' inspection. The ornate fashions that Ortiz describes in *Los negros brujos* are fascinating in and of themselves, but the value of such studies lies in the ability to decode such costumes and correctly identify markers of the underworld's hierarchy. Likewise philological studies, such as Ortiz's *Glosario de afronegrismos* (1924), were aimed at deciphering the cant of criminal organization, thereby facilitating their detection and incarceration. All of these studies were manifestations of the positivist approach that Ortiz adopted from Italian criminologists of the time, most notably Cesar Lombroso, who wrote a preface for *Los negros brujos*. Lombroso's notorious emphasis on anthropometrics and studies of physiognomy helped to shift criminology in the early twentieth century from the study of the *crime* to the study of the *criminal*, who was biologically predetermined toward deviance. Ortiz's early works represent just this kind of anthropological criminology, offering photographs, in profile and head-on, of the *brujos* under examination and illuminating the telltale signs of black "delinquency."

Carpentier was obviously aware of such studies of Afro-Cuban culture. He made use of this archive of material in writing *¡Écue-Yamba-Ó!*, and the illustrations in the novel made no secret of the author's efforts to engage and challenge the work of criminal anthropologists. It is in response to works like Ortiz's *Glosario de afronegrismos* that Carpentier provides his own glossary to the novel. In Carpentier's entry for *ñáñingo* he makes clear that he is engaging with the academic studies on this underworld association, but he also offers a corrective to these studies that attempts to understand the *ñáñingos* apart from their association with criminality. He defines them thus:

> Secret associations of mutual protection, brought to Cuba by black slaves, and which still survive, though transformed, in some of the island's populations. . . . It has been said erroneously that the *ñáñingos* practice witchcraft, and

they have even been implicated in the perpetration of human sacrifices. But if one becomes better acquainted with them and can detach oneself from these magical practices, then sorcery, properly speaking, does not form part of the ritual. In their meetings, the *ñáñigos* observe a picturesque and complicated ceremony, which includes songs, dances and percussions of great beauty. (203–4)

Focusing on the "picturesque and complicated" elements of the music and dances, Carpentier reveals his aesthetic investment in the *ñáñingo* rituals. In order to write about them, though, he must have inevitably made use of the academic studies that criminalized Afro-Cuban culture, even as he was trying to write a corrective to those studies. The novel itself shows Carpentier coming to terms with this archive, which had informed his own understanding of Afro-Cuban culture but which, seen from the inside of a jail cell filled with practitioners of this "picturesque" culture, must have looked horribly flawed. Rather than abandon the work of criminal anthropologists, though, Carpentier met it head-on. Through the material appearance of the book, such as the glossary and the illustrations, he makes direct reference to this body of knowledge, with the ultimate goal of repurposing it to his own ends.

Anke Birkenmaier has presented the most extended analysis of the illustrations in Carpentier's novel. "The photographs included in *¡Écue-Yamba-Ó!*," she remarks, "exhibit surrealist traits that are difficult to overlook," which she ascribes to the "general impression of the strangeness of the photos."[19] The objects photographed, including collections of drums and small *ñáñingo* figurines, in part reflect the surrealist fascination with the primitive, which Carpentier encountered in Paris. However, these are not random objects of exotica but are instead woven into the story of the novel, with short phrases from elsewhere in the text serving as captions. While this may suggest that the photos simply illustrate the novel, the relationship between text and image is not so straightforward. Of this relationship Birkenmaier observes, "In the case of Carpentier, it is almost as if there were a division of perspective between text and images, in the sense that the text explains the divine African names of some Christian statues and thus makes 'visible' the African culture, but the photos remain enigmatic and keep its secret."[20] This notion of the photos keeping the secrets of Afro-Cuban culture is compelling, especially since many of the cultural practices they reflect were illegal at the time and under the close scrutiny of the Cuban state. While the illustrations in *Écue* reflect the influence of European surrealism, the silence and the strangeness of the material book can perhaps be best understood as part of a dialogue with Cuban anthropologists.

The kinds of illustrations that appeared in *Los negros brujos* and *Archivos del Folklore Cubano* are closely mirrored in Carpentier's novel. For instance, Ortiz's illustration of the Afro-Cubans during slavery celebrating El día de Reyes is matched by Carpentier's version. Carpentier also captions these illustrations with excerpts from his own text, in this case adding, "But the blacks of the country ignored the splendor of the Celebration of Kings, which was only celebrated in a dignified manner in the city" (92). By creating this tight interconnection between illustration and text, he furthers the illusion that *¡Écue-Yamba-Ó!* is a work of anthropology. In this case his text seems to follow the same analytical line as Ortiz did, creating a link between the legacy of slavery and the practices of modern Afro-Cubans. It is in the book's photographs, however, that *Écue* departs from the anthropologists. Again the subject matter is strikingly similar, but the medium serves as a reminder of the criminological roots of such academic studies.

These photos allude to the forensic practices of Cuban anthropologists and the source of their material evidence—objects that police had seized during arrest. The photos that Carpentier includes in *¡Écue-Yamba-Ó!* are closer to those that Cuban police would take as evidence than any image the criminal anthropologists would care to include in their works. Ortiz's claims about the intimate objects of Afro-Cuban life are supported by a sanitized line drawing of an altar scene from the home of a *brujo*, whereas Carpentier includes photographs of similar objects and captions them with explanatory material that echoes the fascination of the criminal anthropologists (fig. 12). His presentation of these objects in photographs is ultimately a satirical gesture aimed at exposing the true sources of these "scientific" studies. Photographs do appear in Ortiz's book, but only in the form of booking photos of black men. The objects of supposed *brujería* are represented in more benign, academic drawings that attempt to conceal their origins and present them as objects suited for the museum rather than the police station. On the other hand, the orishas in Carpentier's photo seem to form their own police lineup, parodying the study of Afro-Cuban men and women and emphasizing that the source of these objects was the criminal justice system.

In his studies of the criminalization of Afro-Cubans, Stephan Palmié argues that when police and anthropologists approached these "ill-understood heaps of de-contextualized objects," the goal "was not to understand their meaning, but to create evidence of something which had no meaning."[21] We can see further evidence of this process in some

Figure 12. Photograph from Alejo Carpentier's *¡Écue-Yamba-Ó! Novela afrocubana* (Madrid: Editorial España, 1933). The captions reads, "Babayú-Ayé, Yemayá y Obatalá (este último, dios andrógino, aparece aquí en su representación femenina) [Babayú-Ayé, Yemayá and Obatalá (this last one, an androgynous god, appears here in its feminine representation)]."

of the illustrations in *Archivos*, especially in articles by Israel Castellanos, who, as the director of the Laboratory of Penitentiary Anthropology, had direct access to confiscated material. In an article on the *diablito* (a figure in the *ñáñigo* hierarchy) Castellanos included an illustration of a *diablito* costume and noted in the caption, "Model extant in the Criminological Museum of the University of Havana's Academy of Medicine" (fig. 13). In *Écue* Carpentier includes his own *diablito*, a doll photographed by the police as though it too is being booked and

Figure 13. Illustration from Israel
Castellanos's "El 'diablito' ñáñingo" in
Archivos del Folklore Cubano (1925).
The caption reads, "Traje de diablito
hecho de cotí, a rayas transversales de
diversos colores y adornado con fibras
vegetales [Diablito suit made of ticking,
striped horizontally with diverse colors
and decorated with plant fibers]. (Modelo
existente en el Museo Criminológico de
la Cátedra de Medicina Legal de la Universidad de la Habana.)"

jailed (fig. 14). So while the material construction of *¡Écue-Yamba-Ó!*
placed it in conversation with the academic studies of Afro-Cuban culture of the time, Carpentier consistently undercuts that work by insisting on the inseparable nature of anthropology and criminology in Cuba.
By emphasizing the prison as the original archive for these academic

Figure 14. Photograph from Alejo Carpentier's *¡Écue-*
-Yamba-Ó! Novela afrocubana (Madrid: Editorial
España, 1933). The caption reads, "El Diablito se
adelantó, saltando de lado . . . [The Diablito moved
forward, jumping from side to side . . .]."

studies, he offers an alternative anthropology of Cuba culture, one that
assumes the perspective of the incarcerated and scrutinizes the rest of
society from behind bars.

From the Measure of Industry to the Measure of Science: Inside Havana's Jail

Perhaps the most frequently overlooked of Ortiz's works was the one
most fully embraced by Machado's government: the *Proyecto de código
criminal cubano*, which Ortiz published in 1926. After years of studying

Cuba's criminals and documenting their distinctive traits, this book-length plan for reforming the prison system was the ultimate application of all Ortiz's theories about criminology. It laid out in detail how various criminals should be punished based on their mental status and "responsibility"; it defined the conditions of the new "modern" prisons; and, most important, the *Proyecto* introduced the idea of the "delinquent" into the lexicon of Cuban criminal justice. Ortiz writes that "delinquents" are "dangerous persons" who "show by their external conduct, notoriously contrary to the good customs or laws of public security, a state of extraordinary mental, moral, or legal maladjustment that has created in them a proclivity toward delinquency and social fear."[22] Again, this "maladjustment" is located entirely within the individual under scrutiny, precluding any discussion of how the "good customs" of Machado's Cuba and its reliance on foreign capital might have produced and even necessitated delinquency.

In her essay on the *Proyecto* and its place within Ortiz's larger body of work, Bronfman points out that the book received wide recognition and was endorsed by Machado's government.[23] Ortiz distributed his book to fellow scholars and to newspaper editors, both in Cuba and abroad, who published favorable reviews. Thus, according to Bronfman, "the *Proyecto* was widely publicized, and generated a variety of responses."[24] She quotes from a glowing letter that makes clear the extent to which Ortiz's views represented the mainstream of criminology as well as the "regenerative" aims of the state: "General Gerardo Machado y Morales, like you suffers the most intense, incurable, and beneficial fever in favor of the advancement, morality, and progress of the Republic. . . . Your Penal Code will be from now on in Cuba THE CODE OF MACHADO!!"[25] The fascinating medical language of this letter, in which Ortiz and Machado share the same reformist disease, demonstrates how prevalent this biological rhetoric actually was among Cuban intellectuals. Everyone, from the dictator to the prisoner, was to have his symptoms diagnosed.

As a consequence of Ortiz's *Proyecto*, Cuban prisons refocused their attention on the external criteria of the criminal. This positivist methodology was finally realized all across the island when Ortiz's recommendation for an "anthropological exam" was implemented in all of Cuba's prisons. He states in the *Proyecto*, "Each inmate will be submitted to an anthropological exam according to the conditions established in the Criminal Ordinances."[26] Behind this discrete sentence lies an entire system for measuring and studying the Afro-Cuban. Its simplicity conceals the countless scenes of horror and humiliation involved in conducting such exams.

It is at the site of criminal examination that Alejo Carpentier most directly engages the academic discourse of his day and critiques the system that has reduced his characters to objects of study. In his version of the "exam," Carpentier offers us the humanizing details of these scientific practices. At the climax of *¡Écue-Yamba-Ó!*, Menegildo has been arrested for murder and brought to the city, where he finds himself in the Prado jail. By way of being processed into the carceral system, "he was subjected to an anthropometric exam. Each scar, each sore on his body was located without delay. His description, in feet and inches, cranial capacity and enumeration of decayed molars, were all plotted with astounding exactitude" (131). The similarity between Ortiz's language in the *Proyecto* ("estará sometido al examen antropológico") and Carpentier's language ("se le sometió al examen antropométrico") is striking. The important change that Carpentier makes, from "anthropological" to "anthropometric," signals the dubious nature of this inquiry, more intent on acquiring "measurements" than knowledge. It may be that Carpentier is differentiating this act of criminal anthropology from more affirming studies of Afro-Cubans, among which he no doubt included his own novel.

What is remarkable about Carpentier's portrayal of the exam is that he presents it from the perspective of the inmate. After Menegildo's body is scrutinized and measured, he is, astonishingly, flattered. Carpentier satirizes, though not without a certain pathos, the sense of importance Menegildo feels at having this much attention paid to him: "In spite of his confusion, he began to wonder at the importance granted to his person. Who until now—except Longina—had devoted even a moment of attention to him? It had never happened in his entire life as just one more black man in the village" (131). By narrating the anthropometric exam from the perspective of the subject, Carpentier highlights the inherently dehumanizing nature of contemporary scientific studies. Even though Menegildo's impulse to admire himself is naïve, he is right to ask: Who has paid attention to him until now? While Menegildo is made visible to the Cuban state in terms of measurements and profiles, no doubt to see whether he fits any of the criminal types, the exception that he provides—Longina—ends up being the vehicle for Carpentier's critique of eugenics and his parodic "antidote" to the sterile culture of "Wall Street." In addition to the plotline that traces Menegildo's path into the Havana underworld, the novel also traces a reproductive plotline.

Menegildo's sexual encounter with this Haitian immigrant is as crucial to his development as the other "initiations" of the novel, and the child they produce, outside of marriage and the legal and medical surveillance that would go with it, flies in the face of contemporary eugenics and the immigration laws. Before turning to this reproductive plotline, and the rest of the novel, in detail, I first want to explore the importance of eugenics within the context of Carpentier's composition. The work of early Cuban criminal anthropologists, such as Ortiz and Castellanos, was part of a much larger international movement. It is by reading *¡Écue-Yamba-Ó!* against the backdrop of Pan American eugenics that we see the connection between science and transnational capital that Carpentier was trying to expose.

Havana 1927: The First Pan American Conference on Eugenics

Just weeks before its large and public conference at which Machado's government was toasted, the Pan American Union had held a much quieter meeting in Havana. This was the First Pan American Conference on Eugenics and Homiculture of the American Republics. While it was a small proceeding, the Eugenics Conference was not a niche interest unrelated to the larger Pan American conference held after it. Rather the effort to bring the rest of the Americas into the fold of U.S.-defined modernity was contingent upon such scientific endeavors. The work of these scientists was therefore not distinct from the larger aims of the Pan American Union. As Cuba's secretary of state Rafael Martínez Ortiz declared when he welcomed the delegates on behalf of President Machado, the countries of the Americas needed to track individuals with "hereditary pathological defects" and curtail their migration as a crucial step in the economic advancement of the hemisphere. He made clear that the work of regulating populations, which the delegates were setting out to do, was essential to the "material progress" of all nations.[27]

While the U.S. delegation was interested in extending its eugenically informed Immigration Act of 1924 beyond its own borders, both the U.S. and Cuban delegations saw the link between the work of the eugenicists and the production of a viable workforce to sustain the economic systems of the Americas. The creation of this workforce would require stricter immigration policies, but it would also necessitate that the states supervise procreation, applying what the delegates termed "marital prophylaxis." As the head of the Cuban delegation, J. A. López del Valle, argued, it was the duty of scientists and lawmakers to prevent the union of undesirable individuals who lacked the "vital capital" to thrive.[28] López del Valle's telling phrase indicates a kind of biopower avant la lettre, suggesting the way the hemisphere's underclasses were valued for their labor and that even their hereditary traits could be understood as an economic investment. Likewise in *¡Écue-Yamba-Ó!*, Carpentier's black characters have been reduced to their value as "vital capital," and it is only by circumventing the systems of production and reproduction into which they have been circumscribed that they assert their individuality. The union of Menegildo and Longina, two such "vicious" individuals, becomes a defiant act in the face of such state regulation. However, Carpentier was not the only one resisting these policies. Between the opening and closing remarks of the Cuban delegates, which I have quoted, the conference involved contentious debate and resistance on the part of the other Latin American delegates to the racialized immigration policies being proposed.

The debated text of the "Pan American Code of Evantropy" had been authored by Dr. Domingo Ramos, head of the Cuban delegation and secretary-general of the conference. Ramos spent much of the conference defending his text, which would have mandated that each nation classify its population according to whether individuals were "germinally good," "bad," or "suspicious or doubtful." The Code itself provided no specific criteria for making such distinctions (that was to be worked out, unsuccessfully, at the conference), but it did assert that only the "germinally good" and "somatically responsible" would be free to migrate from one American nation to the other. While Ramos took ownership of the Code, it was very much the result of his relationship with the U.S. eugenicist Charles Davenport.

In her definitive study, *"The Hour of Eugenics": Race, Gender, and Nation in Latin America*, Nancy Stepan demonstrates the influence that Davenport had in international eugenics circles and the key role he played in forming Cuba's nascent eugenics research. His Cold Springs Institute had become a beacon of eugenics research and he had been instrumental in organizing the Second International Eugenics Conference held in New York in 1921. Davenport's views concerning racial "vitality" and "degeneracy" (views he would reiterate in the lecture he gave in Havana) developed within the same positivist framework that structured criminologists like Lambroso and Ortiz. His work was aimed at the decidedly practical application of biological criteria to immigration law. Indeed it was Davenport's main partner, Harry Laughlin, who had testified before Congress in order to promote the Immigration Act of 1924.[29] However, while that act was based on a strict quota system, by 1927 Davenport believed that the reach of eugenics should extend even further. In his lecture "Immigration and Race Crossing," he told his fellow delegates in Havana that they should now concern themselves with the "quality rather than the quantity of immigration."[30] It is no wonder, then, that delegates to the conference recognized in the proposed Code the efforts to extend this immigration policy throughout the Americas.[31] This goal was, of course, couched in terms of "progress" and "improvement" of the hemisphere.

The eugenics conference anticipated the lofty transnational rhetoric of the upcoming Sixth International Conference, and both of these meetings thinly concealed the efforts of U.S. scientists to spread their influence and the eagerness of Cuban statesmen to adopt and enforce these new ideas of biological control. It should be noted that U.S. scientists and intellectuals were not alone in articulating biological definitions of race and nationality during this period. Around the same time José Vasconcelos developed his notion of a racial utopia in *La raza cósmica*, which, as discussed in the previous chapter, was predicated upon the cultural and biological assimilation of indigenous peoples into a mestizo nation.

Even earlier the Guatemalan writer Miguel Ángel Asturias had articulated a similar solution to the "Indian problem" in his *Sociología Guatemalteca* (1923). Although the Nobel Prize–winning author is now remembered for his avant-garde celebrations of indigenous culture in such works as *Leyendas de Guatemala* (1930), such ideas developed later, during his stay in Europe, where primitivism was then in vogue. In the early 1920s, however, Asturias had concluded that Guatemala's indigenous population had become genetically debased and required an influx of European immigration to balance the country's genetic makeup.[32] While Carpentier's *¡Écue-Yamba-Ó!* and Asturias's later writings point out the colonial nature of eugenicist projects, it is important to remember that Latin American intellectuals frequently authored such projects themselves.

And so, if Davenport produced the eugenicist knowledge behind the proposed Code (his paper at the conference, "Immigration and Race Crossing," hints at his methodology), then his disciple Ramos was just as culpable for supplying the Cuban face to this proposal and couching it in the rhetoric of "progress." In his opening remarks he impressed upon the delegates the historical importance of the work they were undertaking and how it fit into the hemisphere's march toward modernity. Ramos proposed that the history of the New World could be divided into three periods: "The Conquest and Colonization, the Freedom and Independence already obtained, and the Improvement which we are now experiencing. In this last one there are two aspects: the Improvement of the environment and the Improvement of man."[33] Ramos went on to stress the important part that the scientists at the conference would play in this "Improvement." While the first two stages of history were led by "the soldier and the apostle," now "the jurist and man of science, represented by the brotherhood of physicians and naturalists, [were] the ones to effect the Improvement of América."[34] The work of these scientists was therefore not distinct from the larger aims of the Pan American Union, nor was it all that different from Machado's goal of "regeneration." The vision of hemispheric cooperation, which we see time and again during this period, is that of U.S.-defined modernity. Below this utopian rhetoric, though, there always resided a more practical and immediate plan for the Americas, a plan that allowed capital to circulate while it restricted the movements of people of color.

It is no coincidence that the most propitiatory of the Latin American and Caribbean delegates represented the nation with the strongest ties to the United States. Indeed Ramos made no secret of his desire to proliferate U.S. immigration throughout the hemisphere. One of his key tenets for moving the hemisphere forward was that the delegates agree upon a "migratory policy, like the one adopted by the United States of America." Other delegates at the Havana conference, however, were less willing to have U.S. conceptions of race categorize their populations. As Stepan rightly argues, Latin American eugenicists, rather than merely "copying" their U.S. counterparts, actively shaped the way eugenics was understood in the rest of the world.[35] The delegates at the Havana conference presented their own ideas of what constituted "public hygiene" and opposed the underlying politics of empire that they recognized in the Pan American rhetoric of the U.S. and Cuban delegations.

On the first day of the conference, the delegate from Mexico, Dr. Rafael Santamarina, raised objections to the kinds of testing that would be employed to determine "mental condition." He pointed out that such tests would be administered in the language of the state and would therefore be testing an individual's command of that language rather than actual mental ability. Santamarina used the example of the U.S.-Mexico border, where Spanish-speaking schoolchildren had been labeled "mentally inferior" based on the results of English-language tests. This insightful objection to Ramos's plan and to the overall aims of the conference was quickly squelched by other members of the Cuban delegation, who redirected the discussion and effectively silenced the criticism. Santamarina's objection set the tone, however, for later objections by other Latin American delegations, which ultimately put Davenport and Ramos on the defensive and derailed the conference proceedings. The most outspoken of the critics was the Peruvian delegate, Dr. Carlos Enríquez Paz Soldán, who challenged the core assumptions about race that the proposed Code had made. It is worth looking at Paz Soldán's objections in detail because the explicit connections he articulates between science, immigration, and imperialism make it possible to understand Carpentier's more subtle literary critique of the same system in ¡Écue-Yamba-Ó!

Paz Soldán was then a prominent figure within the PAU, serving as subdirector of the Pan American Sanitary Union, as well as an intellectual and political voice within his own nation. His vision of "public hygiene" ran counter to the biological assumptions about race that informed eugenics, namely that the Anglo-Saxon race was the purest and best race, followed by the "Latin" or Spanish race. Instead Paz Soldán frequently advocated for the indigenous peoples of Peru and offered social and political rather than biological explanations for their conditions. For instance, in the 1930s there was a remarkable rise in coca addiction among Peruvian Indians, which most observers explained as a medical or social problem, reflecting the degeneracy of the Indian. Paz Soldán's explanation, however, demonstrated his global thinking on such issues. The demand of foreign nations—the United States, Japan, and several European countries—had created the cocaine industry in Peru, but when these nations passed legislation to make the drug illegal, Peru lost its outlet and was left with large amounts of cheap, unused coca. The Indians' addiction was thus a product of political and economic conditions rather than their inherent biological makeup.[36]

The kinds of objections that Paz Soldán raised at the 1927 eugenics conference beggar belief, with their bold and prescient challenge to the racism of the day. He begins his assault on the section of Ramos's Code that concerned definitions of race. Paz Soldán asks the delegates to consider this section from "the American point of view" and challenges them with this question: "In America, what races are there? Which are the American nations that can speak of their races as something concrete?"[37] He goes on to recount the history of Peru's racial diversity—its indigenous population meets the white blood of "The Conqueror," slaves are imported from Africa, and even British pirates are factored into the gene pool. Paz Soldán thus concludes, "I am of the opinion that notwithstanding all that has been said about races, there is no determined race." He then points the accusatory finger at all the other American nations, composed as they are of immigrants: "If I were to say that in Peru there is [a determined race], really I would be lying; as it cannot be said that there is a Cuban race, and the same applies to the United States, Argentina, Chile. . . . "[38] This critique points out the arbitrary nature of racial categories, which have been produced by history, not biology. Since there is no scientific reasoning that supports their work, Paz Soldán suggests that the distinctions that Davenport and Ramos are so invested in defending must be motivated by something else.

At the end of his diatribe, once he has dismissed the scientific merits of the conference and argued persuasively in favor of rejecting Ramos's plan, Paz Soldán arrives at the political implications of a eugenics code. To discuss such racial distinctions as an intellectual debate was one thing, but to turn the Code into law, as Ramos proposed at the outset of the conference, was, in Paz Soldán's view, truly dangerous: "We should not forget that legislation on this matter, despite our good intentions, would only revive racial pride and would bring with it, as a consequence, what is worse—imperialism, political conflicts, and bitter struggles."[39] The notion of categorizing races could not have been a surprise to the Peruvian delegate (he was, after all, attending a eugenics conference!), but the codification of those categories based on existing U.S. laws raised the all too familiar specter of Yankee imperialism. Paz Soldán's ire reflects the sustained suspicion of Pan Americanism that was held by intellectuals in Latin America, even those who worked closely with the PAU. The 1927 eugenics conference was an important site of contestation for determining U.S. hegemony in the hemisphere, and Paz Soldán's argument exposes the relationship between academic discourse and political realities in clearer terms than I could hope to articulate: "The quota of immigrants in the United States is more than anything else an economical solution with the help of science, but not a biological solution because it has no foundation."[40] While matters of trade and foreign policy were debated overtly at larger Pan American conferences the next month, Paz Soldán's critique identified the proposed eugenics Code as playing a fundamental, though unstated role in those policies.

Lest I valorize the Peruvian delegate too much, it should be remembered that in one regard he was in line with the racism of his day. Paz Soldán believed firmly in "the defense of the American continent against yellow immigration."[41] The critiques of eugenics made by Paz Soldán and by Carpentier share many similarities, especially in their indictment of U.S. policy as the science's driving force. However, Carpentier's critique also reimagined the Chinese immigrant, turning the target of immigration laws into the locus from which the American continent could be defended from transnational capitalism. As becomes clear in Carpentier's meditation on eugenicist discourse, any attack on transnational capitalism must recognize that the politics of material production are inseparable from the politics of reproduction.

Production and Reproduction in *¡Écue-Yamba-Ó!*

Menegildo's relationship with his Haitian partner, Longina, is at the core of the novel's critique of eugenics and the immigration policies that eugenic science had informed. Their union takes place outside the surveillance of the state, whose policy of "marital prophylaxis" would surely have prohibited two such "doubtful" individuals from reproducing. As such the birth of their child has the potential to be an act of political defiance equal to the alternate epistemology of the "doctrine of the sun." But even before that, Carpentier frames the relationship between Menegildo and Longina as one founded on evading the anthropometric study of Cuba's black population.

As they meet and the romantic plotline proceeds, their relationship becomes increasingly less personal, dissolving Longina into an anonymous archetype. Later, in prison, Menegildo thinks back, trying to remember her: "What was it like, in reality, Longina's face? Worn down by the effort of memory, it was no more than an obscure form, without a nose and without a mouth" (143). While the erasure of Longina's face does alarming violence to the main female character in the novel, Carpentier seems to offer this as an image that resists state surveillance. Menegildo imagines her "without a nose and without a mouth," two of his own body parts that were measured when he first entered the prison, without which she would be invisible to the penitentiary apparatus. Indeed the same criminal anthropologists who intently studied Menegildo and other Afro-Cuban "delinquents" were also occupied with the study of "feminine delinquency," as Israel Castellanos titled his 1929 book. Black and Haitian, Longina would surely have been of interest to Castellanos and others, who would have accordingly documented her race, complexion, hair, eyes, nose (tip and base), lips, mouth, ears, and tattoos.[42] Menegildo, however, works against anthropometric criteria to create an "obscure form," hidden from the gaze of the scientists. His is an act of forgetting, but it is also a politically charged act of concealment.

This one moment of misremembering counters the systems of surveillance articulated in Ortiz's *Proyecto* and the positivist methods of Cuban anthropology in general. However, the novel also uses the body as a means of resisting the transnational forces of eugenics. *¡Écue-Yamba-Ó!* offers the reproductive potential of Menegildo and Longina as a defiant response to the science of the Pan American Conference on Eugenics. From conception to birth, Carpentier continually links the sexual reproduction of his characters with the material production of transnational capitalism, which continues unabated in the background.

The music and the "rhythms" of Menegildo and Longina's relationship are repeatedly measured against the hum of the *ingenio*. However, the real "triumph" comes later, when their union, and Longina's pregnancy, mute the hum of the *ingenio*: "Longina's belly grew day in and day out. The marriage prospered. The memory of the Central San Lucio was being lost in veils of fog. . . . The *ingenio* remained mute. The clocks struck twelve. They listened to the secrets of the breeze and their bellies tightened" (179). Thus it is the reproduction of Carpentier's Afro-Cuban characters that serves to counter the material production of the *ingenio*, churning out tons of processed sugar for the U.S. market and facilitating the incarceration of Cubans, both as prisoners in Machado's jails and as workers tied to the *ingenio*'s clock. The tone of anti-imperialist victory, though, rings hollow. While the image of Longina's "belly" (*vientre*) growing is an optimistic one, suggesting that even after Menegildo's death the Cués will live on, Carpentier's counterpoint is the family's clenched bellies as they anticipate hunger. The relentless churn of the *ingenio* has indeed been silenced, but the fate of these characters is so inextricably bound with the factory that if its pistons do not turn, the characters will not eat. Even at the end of the novel they are *still* victims of the labor economy, which produces everything for foreign markets and leaves them just enough to survive. It remains unclear how the life of Menegildo's son will be different from that of Menegildo, as both grow up in the shadow of the *ingenio*. The reproductive plotline of the novel suggests resistance to the discourse of eugenics, but its oppositional potential is ultimately disappointing. If we look at Menegildo's time in prison, though, we can see the one brief reprieve from transnational capitalism that Carpentier offers his characters.

Modernity and Its Incarcerated Other: Carpentier's "Antidote to Wall Street"

As Carpentier wrote the first draft of his novel, it must have been evident that the "primitives" alongside him in prison had already been incorporated into modernity—that of Cuba's prison system. In his 1977 preface to *Écue*, he indicated that the "surrealism" of the novel was very much invested in the present moment as he described the scene of its composition: "Imprisoned by Machado's police in 1927, [he wrote] to circumvent the tedium of confinement in the prison which stood then at Prado No. 1 (given the unique situation, surrealist if you look closely, in which the sinister building was installed on the beautiful avenue which was the preferred walking place for the Havana bourgeoisie of that time)" (8). Although there may be similarities between Carpentier's anthropological bent and those of European Surrealists whom he encountered while living and working in Paris, *Écue* is more directly invested in the injustices of Machado's Cuba and the U.S. wealth that backed up the regime and made possible the close proximity of prisons and "bellas avenidas." We might think of this as a kind of "Havana surrealism" that Carpentier presents us with, whereby modernity and its barbaric underside are continually present on the same city street. This biographical experience with Havana's prisoners and bourgeoisie is echoed in Carpentier's novel, in which the close proximity of *ñáñingo* prisoners and North American tourists brings together the author's concerns with policing the Afro-Cuban body and the transnational forces (like the Pan American conferences) behind their containment.

Once in prison Menegildo encounters an entirely different world, in which he achieves a new autonomy and ultimately inverts the politics of surveillance that has dominated the novel thus far. After the anthropometric exam has made him visible to the state, his initiation into the *ñáñingo* underworld makes him socially visible, so that the jail serves paradoxically as an alternative space where Carpentier offers a vision of social constructions that resist Machado-era surveillance. The prison world that Carpentier presents in *¡Écue-Yamba-Ó!* is, oddly enough, one of carnivalesque liberation in which Menegildo finds a new language as well as a reprieve from pressures of labor and production and inverts the power dynamics of anthropology by turning his scrutinizing gaze back upon white society.

In the three chapters entitled "Rejas," or "Bars," he is introduced to the underworld run by the *ñáñingo*, who create their own alternative language and alternative economy, both of which evade the gaze of mainstream Cuban society. When he first enters the cell, Menegildo is reassured by Güititío, the "president" of the *ñáñingo*, "You'll soon get used to jail, the jail was made for men!" (133). Indeed it was made for a certain kind of man who, thrust under the wheels of Machado's forward-moving society, has created an alternative world that reflects all too accurately the world outside the jail. In this polyglot and multinational jail cell, there were "creoles, mulattos, French, Poles, [all of whom] lived under the domination of a few strong men, Radamés and the Chinese Hoang-Wo who presided over the trust of nations" (137). While Havana's jails were certainly a place where all sorts of nonwhites could meet, Carpentier's creation of a "trust of nations" is a timely parody of the international conferences going on outside the prison. The composition of the prisoners opens up the seemingly local issue of how Afro-Cubans were policed and studied in Havana to a larger conversation about the ways race operated within the hemisphere. And the fact that all these prisoners are presided over by "the Chinese Hoang-Wo" signals a clear inversion of the racial hierarchies enforced by the immigration laws of the Americas. In the *ñáñingo* prison community, then, Carpentier offers an alternative vision of transnational cooperation to the one being articulated by the Pan American Union.

The principal attribute of the *ñáñingo* is their cant, developed as a mix of Afro-Cuban dialect and physical gestures called "the Chinese Charade." This system of communication, designed to elude the surveillance of police and prison guards, makes use of the riddles and codes that Chinese Cubans used to run Havana's underground lottery. The very target of immigration restrictions, the Chinese criminal, is thus reframed as a useful figure who provides an alternative to the transnational economy. Carpentier demonstrates his claim that "The inventors of the [Chinese] Charade had needed only 36 figures to capture the essential activities and desires of man" (137) by providing the most curious illustration in the book (fig. 15). The body of this Asian man is covered with a confusing array of iconography—from the horse that rides across his head to the snake that crawls down his ankle—all of which is paired with numbers and Chinese characters. Presumably these parts of the body would be touched in a certain sequence to relay a message to someone conversant in "the verses" of the Charade. However, if we place this diagram of the body alongside the discourse that contemporary criminologists and eugenics were producing around the body of inmates, the illustration takes on greater significance within the novel. Just as the body of the

Figure 15. Diagram of the Chinese Charade.
Illustration from Alejo Carpentier's *¡Écue-Yamba-Ó!*
Novela afrocubana (Madrid: Editorial España,
1933). The caption reads, " . . . Los inventores de la
Charada China solo habían necesitado 36 figuras
para resumir las actividades y los anhelos escenciales
del hombre . . . [. . . The inventors of the Chinese
Charade had only needed 36 figures to sum up the
activities and desires of man . . .]."

immigrant had been inscribed by the state with labels like "doubtful"
and "bad," this figure suggests an alternative inscription by which that
same body is used to create meaning indecipherable to the state. Carpentier thus refashions the archive of anthropometric data to suit his own
anti-imperialist project in the novel.

When Menegildo learns these "charades," he gains a new way of looking at the society around him: "The words of his companions revealed

to Menegildo the habits and mysteries of the city" (136). The gestures of the Chinese Charade provide him with a new way of thinking about his body, as something that creates meaning rather than something that is measured and translated into raw data for the criminologist to make meaning of. Yet the original use of the Charade—to conduct under-ground gambling—also provides him with a means of income outside the labor system of the *ingenio*.

Menegildo's first real wealth comes to him, oddly enough, while he is in prison as he gambles with his *ñáñingo* companions. His work outside the prison placed him at the bottom of the economic pyramid, whereby the labor was extracted from his body for the profits of Cuban elites and for-eign corporations, but the prison in *¡Écue-Yamba-Ó!* is outside that labor economy. Here the men play games, develop cryptic languages, and build alliances that they will translate to the world outside of the Prado's bars. For Menegildo the transformation from laborer to delinquent is complete. Upon his release, his cousin will remark, "Just a few weeks of obliged pro-miscuity with men of other customs and other habits had scraped away the crust of original clay that armored the country peasant against a series of temptations" (142). Not only will this "peasant" layer be removed, but he will also have disposable income for the first time: "With the money won in the Charade he had just bought himself a shirt resplendent with blue and orange squares" (142). This rebirth of Menegildo behind bars is a product of his association with the *ñáñingo* and the new language he acquires. Therefore Hoang-Wo's underground economy accomplishes what the birth of Menegildo and Longina's son cannot. While the cou-ple merely produces "one more black" to serve the *ingenio*, Hoang-Wo, even though he is in prison, has allowed Menegildo to move outside of the labor economy for the first time. Carpentier inverts our expectations for the novel of development since it is not procreation that marks the turning point in Menegildo's narrative but rather his incarceration.

Carpentier makes clear the social inversions of his prison when he depicts his characters looking through the bars at the outside world. Driving home the kind of surrealism that Carpentier found in the juxta-position of Havana's jails with its "bellas avenidas," the prisoners look out from their cells into an adjacent hotel room, fully lit. There they find a blond North American woman undressing:

> The prisoners got up in a tumult, going to frame their faces between the bars in order to contemplate the interior of the lighted room. Separated from them by but a few meters of air redolent with asphalt, a blond woman, American

without a doubt, was slowly stripping her lace bodice. Her hands, going to reunite with one another between her shoulder blades, made her arms into an arabesque of wings. Later, with a gesture that seemed to be launched from her hips, the woman began to escape from a wide girdle, which two fingers threw to the floor. She closed the wardrobe, and the mirror, positioned at a new angle, revealed the presence of a man, lying down and reading a newspaper. The blond, nude, came over to his side, with a sudden jolt to the bed frame. Fifty anxious looks converged on the thigh that was being lightly scratched by a thumb. A breast rubbed several times against the elbow of the man without him abandoning the printed page. Disarmament conference? Cooperativism? The woman's fingers traced pantomimes that didn't have the least effect. She then returned to a mound of caramels that rested on the little night table. In chorus the prisoners howled

"Take her . . . ! Pig . . . ! What are you waiting for . . . !" (143–44)

Though behind bars, these prisoners are able to see and study the most intimate details of this white North American couple. Their voyeuristic appetites are certainly fed by the blond woman as she undresses, removing the artifice of her girdle and bodice. From their perspective, this woman, her arms shaped into an "arabesque of wings," is no less exotic than the hypersexualized images of black women continually consumed by tourists and scientists alike. It is from this alternative space, which Carpentier has constructed within the prison, that the power relationships of anthropology in Cuba are finally inverted.

As engrossed as they are in looking at the American woman disrobing before them, the prisoners also take note of the languid man buried in his "printed page." Looking from the prisoners' perspective, Carpentier offers a stale and flaccid image of white society, immersed in its conferences and its Wall Street economies but ignorant of the sexualized "rhythms" in which Menegildo is fluent. When the American woman's sexual advances are not returned by her male companion, she retreats to her "mound of caramels," a product of the sugar industry and of Afro-Cuban labor, to satisfy her needs.[43] As she consumes the material goods that many of the prisoners across the way have produced, the realities of transnational capitalism become eminently clear. North American luxury is possible only because the workers of Cuba live under a police state. Likewise money and sugar circulate freely because the more "doubtful" members of the hemisphere are restricted in their movements. Beyond the taunting and howling of the prisoners, Carpentier has made the very serious suggestion that the worlds inside and outside the prison are interdependent, and it is no coincidence that in Havana one finds the jail so close to the "bellas avenidas."

The image of the North American woman lying in her hotel room, consuming the Cuban caramels, returns us to the beginning of the novel, where the "gigantic diabetic" that is the sugar industry consumes both sugar and human labor. Such anti-imperialist and anticapitalist moments place *¡Écue-Yamba-Ó!* within a history of Latin American writers who opposed the "Colossus of the North." We need only think of the works of Ruben Darío or Carpentier's Cuban contemporary Nicolás Guillén to see that his politics were shared by others. What makes Alejo Carpentier's first novel distinct, though, is his engagement with the academic discourse that made such imperialism possible. By incorporating the discourses of anthropology, criminology, and eugenics into *¡Écue-Yamba-Ó!*, he makes clear that by the 1920s and 1930s U.S. hegemony in the Americas was very much an empire of knowledge production. As was evident at the Pan American conferences of the time, the utopian rhetoric of transnational cooperation often masked these pursuits to study and contain the Americas by amassing an archive of information about the region. Carpentier, however, incorporates this archive into his novel and deploys it for his own anti-imperialist ends. The way he engages the discourse of the eugenics movement and reframes that discourse presents Afro-Cuban culture as an alternative vision of transnational community counter to the one being articulated by the Pan American Union.

4 Pan American Progress

The Crime of Cuba, Economic Development, and Representations of the "South"

Already a large portion of Alabama's population has reached a Central American level in its living standards, with even less food available.
—Carleton Beals, "Red Clay in Alabama: 'Rehabilitation'"

But why make Mexico city, or Guadalajara, or—the thought blanches me—Oaxaca, into a second-rate Memphis, Tennessee? Be yourself, hombre.
—Stuart Chase, *Mexico: A Study of Two Americas*

WITH VIOLENCE IN THE STREETS, mass incarcerations, and finally the overthrow of the Machado regime, 1933 marked a significant turning point in Cuban history. But it was also an important year for understanding the way U.S.-centered conceptions about economic development and about racial difference proliferated throughout the hemisphere. In the previous chapter we saw how Alejo Carpentier exposed the interrelation of eugenics and foreign capital as a means of disciplining Afro-Cuban laborers, and, I have argued, *¡Écue-Yamba-Ó!* challenges the scientific racism underlying Pan Americanism. And yet the way knowledge production was used to reinforce U.S. dominance was rarely so obvious; there was not always a eugenics conference where these ideas were so openly discussed and recorded. Instead the logic of Pan Americanism was often reinforced through the representations of Caribbean and Latin American peoples.

While Pan Americanism was centered on the supposedly common characteristics of all American societies, when it came to their economies they were rarely represented as equals. Instead the *Bulletin*'s regular series "Pan American Progress" pointed out where the member nations of the PAU fell short of U.S. standards of technology and infrastructure as well as how they were struggling to catch up. There were, as Stuart Chase suggested in the subtitle to his 1931 book, "two Americas." Such texts were part of a larger Pan American project of representation that marked the different realities of the hemisphere's present and simultaneously imposed the allegedly shared goals for future development. The documentary form was central to this project of representing the hemisphere since a fundamental conceit of the form is that it presents the "true" version of its subject, a problematic presumption I will explore. Although it is not an academic discipline, documentary is still a way of organizing knowledge and of shaping how those who control that knowledge perceive the subaltern. In addition to tracing the development of the documentary as a form that grew out of complex exchanges between U.S. business interests and writers and visual artists I argue that much early documentary was devoted to demarcating the "developed" from the "underdeveloped" world years before these terms came into common use. With their focus on recording the poverty in parts of the Americas, many documentary texts and photographs ended up conflating parts of Latin America and the Caribbean with the U.S. South as similarly "backward" lands that were decidedly outside of Pan American progress.

The more familiar version of documentary usually begins in the U.S. South. In the 1930s the Farm Security Administration (FSA) dispatched writers and photographers throughout the United States to capture images of the nation's farmers suffering through the Depression along with evidence of the ameliorative work being done through the New Deal. Much of the focus was on the plight of farmers in the South and the (often ineffectual) efforts of the federal government to counter both economic and natural disasters. The hardships of the Depression had become familiar to residents of the North, but as these reports on tenant farmers brought home the faces of rural suffering, such images from the South increasingly evoked a pre-industrial, foreign land. The region's otherness, its seeming incongruity with the rest of the nation, led Erskine Caldwell and Margaret Bourke-White to ask in the title of their 1941 portrait of rural America, "Say, is this the U.S.A.?"

This perceived foreignness led some observers to view these regions as belonging less to the United States than to the other, more distant regions of the Western Hemisphere. The nations of Latin America became frequent points of comparison and served as a way to measure poverty in the United States, as areas of the South sank into uncharted depths of hardship. Writing for the *Nation* in 1936, the only way that Carleton Beals could make clear the acute struggle of life in Alabama was by looking farther south. Amid the Depression and a crisis in cotton production, he writes, "already a large portion of Alabama's population has reached a Central American level in its living standards."[1] In other instances the U.S. South and Central America became interchangeable benchmarks

Figure 16. Walker Evans, Untitled. In James Agee and Walker Evans, *Let Us Now Praise Famous Men* (1941; New York: Houghton Mifflin, 2001). Bud Fields and family in bedroom, Hale County, Alabama, 1936. (The Metropolitan Museum of Art, Walker Evans Archive, 1994.258.310; © Walker Evans Archive, The Metropolitan Museum of Art)

for poverty. Writing just before the U.S. entry into World War II, Beals assesses the life of peasants in Eastern Europe: "They had less chance to wrest a livelihood from nature than the highland Indians of Guatemala. They were subject to atrocious economic and political tyranny. Nothing was more sickening (except parts of our own Georgia and Alabama)."[2] For Beals, and for the U.S. readership he presumes here, indigenous communities in Guatemala and the sharecropping regions of the South are part of the same Global South.

In photographic representations the people of these two regions could be just as interchangeable. Two Walker Evans photos (figs. 16 and 17) suggest how closely related such representations actually were. The first photo was taken by Evans in Alabama in the summer of 1936, published preceding James Agee's text in *Let Us Now Praise Famous Men* (1941), and is now an iconic, frequently reproduced image of southern tenant

Figure 17. Walker Evans, *Havana: Country Family*. In Carleton Beals, *The Crime of Cuba* (Philadelphia: Lippincott, 1933). (The J. Paul Getty Museum, Los Angeles; © Walker Evans Archive, The Metropolitan Museum of Art)

farmers. The second photograph was taken in Havana in the spring of 1933. It appeared, along with thirty other photos, at the end of Beals's exclamatory exposé of the Machado dictatorship, *The Crime of Cuba* (1933), and was then forgotten by all but Evans scholars. The contexts of the two photographs, both in terms of physical location and the books in which they were published, were undeniably different, yet their representation of poverty was strikingly similar. Evans glosses over none of the evidence of his subjects' hardship, from their tattered clothing to their weather-worn faces, but neither does he exploit these details in sensational fashion.[3] Rather these families are aware of the photographer's presence and allowed to represent themselves to the camera. In the years that followed these two photographic projects, Evans would pair even more of his images from Cuba and Alabama, finding similar faces and similar conditions of poverty in these regions separated by a mere eight hundred miles.

By beginning with examples from the work of Beals and Evans, I hope to illuminate a tendency among left-leaning U.S. travel writers to conflate the U.S. South and Latin America. *The Crime of Cuba* is in itself a complicated text, and my reason for examining it in detail is that it is the point of intersection for much larger issues during this time. First, the work is a pivotal step in Walker Evans's career, and thus it causes us to reappraise the standard genealogy of documentary photography, which places its origins in the FSA projects in the U.S. South. Second, the conflation of parts of Latin America and the U.S. South (in the case of *The Crime of Cuba*, Cuba and Alabama) suggests the way Pan American ideas about economic development and race were often imposed on peoples abroad. Third, and especially relevant to *The Crime of Cuba*, is the way U.S. writers participated in constructing this vision of Latin America and the Caribbean. As much as writers like Beals championed the cause of the Cuban people and railed against the forces of U.S. imperialism, Cuba is still presented in these texts as a decidedly unmodern place whose inhabitants behaved according to racial stereotypes. This critical posture, what I call radical paternalism, is certainly present in *The Crime of Cuba*, but the work of Beals and Evans also opens up one of the central tensions of Pan Americanism. That is, how does one speak for all of the Americas from within the United States? And, in the case of Beals, Evans, and many of their contemporaries, how does one advocate for the exploited peoples of the Americas from within the United States? Even critics of the U.S. Empire had to negotiate these contradictions.

For many U.S. writers and intellectuals during the Depression, the exclusion of southern regions (whether Alabama or Guatemala) from the promises of modernity represented the failure of capitalism, which the 1930s had made irrefutable. By looking south, writers and artists, particularly those on the left, found evidence for their critique of the U.S.-centered economy that dominated the hemisphere. Years before the terms *developed* and *underdeveloped* came into common use and decades before critics noted the way underdeveloped nations came into being through their contact with developed nations, many on the U.S. left were striving to make clear the pitfalls of the modern narrative of progress.[4] Despite the radical declarations on behalf of the people and regions on the losing end of this progress, U.S.-based critics often framed their arguments in condescending, paternalistic terms. The victims of poverty were premodern peoples who needed righteous critics in the North, such as Beals and Evans, to critique the capitalist system from within.

Among the iconic examples of the documentary book, *The Crime of Cuba* may not initially seem to fit. Landmark works such as Margaret Bourke-White and Erskine Caldwell's *You Have Seen Their Faces* (1937), Dorothea Lange and Paul Schuster Taylor's *An American Exodus: A Record of Human Erosion* (1939), and James Agee and Walker Evans's *Let Us Now Praise Famous Men* (1941) significantly shaped the way those in the United States saw the face of poverty in their own nation, and they have since become touchstones for popular conceptions of the Depression. But before any of these volumes landed on the shelves, *The Crime of Cuba* had already pioneered the combination of image and text that became the trademark of the documentary book. Although the form has now become closely associated with the U.S. South, documentary's origins can be traced to a much broader interest in representing economic injustice throughout the Americas, which we see in the work of Beals and Evans. Because their work stands at the center of so many hemispheric currents, they offer a crucial site for thinking about the distribution of wealth in the Americas and how to represent those who live on the underside of modernity.

Representing Modernity in the Americas

There is, of course, a long history of Europeans and North Americans writing about Latin America and the Caribbean, and this chapter traces only a very small part of that history. For explorers from Spain, France, and England, the Americas occasioned exaggerated reports of gold and exotic peoples meant to fulfill the fantasies of early modern Europe and to keep at bay both monarchs and anxious creditors. In the eighteenth and nineteenth century this was followed by a more rigorously empirical kind of report in which amateur scientists described, catalogued, and, if possible, brought back samples of this new colonial frontier. Mary Louise Pratt has revealed the way the "descriptive apparatuses of natural history" worked to categorize the peoples and regions of Latin America at the same time that they naturalized European Enlightenment thought as the dominant method of organizing the world's knowledge.[5] However, these texts performed a third function: they speculated about the region's potential wealth. This tradition continued in *Pan American Magazine* and other contemporary publications that provided U.S. businessmen with exotic descriptions of Latin America while reinforcing their belief that such lands were primarily investment opportunities. The ideological work done by "descriptive apparatuses" is common to all travel writing, and in the Pan American era of the early twentieth century the way Latin America and the Caribbean were described by writers from the North also naturalized the paternal role that the United States would play in any hemispheric relation. This generation saw the emergence of what would later be called Latin American studies within the U.S. academy, and, no matter how specialized the subject matter, from Mayan archaeology to Cuban sugar production, such studies operated on the presumption that the regions south of the United States were all moving inevitably along the path of progress that it had defined. Yet much of this ideological work also took place outside the academy, and the textual and visual representations of Latin America contributed to the construction of two Americas, one "modern" and one "premodern."

The rise of the photomagazine in the 1930s served as an important vehicle for these narratives of progress since this medium was able to align the values of U.S. corporations with this longer tradition of representing the Americas. While they were not strictly documentaries, these magazines represented a key step in the development of the documentary book because of the way they merged text and image. Advances in printing technology as well as the high budgets of magazines like *Fortune* made photographs something that readers came increasingly to expect. Indeed *Fortune* was where many of the decade's most notable photographers had their start; Bourke-White was for years its feature industrial photographer (and the only photographer to receive a byline), and Evans, whose early work was featured there, later became the magazine's photography editor. And of course, this was the magazine that contracted Agee and Evans to report on tenant farmers in Alabama, which, though the report never appeared in the magazine, would later be developed into *Let Us Now Praise Famous Men*.

Fortune was aimed at businessmen who both invested in Latin America and vacationed there. Therefore its representation of Latin America captured both the exoticism and the investment potential of the region. Alongside glossy photos of beaches and aerial photos of green valleys were articles on the growth of U.S. capital in the hemisphere. Pan American Airways was a favorite subject in the 1930s since Juan Trippe represented the kind of success story that *Fortune* liked to promote and his airline offered exciting new destinations and new trade possibilities. The magazine described Pan Am as "an organization which had come to represent the North American continent" and whose prestige "was inextricably—if sometimes intangibly—bound up with U.S. trade."[6] Not only could Pan Am take businessmen nearly anywhere in the hemisphere, but, *Fortune* claimed, it also took an active role in promoting U.S. business: "If you want to sell shoes in Ecuador or Brazil or Uruguay, Pan American will collect data for you on prices, competitors, politics, and shoe consumption, will offer suggestions as to the best way to exploit the market, and hold your hand when you get into trouble."[7] Sentiments like this, along with the lush photographs, enticed readers to make themselves and their capital at home in the region.

While Latin America made only an occasional appearance in *Fortune*, it was the focus of *Pan American Magazine*, a journalistic hybrid of the time, which shared many attributes of the official *Bulletin of the Pan American Union* and the pro-business *Fortune*. Eventually adopted and published by the Geographic and Historical Society of the Americas, *Pan American Magazine* had a thoroughly academic editorial board, run out of the Smithsonian, and notable members such as Hiram Bingham. However, its intended reader was certainly not the scholar or the diplomat. With advertisements exclaiming "Ship now to Salvador via International Railways" and promising that All American Cables was "turning the Americas into a neighborhood," the magazine was aimed at business executives who might also have a copy of *Fortune* in their offices. To more fully understand *Pan American Magazine*'s purpose and its intended readership, we can look to its "Call to Subscribers" from a 1933 issue:

> The Pan American Magazine . . . Interesting, informative and well illustrated, featuring pictures of scenes and peoples of the American countries, interprets the Americas to its readers. Its pages are replete with stories of the Western Hemisphere from the earliest times to the present—the history of early American civilizations, the Maya, Inca and Aztec; the flaming achievements of the romantic adventurers who came after Columbus; the struggles of the first settlers in the various parts of the Americas; the present day progress of these countries, their natural resources, the charm and customs of the peoples, their culture and aspirations; their leaders in government, art, science, literature, and industry.
>
> It is invaluable to students, teachers, scientists, travelers, and business executives who desire to keep informed on all phases of the countries of the Western Hemisphere and their 200 million people.[8]

Like so much of Pan American knowledge production, the magazine's focus was on compiling information for U.S. readers. And yet *Pan American Magazine*'s particular emphasis on business reveals the more mercantile interests that were sometimes obscured by the PAU's lofty rhetoric of hemispheric cooperation.

Many of the magazine's features celebrated economic achievements of Latin American and Caribbean nations, such as new benchmarks in petroleum output or new construction projects. While they were occasionally the site of exotic fantasy, in the pages of the magazine these regions were more frequently presented as a new frontier for U.S. business investment. And the more a country emulated U.S.-style development, the more it was praised. A prime example of the magazine's praise of infrastructure and U.S. emulation was the 1931 article "Cuba Completes Two Great National Tasks," which recounted the construction of Cuba's Central Highway and its new capitol, which was an exact replica of the one in Washington.[9] The author describes the recently finished highway and locates it within a history of transportation achievements on the island, including those completed under U.S. occupation. These building projects in many ways symbolized the reign of General Gerardo Machado, whom another article admiringly described as "Cuba's businessman president."[10] The imitation of the capitol revealed the close relationship that Machado desired with the United States despite the decades Cuba had been bound under the Platt Amendment. For Machado, though, a close alliance with U.S. business and with the U.S. government (along with the prospect of economic and military intervention) would help maintain his power since, as Luis Aguilar has suggested, he believed that he could handle his domestic challengers but not a break with the United States.[11] Both the capitol and the Central Highway, by creating thousands of jobs, also helped to cement Machado's early popularity at home and his image as a patriotic savior of Cuba. Such public works projects and concessions to labor groups also led other political parties to adopt the position of "cooperative opposition" that effectively gave Machado political carte blanche.[12]

While the images of material "progress" enticed U.S. investors and solidified Machado's support, both Beals and Evans represented such projects in a way that made clear their hypocrisy. Beals focused on the embezzlement and government corruption that went on behind the scenes of the Central Highway's construction. In his initial article for *Common Sense*, "The Crime of Cuba," he wrote that the capitol and the Central Highway "represented Roman dreams of grandeur which can conceive of perpetuating fame only in material showiness." And the highway, he notes, was built with extensive funds from Chase National Bank and "cost a fabulous hundred million dollars (officially

Figure 18. Walker Evans, *Country Town*. In Carleton Beals, *The Crime of Cuba* (Philadelphia: Lippincott, 1933). (The J. Paul Getty Museum, Los Angeles; © Walker Evans Archive, The Metropolitan Museum of Art)

seventy-five millions)."[13] This is another way of representing "progress" in Cuba that, like *Pan American Magazine*, celebrated the incorporation of Latin American countries into a U.S.-centered economic system while still insisting on the "tropical" details that marked the region as underdeveloped.

Evans's take on material development in Cuba also runs counter to these more mainstream publications. We might compare the celebration of the Central Highway project from *Pan American Magazine* with one of Evans's photos of power lines in Cuba (fig. 18). Photos from *Pan American Magazine* focus on the symbolism of such material development and capture, as do so many of the magazine's images of the Caribbean, an empty exotic landscape awaiting the arrival of U.S. commerce and tourism. Evans, on the other hand, is more interested in how Cubans interface with these new material developments. As with his photos of the Brooklyn Bridge from earlier in his career, the power lines he photographed in Cuba offer the aesthetic pleasure of clean, straight lines cutting across the horizon. But, as always with Evans, the progression of images is the key to our understanding. From the portfolio's first images, which focus on the city of Havana, we follow the power lines out of the city, first to a "small town," then to a "country town," and finally to an "unofficial village of Havana poor" (fig. 19), where modern infrastructure gives way to a shantytown. This "progress," Evans suggests, is a narrative that created two Cubas: a modern destination for capital and a site of underdevelopment, where the workers who made Cuba's bright new future possible were left behind.

The Depression was a crucial period for questioning such narratives, and many intellectuals in the United States were reappraising capitalism's promises of never-ending growth. On the one hand, the Soviet Union's brand of industrialization offered hope that machines could indeed liberate the worker from wage slavery. Before the tragic failures of Stalin's Five-Year Plan became apparent, many in the United States celebrated its achievements, including Bourke-White, whose paeans to Russian industry in *Fortune* magazine and in her book *Eyes on Russia* (1931) predate her representations of southern poverty.[14] On the other hand, many critics of the U.S. market economy came to view industrialization as leading unavoidably to a cycle of economic booms and crashes, and therefore Latin American nations were held up as sensible, pre-industrial economies that could endure the erratic tides of capitalism largely unaffected. Thus while Russia could serve as a vision of the economic future, something that the United States could conceivably aspire to, the economies of Latin America were looked upon fondly as mementos of a past whose loss one might lament but that could never be regained. This kind of nostalgia was nothing new for U.S. writers during the Pan American era, and even the most radical among them still viewed the peoples of Latin America through the lens of paternalism even as they championed their causes.[15]

Mexico: A Study of Two Americas (1931) by the New Deal economist Stuart Chase reflects this view of the nation as the obvious counterpoint to U.S. development.[16] Chase's depiction of Mexicans as "machineless men" ignores the rapid mechanization that was happening in Mexico City and the country's (or at least the avant-garde's) obsession with radios, typewriters, and other tools of the mechanical age.[17] Instead Chase chooses to focus on the rural village of Tepoztlán and draws much of his background knowledge from Robert Redfield's anthropological study published the previous year.[18] Chase also has another recent book in mind as he positions this Mexican village as an explicit

Figure 19. Walker Evans, *Unofficial Village of Havana Poor.* In Carleton Beals, *The Crime of Cuba* (Philadelphia: Lippincott, 1933). (The Metropolitan Museum of Art, Walker Evans Archive, 1994.251.791; © Walker Evans Archive, The Metropolitan Museum of Art)

counterpoint to the increased mechanization of U.S. cities, which Robert Lynd had made famous two years earlier with his study, *Middletown*.[19] The system of peonage still at work in Tepoztlán allows its inhabitants to subsist in the same condition after the stock market crash as it did before—deeply impoverished but not starving—and this provides Chase the occasion to question the "inevitability" of progress. "Precisely why," he asks, "is mass industrialism inevitable in Mexico, or anywhere else for that matter? Machine civilization proper is still incomplete over the United States; the map is spotted with great uninfected areas in the south and west."[20] Whether modernization offers technical emancipation or, as Chase views it, infection, it is clear that in this example Mexico and parts of the United States are linked together as especially unmodern places. With typical condescension and a touch of nostalgia for its handicraft economy, Chase advises Mexico, "But why make Mexico city, or Guadalajara, or—the thought blanches me—Oaxaca, into a second-rate Memphis, Tennessee? Be yourself, hombre."[21] In Chase's earnest advice we see the twin visions of Mexico, as exotic vacation spot and pre-industrial economy, intertwined as part of the same escapist fantasy.

For critics of U.S. capitalism at this time there was perhaps no destination more exotic than a locale that had somehow avoided cheap industrialization, avoided becoming a "second-rate Memphis, Tennessee."

This escapist fantasy of the pre-industrial lands to the south is something that Beals and Evans both wrestle with in their representations of Cuba. Their combined work in *The Crime of Cuba* is in many ways an effort to come to terms with the modernization of the island nation. The two men were on wildly different arcs in the 1930s, but the point at which they briefly intersected, *The Crime of Cuba*, offers many key insights into the larger project of representing economic development in the Americas. The book is explicitly critical of the encroachment of U.S. cultural and economic forces, and it argues instead for an independent Cuba, one that achieves a modernity outside the U.S.-centered path of progress. Yet this vision of Cuba, especially as it is articulated in Beals's text, is still colored by the tropical details of the colonial imagination. As with so much of Pan Americanism, the deep roots of northern paternalism invade every conceptual space and, as we shall see in *The Crime of Cuba*, creep into the work of even the most well-intentioned radicals.

Carleton Beals: Mexico, Cuba, and Beyond

Beals was a prolific journalist and novelist who traveled extensively throughout Latin America and whose work was deeply invested in the region. He came from a family in which radical politics were a given, and, after dabbling in socialism as a college student and working as a journalist for some small papers, he dropped everything and traveled to Mexico in the wake of the revolution.[22] For many North Americans on the left, such as Lincoln Steffens and John Reed, the Mexican Revolution offered a theater in which their radical ideas about labor and proletarian revolution could be played out in real life. While for some the revolution was a brief foray into the political and cultural world of Latin America, the time that Beals spent there began a lifelong preoccupation. It was during his time in Mexico from 1918 to 1923 that he developed as a journalist, and his articles for the *Nation* and *New Masses* demonstrate his devotion to the cause of the worker and his disdain for U.S. intervention.

His first book, *Mexico: An Interpretation* (1923), offered the blend of journalism, activism, and cultural study that would become his trademark. Though its aim was to indict government corruption and class inequality in Mexico, Beals's original intentions in writing the book were notably less political. In a letter to his mother, he said he wanted "to write the finest sociological study ever written in English of Mexico."[23] This book, as well as his other work on Mexico, should be understood within the varied forms of the exotic travelogue, the sociological study, and the journalistic exposé. A decade later Beals employed this hybrid mode on inquiry in *The Crime of Cuba*, combining a sociological study of the Cuban people with a report of the terror and political corruption of the Cuban government.

Beals's decision to write about Cuba was motivated in part by the murder of his close friend Julio Antonio Mella in Mexico City on January 10, 1929. Mella, an exiled leader of Cuba's Communist Party, was believed by many (including Beals) to have been assassinated by the Machado government.[24] Mella had made public his anti-Machado feelings at least as early as 1925, when he dubbed the newly elected president a "tropical Mussolini."[25] This murder put Cuba's internal political conflict in the spotlight and turned the attention of the foreign press to the increasing murders and acts of terrorism, which from that point on dominated any news from Cuba in the years leading up to the 1933 revolution. Indeed in the U.S. literary imagination Machado's Cuba became an island of crime and intrigue, where both Langston Hughes and Ernest Hemingway set underworld narratives.[26]

Beals visited Cuba in September and October 1932 to see firsthand the brutality of the Machado regime. The result was a scathing article he published in the leftist magazine *Common Sense* in December of that year. U.S. readers were forced to look at Machado, this "President of a Thousand Murders," who was running a "'sawed-off shotgun republic' with the support of their own government."[27] The article was eventually published in book form as *The Crime of Cuba* in September 1933, two weeks after Machado was ousted from power. Although Beals's argument was a belated one, the revolution had brought Havana into the headlines and made *The Crime of Cuba*, as its editor had hoped, "the book of the hour."[28] Beals received a great deal of attention from reviewers, who focused understandably on the book's overtly political sections, "The Crimes of Machado" and "American Penetration." However, the book's first section, "Pattern," passed without comment. Here Beals engaged in the kind of "sociological study" he conceived of in Mexico. This portrait now seems unconnected with the rest of the book, which includes Beals's critique of U.S. policy, Cuba's struggle for independence, and the violence of Machado's rule. However, it is the "Pattern" section that demonstrates Beals's efforts to locate the Cuban people on the cusp of modernity and to make sense of their complicated racial history in terms that his U.S. readers would understand.

Beals isolates the competing and, in his view, complementary elements of Cuba's racial landscape in which "colors flow into each other."[29] This image will serve as the key to Cuba's advancement, as he later concludes: "Out of this melting pot is emerging the true Cuban type, into whose hands the destinies of the island must ultimately come. Between these racial, economic, and cultural extremes is encountered the Cuban in the making—in this mestizo middle ground" (81). But this romantic vision of hybridity becomes more complicated when Beals shifts from discussing abstractions of "black" and "white" and focuses his study on actual Cubans.

While, in the opening sections, Beals expands on the symbolism of the landscape, in the chapter "Black Joy" the dancing bodies of Fela and Toñico, two Afro-Cubans he observes in a nightclub, serve a similarly symbolic purpose in his argument. Fela, an "octoroon," sits in a hot bar staring at Toñico, whose "black pulpy mandible and fig lips stuck forward fiercely" (40). In spite of the gallingly racist description of Toñico, Beals actually does imagine himself as an advocate for these two. His portrayal, heavy on pathos, is intended to cast them as victims of U.S. imperialism. After relating how the meager wages Fela earns dancing with tourists must support her mother and five siblings, Beals chastises those tourists:

> None of the hale back-slappers at her table who bought drinks, exhausted her dozen words of English, then went their way, came to know her arduous personal history or to know the rhythms—so far from commercialized tunes—locked in her lovely tan and gold body. Doubtful if they even noticed—because of her finely chiseled features—that her grape-snug olive skin covered over a complex heritage much more incontiguous than merely that of Navarro in Old Spain. But any one more sensitized to Antillean racial vagaries [presumably Beals] would have noticed now in the way she sat poised of loin and limb not Spanish but African; would have caught the significance of the haze gathering in her ebony eyes as she watched the black man in front of her, a smoldering stare that revealed her terrific duality— boiling in the cross-current of her unfused blood-streams—of utter distaste and profound attraction. (40)

Even while Beals positions himself as sympathetic to Fela's struggle, his own interests lie less with her "arduous personal history" than with her "grape-snug olive skin." Indeed the fecund and ripe fruit imagery persists in this section, offering up Fela as a kind of crop. As Toñico plays, she takes to the dance floor alone, in what is meant to be a more authentic cultural expression than the way she dances to the "commercialized tunes" played for tourists. As the pace of the dance increases, "Fela breathed heavily; her large breasts, distended like ripe fruit, heaved; and her sweet warm voice—like a low dark cloud in the azure sky of a tropic afternoon—came back with an answering chant, at first soft and warbling, mellifluous, as though she were struggling to remember something long forgotten. A feline glide—she was on her feet dancing. Strips of olive flesh showed through her negligee" (41–42). The anxious rhythms of these sentences betray Beals's own excitement. While he distances himself from the tourist in the cabaret, he is also complicit in this sexualized economy, a customer who not only consumes for his own pleasure but also panders Fela's image to the reader.[30]

As tropical and "ripe" as the image of Fela is, the rapture of Beals's exotic description pauses for a parenthetical aside much closer to home. Her dancing becomes empty and joyless, undercutting the section's title, until "her face had grown deathly expressionless, vacant eyes rolling up in mesmerized inwardness, lush red lips drawn down in a half-curve of symbolized suffering; her arms were stiff, elbows crocked out, hands rigid, fingers tight together pointing, thumbs sticking up" (42). Then, to drive home the image, Beals asks the reader in a parenthetical aside, "(Have you ever seen a black mammy munching an apple held in the full palm?)" (42). The absentminded and indeed alienated motion of Fela's body links her labor on the dance floor to that of a black house servant in the United States. What is confounding about Beals is the jarring mix of condescension alongside the critique of hemispheric capitalism and the ways it has racialized labor. This is a text of two minds and many irreconcilable claims.

The analogy between the Cuban dancer and a racist tableau from the U.S. South is a strategy for making the foreign legible, an underlying aim of all documentary. But Beals simultaneously interpolates Fela into U.S. racial identities, committing an act of cultural misinterpretation far more violent than the U.S. tourists whom he chastises. For all his simplifications, though, what Beals has articulated in this passage is a transnational black identity (a worthy reminder that not all such formulations are empowering). As he links Fela with the stereotype of the southern mammy, he constructs an identity based on labor, one in which the female body of color has been so thoroughly commodified that, whether dancing or nursing, its every purpose has been preordained for white consumption. Understanding Beals's racial politics and the link he suggests between Cuba and the U.S. South is significant not only for understanding *The Crime of Cuba* but also for understanding the paternalism at work in many of the representations of Latin America and the U.S. South.

However, this was not the only way of thinking about labor and about the new economic realities encroaching on both regions. Even within the same volume Evans's photographs provide a counterpoint to Beals's exotic portrait of Cuba and his essentializing racial categories. To be sure, Evans suggests similarities between the material realities of Afro-Cubans and African Americans, but the important difference is that he largely allows his subjects to represent themselves. Since Evans took his evolving visual aesthetic from Cuba to Alabama, it is crucial that we understand the quite different manner in which his photography conflated the two regions.

Walker Evans: New York, Havana, Alabama

Evans is now best known for the photographs of the U.S. South he took for the FSA in the 1930s and for his collaboration with Agee in *Let Us Now Praise Famous Men*. Even though *Famous Men* was not published until 1941, after many of the other important documentary books, Evans's work at the FSA had already influenced the generation of photographers who worked with him during the 1930s. His aesthetic shaped the work of contemporary photographers, and since that time it has defined historic representations of the Depression. As William Stott has noted, "Evans' version of the thirties, his cool yet disquieting vision of America, has prevailed" as the dominant mode of representing the decade.[31] But often this mature work serves to obscure Evans's early years.

Having left college after one year to chase his bohemian ambitions, Evans spent much of 1926 in Paris, soaking up avant-garde art and spending his days photographing street scenes. He then returned to New York, where he worked during the late 1920s and early 1930s documenting city life and experimenting with photographic techniques. His photographs of the Brooklyn Bridge, Coney Island, and city billboards and numerous candid street portraits have surprising visual resonances with his later Cuban photographs. His work in Havana in 1933 stands at a midway point between the New York photos and those from *Famous Men*, and thus a closer look at the Cuba portfolio, at the sequencing of its images and the way individual photos resonate with his earlier and later work, reveals Evans's artistic and political development during the decade. But apart from revealing the development of one photographer, *The Crime of Cuba* is a crucial document for understanding Pan American modes of representation because as Evans moved about the hemisphere, from New York to Havana and Alabama, he brought his style with him. The development of documentary photography, then, and the iconic images of *Let Us Now Praise Famous Men*, was a process of transculturation that, like Beals's writing, conflated representations of Latin America and the U.S. South. The critique that each was struggling to articulate in his own way attempts to unravel one of the fundamental presumptions of Pan Americanism, namely that the rest of the hemisphere longed to emulate U.S. consumerism. However, for two U.S. artists articulating that criticism for a U.S. audience, the resulting argument was not at all straightforward.

The photographic projects in Havana and Alabama each began as very specific assignments (with outside funding from the FSA and *Fortune* or from Beals's publisher), but in each case Evans made the project his own. In later years he confessed that his photographs of southern tenant farmers were not done to meet the expectations of his employers: "I was just in a sense taking advantage of the FSA and using the government job as a chance for a wonderful individual job. I didn't give a damn about the office in Washington—or about the New Deal, really."[32] In giving him his assignment in Cuba, the editor at Lippincott had given him the clear task of providing photos for Beals's text, and he had a preconceived vision of the role Evans's photographs would play in the final book. Evans, however, claimed never to have read Beals's text. If neither pleasing his employers nor "illustrating" a text was his concern, then what *was* his purpose? Reflecting on his Cuban photographs nearly forty years later, Evans concluded, "I was sure that I was working in the documentary style. Yes, and I was doing social history, broadly speaking."[33] It remains to be seen, though, what kind of "social history" this was and how it intersected with Beals's own pretensions to conducting a "sociological study." Despite the exotic representations of Latin America, among them the "Pattern" section of Beals's *The Crime of Cuba*, and representations of Cuban "progress" such as *Pan American Magazine*'s depiction of the Central Highway, in these photographs Evans locates the common elements of city life. His years of photographing the cityscape of New York had trained him to look for similar images in Havana. Despite being sent there to document a country embroiled in political violence and imminent revolution, Evans was still inclined to see the "New York" in Havana.

The time that Evans spent in New York certainly influenced this later work. There are, for instance, obvious similarities between photos he took at Coney Island and some of those he took in Havana, where he still had an eye for people sleeping on park benches. Not only did Evans continue his fascination with these candid moments, but he also returned to one of his favorite subjects: signs and movie posters, especially those adapting novels by Hemingway, with whom Evans was carousing in Havana. Evans was certainly interested in visual signs of modernization, but what that looked like in Cuba was unique and was inseparable from imperialist policies Beals decried and from the oncoming revolution.

Evans would later insist that his worked aimed at documenting its subject but with "NO POLITICS whatever," and indeed we have a hard time pinning down his politics in *The Crime of Cuba*.[34] Certainly he responds to the same state violence that sent Beals to Cuba and depicts, through found photographs, the dead bodies that this conflict produced, even though U.S. culpability is not as readily available as it is in Beals's text. However, I agree with Jordan Bear that the Cuban photographs offer the occasion to "reevaluate the surprisingly durable portrayal of Evans's political indifference."[35] For instance, Evans's photographs of power lines, which he seemed to find in even the most rural parts of Cuba, demonstrate his work's potential for political ambiguity. Are they evidence of the photographer's continued fascination with cityscapes and the pleasing lines that they make through his composition, or do they point out the encroachment of General Electric and other U.S. companies into the island's economy?[36] Evans's argument emerges through his arrangement of the Cuban portfolio. It is the juxtaposition of hard and contradictory truths as well as the impulse to create meaning through the sequence of photographs that first appeared in his work after his time in Cuba.

The thirty-one images that Evans arranges at the end of the book consistently undercut any notion of an exoticized Cuba and present the viewer with the encroachment of modernity at every turn. The series works mainly by presenting counterpoints, as with the central section of the portfolio, which presents images of development and underdevelopment, the promise of modern Cuba and the disappointment Evans saw in its streets. Evans's artistic project, then, is to turn the lens of anthropology back upon the developed world. He stated in his 1931 essay "The Reappearance of Photography" that he admired "a photographic editing of society, a clinical process; even enough of a cultural necessity to make one wonder why other so-called advanced countries of the world have not also been examined and recorded."[37] Even if Cuba and Alabama are still defined as unmodern, they are undeniably part of the same social and economic system and not images from which affluent U.S. readers can completely divorce themselves. Rather than represent Cuba as a benchmark for underdevelopment against which U.S. industry can be understood, Evans's photography of the 1930s points out the shared humanity of Cubans and North Americans.

More than anything, Evans wanted to convey a sense of fraternity with his subjects. It was in Havana that he began to move away from his typical candid shots, catching his subjects off guard, and he also began to allow his subjects to pose themselves and to choose the manner of their representation, as he would do later in *Famous Men*. Writing of the similarities between Evans's work in Cuba and in the U.S. South, Giles Mora has noted his desire to undermine the power dynamics of representation: "This anthropological way of approaching social problems confirms the familiarity rather than the distance between Evans and the lower classes."[38] Evans's ability to break down the class barrier between photographer and subject stems from his abandonment of the candid shot. He wrote in a dust-jacket blurb for *The Crime of Cuba*, "None of the pictures with people is posed."[39] Indeed the Cuban subjects in these photos are not posed by Evans but are instead allowed to pose themselves. This is the first glimpse we have of Evans's mature style, the kind we will ultimately see in the portraits for *Famous Men* he did three years later, but it was in Havana that he first developed this approach.[40]

Evans desired to trace a shared humanity across national boundaries, pointing out that these individuals from different cultural and racial backgrounds were united by their poverty and their exclusion from the promised land of modernity. This connection is evident in a few of the photos that made their way into *The Crime of Cuba*, such as *Stevedore*, but there is even more evidence in other Cuban photographs that he kept for later publication. After years of having his photographs appear in other people's books and articles, he finally arranged his own survey in 1938, titled simply *American Photographs*. These photos were American in the broadest geographical sense, and it was here that some of the unpublished Cuban photos surfaced, as well as some of Evans's Alabama photos (which were languishing unused as Agee wrestled with the text for *Famous Men* until 1941). What is especially striking about *American Photographs* is the manner in which Evans, as always, creates meaning through his sequencing of images. Looking back over his work of the 1930s, he seems to make connections across photographic

Figure 20. Walker Evans, *Coal Dock Worker, 1932*
[*sic*]. In Walker Evans, *American Photographs* (New
York: Museum of Modern Art, 1938). (The J. Paul
Getty Museum, Los Angeles)

projects and across national boundaries. Through his juxtaposition of
images, he, like Beals, suggests connections between Afro-Cubans and
African Americans, but he does so for quite different ends. If we look,
for instance, at the pairing of a Havana coal dock worker (fig. 20) and
Minstrel Showbill (fig. 21), transnational resonances emerge. Evans must
have noticed the similarities between this white-bearded dock worker
and the central figure in the show bill. Apart from that, however, the
tone of each image is set up to contrast the other. While the show bill
captures all of the degrading representations that Beals's mammy reference evokes, the Havana worker is not a figure of entertainment. Evans

Figure 21. Walker Evans, *Minstrel Showbill*, *1936*. In Walker Evans, *American Photographs* (New York: Museum of Modern Art, 1938). (The Metropolitan Museum of Art, Walker Evans Archive, 1994.258.91; © Walker Evans Archive, The Metropolitan Museum of Art)

represents him, not dancing for tourists like Fela, but instead composed after a day's labor. His blackface comes from a lifetime of handling coal, not from the blackened cork of the Vaudeville circuit. By juxtaposing these two images, Evans opens up important questions about the status of black labor in both Cuba and Alabama as they both work to bring about the progress from which others will benefit.

The "Southern" Analogy: The Left and the Politics of Colonialism, at Home and Abroad

The connections that Beals and Evans make between Cuba and Alabama as unmodern places are part of a long heritage of "othering" the U.S. South, of establishing it as a foreign, subaltern place. After the failed project of Reconstruction, the northern view was that the South was a backward region, which had not caught up with the industrial developments of the rest of the nation nor with its modern standards of democracy. From the late nineteenth century through the civil rights era, the dominant cultural image was of heroic federal troops from the North coming into the South to prevent lynchings, segregation, and disenfranchisement. Harilaos Stecopoulos argues that the creation of a dominant, industrial North and an underdeveloped South in the nineteenth century provided the United States with a template for advancing itself as an imperial power abroad: "The federal government's decision to abandon the onerous task of building democracy in the region didn't only devastate the African American South, but also laid the groundwork for the U.S. betrayal of many other communities of color overseas."[41] The rest of his study usefully pairs the national and international effects of Reconstruction's failure, particularly the way it shaped the U.S. paternal role in Latin America and the Caribbean in the following century. Along with battalions of marines landing in the Dominican Republic and platoons of U.S. millionaires buying up Cuban industry came the rhetoric of aid that still lingered from Reconstruction, what Stecopoulos calls the "compromised, if not hollow, promises of democratic uplift on a host of subaltern peoples."[42] It is the creation of coloniality in both Alabama and Cuba, as well as the hypocritical talk of "uplift" masking both cases, that ignites Beals's anti-imperialist sentiment.

Beals, of course, also participates in this subaltern depiction of the South, comparing living conditions in Alabama with those in Central America and linking the poverty of indigenous Guatemalans with that of rural southerners. However, as condescending as his references to "Central American living conditions" may be, he views both regions as products of U.S. economic imperialism. In the same *Nation* article in which Beals links Alabama to Central America, he also describes the state as "this colonial fringe of the nation," thereby making clear that northern industry relies on the hegemonic structures of empire, creating subaltern populations both within and outside the national borders.[43] Anti-imperialism is one of the unifying themes of Beals's diverse body of work, and his analysis of social injustice from Alabama to Mexico, Nicaragua, and Cuba is rooted in an attack on the structures of capitalism that have created such inequalities. For instance, when he writes of the "backward" and complacent character of Mexico in *Mexico: An Interpretation*, he is quick to point out that "the Mexican is not wholly to blame. . . . It is a reflection of centuries of foreign domination by governments, religions, and cultures alien to his genius, during which time he has been betrayed, plundered, and his spirit profaned and exhausted. We, in our economic conquest, our intriguing politics, our failure to promote social reconstruction, bear our share of responsibility."[44] The anti-imperial self-lacerations continue even as he catalogues the inherent cultural deficiencies of Mexico and the supposed character flaws of Mexicans that prevented them from attaining U.S.-style progress.

Mexico: An Interpretation relies on precisely this kind of essentialism. The volume is devoted to explaining Mexican history to U.S. readers, everything from the Conquest to the Revolution and the more recent conflict between the new government and the Catholic Church. However, there is one chapter, "The Mexican as He Is," in which Beals indulges in the "sociological study" that he intended the book to be. He concludes that the "Mexicans are a dislocated, backward, oppressed and exploited people, lacking stamina."[45] Here the condition of backwardness is constructed as the result of exploitation, but the Mexican people are presented as backward nonetheless. Eight years later Beals wrote in *Mexican Maze* that the system of global capitalism "forges the chains of subjection for the exploitation of backward peoples."[46] Even as he takes their side and advocates justice in the face of hemispheric exploitation, he continues to see these people as essentially backward. Later on in *Mexican Maze* he suggests that the Mexican character can be summed up by the single word *vacilada*. "The major portion of the Mexican world," he writes, "is subject to the *vacilada*, which is characterized by irresponsibility, recklessness, whimsicality, irrationality, passion, daring, Caesarian ambition."[47]

Nevertheless descriptions such as these did not mean that Beals condemned the Mexican people. This is the thing that is so striking about

Beals—he is able to oppose social injustice with extreme conviction while simultaneously viewing the subjects of that injustice as racial inferiors. This contradiction, seen most glaringly in his description of Fela in the Havana nightclub, presents a problem for any reader of Beals. While his anti-imperialist critiques are insightful, they mask a deep-seated paternalism and sense of racial and national superiority, all of which tangle our understanding of his leftist advocacy and its attitude regarding the Global South. His description of Fela as a mammy suggests that he transposed ideas about race from the U.S. South onto Cuba, but I want to consider another example of his writing that deals with African Americans in the South in order to understand that troubling passage from *The Crime of Cuba* and the larger contradictions of northern advocacy journalism.

A series of antilynching articles he cowrote for the *Nation* in 1935 demonstrates the contradiction of Beals's racial politics. As always his vitriol is aimed at government corruption and the abuses of business. The villain of the ironically titled "Louisiana's Black Utopia" is Huey Long and the "so-called civilization of Louisiana," which, Beals and his coauthor Abel Plenn point out, "rests on a black cushion."[48] The article is devoted to a detailed and impassioned account of recent lynchings in the state and the legal corruption that allowed these murders to go unpunished. This was not solely the work of a few sheriffs and vigilantes: "The submergence and exploitation of the Negro condition all social phenomena, shape all institutions and determine Southern reaction to significant problems. . . . His life at any given moment hangs on the slender thread of white emotional stability."[49] The authors thus encourage identification with these victims rather than an awareness of their racial difference.

In 1936 Beals wrote another series for the *Nation*, this time on Alabama, in which he advanced an argument remarkably similar to the one that Agee was making that same year. Both men sought to expose the hardships of tenant farming and the inadequacies of federal relief; however, Beals's work focused exclusively on black farmers. Like Agee, he offers detailed portraits of individual farmers, and, again like Agee, Beals gives his farmers pseudonyms (though this protects them from the very real threat of lynching from which the subjects of *Three Tenant Families* were immune). The central farmer of Beals's articles "is intelligent and independent of spirit, qualities which are terrible handicaps for a Negro in the South."[50] Regardless of such intelligence and independence, the relief programs of the New Deal habitually paid white farmers a higher amount than black farmers in the same region, reinforcing the system of segregation with federal dollars. As he describes black tenant farmers being squeezed between the federal government and their landlords, Beals concludes that "many 'rehabilitation' farmers have merely exchanged one bad master for two worse ones."[51] In his analysis of the economic injustices at work in Alabama, he frames federal relief as an extension of the plantation system, thus offering, as he does in many of his works, a deep historical context for understanding present-day political situations.

One way of thinking about the contradictions in Beals's writing is by acknowledging the deep-seated patriotism at work in even his most scathing attacks on the U.S. government and U.S. corporations. His vision of a hemispheric community is always one in which U.S. democratic values lead the way and those same enlightened North Americans lift up the regions of the hemisphere—but from a distance. And so in this way even as he opposes the narrative of Pan American progress, Beals cannot help but repeat its U.S.-centered view. We see an example of this latent patriotism in the concluding chapter of *Mexican Maze*, "Mexico and the Machine Age." Unlike Stuart Chase, he has concluded that the arrival of mechanization in Mexico is inevitable, and he describes the encroachment of U.S. capital and Mexico's coming transformation into an industrial society. While Beals made a career out of attacking the Dohenys and Morgans of the world, he was certainly not opposed to a capitalist economy or the influx of U.S. capital into other countries in the hemisphere. In this chapter he describes how the Mexican system of peonage will be abolished in favor of "labor freedom," but the uplift for the Mexican worker, he argues, can be achieved only with the help of outside investment. Mexico "will adopt the factory system. That system is inevitable. But it is a system which can only be successfully implanted by foreigners wielding foreign capital."[52] The contradiction inherent in this view of industry is a function of Beals's belief in the promises and perils of modernization, in its potential to emancipate the workers as well as to create an oppressive capitalist modernity whose progress depends economically upon the subjugation of an underclass and geographically upon the creation of underdeveloped regions.

Modernity, Documentary, and Radical Paternalism

"Mexico and the Machine Age" gets to the core of Beals's dual vision of modernity in the Americas, and it also suggests the contradictions of Pan Americanism. Although Beals virulently attacked the advance of the U.S. Empire in the hemisphere, in much of his writing certain presumptions of U.S. superiority persist (as do U.S. racial hierarchies) so that it remains difficult to view this self-described anti-imperialist as a true champion of autonomy for any nation in Latin America. His colonial gaze simultaneously normalizes those same oppressive forces. We might approach this seeming contradiction as a latter-day example of what Pratt has termed the "anti-conquest" narrative. Writing with regard to the era of Enlightenment, Pratt deploys this term to describe "the strategies of representation whereby European bourgeois subjects seek to secure their innocence in the same moment as they assert European hegemony."[53] In a way all of Pan Americanism was an anticonquest narrative. The rhetoric of a cooperative hemisphere made up of equal nations was a way for institutions like the PAU and for U.S. corporations to continue their economic dominance while still feeling like "good neighbors." It was an essential component of the Pan American project, but this righteous stance also factored into the critique of Pan Americanism. In the context of the 1930s the posture of innocence among U.S. intellectuals became a kind of radical paternalism, a fiery anti-imperialism mixed with the residue of racial and national superiority. The truly sympathetic U.S. observer had to insist that he was not just another condescending gringo, that he had *experienced* the land itself. For instance, Beals's claim to understanding Cuban culture derives from his insistence that he is not just another American tourist in a Havana cabaret. By differentiating himself from the "hale back-slappers," he casts himself as an expert and offers his interpretations as unimpeachable "truths" about Cuba.

This anxiety and constant need to prove the veracity of one's account can also be seen in the documentary writing of the time. Clearly in the pages of *Let Us Now Praise Famous Men*, Agee wrestles with the question of his own "innocence" and continually expresses the guilt he feels because the subjects of his book were "dwelt among, investigated, spied on, revered, and loved, by other quite monstrously alien human beings, in the employment of still others still more alien."[54] Evans later remembered, "You notice that Agee is saying ad nauseam almost throughout the book: 'For God's sake, we must *not* exploit these people, and how awful it is if we are. And we *are* working for this goddam profit-making corporation that's paying us, and we feel terrible about it.'"[55] While *Famous Men* presents a look into the lives of southern sharecroppers in the 1930s, it is perhaps foremost a documentary account of Agee's own anxieties and liberal outrage. Yet the most important thing for Agee to convey to his reader is the idea that he and Evans are not mere tourists and that, innocent or guilty of exploitation, they have experienced the reality they represent and are thus authorized to document that reality.[56] While Agee's writing was certainly more self-reflective than anything we see in Beals, both exhibit a similar conflict between advocacy and exploitation, between anticapitalist critique and the condescension of the outsider.

While that "goddam profit-making corporation" never published the record of their time spent with three tenant families in Alabama in 1936, *Fortune* did publish another collaboration of Agee and Evans, a little-remembered documentary of a cruise to Havana. It is in this text that the contradictions of this performed innocence are perhaps most clear, as Agee and Evans insist upon differentiating themselves from their fellow travelers and making it clear that they are *not* tourists. Published in 1937, "Six Days at Sea" marks a bridge between Evans's previous trip to Havana to work on *The Crime of Cuba* and the work he and Agee would publish from their time in Alabama. *Fortune* hired Agee to take a cruise from New York to Havana for its upcoming issue on "U.S. shipping" (demonstrating yet again the central role that U.S. commerce played in representing the rest of the Americas), and so Agee brought along his wife and conscripted his good friend Evans to take the accompanying photos. The resulting article had little to do with Cuba or the horrors of political unrest that Evans had seen four years earlier; it was instead a "human document" (as the editors called it) of middle-class American leisure. While Agee's portrait of the three tenant families neared hagiography, the way he described American tourists was condescending and often cruel. A few of the passengers were Cubans using the ship for the "normal" purpose of transportation, but "the others were creatures of a different order. They were representatives of the lower to middle brackets of the American urban middle class and they were on a cruise."[57] Although he would feel guilty about prying into the lives of the "undefended and appallingly damaged group of human beings" he met in Alabama, Agee seems to feel nothing but disdain for the petit-bourgeois tourists.[58] These subjects have, after all, not been excluded from modernity and therefore merit the full force of Agee's resentment.

Their stay in Havana lasted for only eighteen hours, but one cannot help but speculate about what Evans might have shown his friend of his previous trip. Did he introduce him to his few journalist acquaintances (the even fewer who had survived the revolution)? Did he take Agee to the dock to show him the stevedores? Did they both wonder at the prospects of this new Cuba, now under the control of Fulgencia Batista? Aside from the *Fortune* article, there is no other published record of the

time that Agee and Evans spent in Havana, so this will remain speculation for the time being,[59] but there is some indication that those eighteen hours tinted ever so slightly their portrait of Alabama. By the time
Famous Men saw publication, Agee still recalled "the lower American
continent": "Beneath, the gulf lies dreaming, and beneath, dreaming,
that woman, that id, the lower American continent, lies spread before
heaven in her wealth. The parks of her cities are iron, loam, silent, the
sweet fountains shut, and the pure façades, embroiled, limelike in street
light are sharp, are still."[60] Agee's image is a typically exotic depiction
of Latin America and is in keeping with the history of North American writing about the region. However, the more specific detail that the
"parks of her cities are iron" could be a memory from his brief visit to
Havana in the summer of 1937 (the only time he spent in any place that
could be considered the "lower American continent").[61] If so, his memory is filled not with the violence of the recent revolution but rather, as
the *Fortune* article demonstrates, with the tourist's version of Havana.
Even if Evans did not have the time or the inclination to show him traces
of the violent Havana he had seen, in "Six Days at Sea" Agee nevertheless expresses his own critique of U.S. imperialism: "At the Main Monument, which is capstoned by the quaint word Liberty, the hog [their tour
guide] reminded his little charges how the U.S. gave Cuba Hobson's (not
by any chance Iscariot's) Kiss and made our little brown boy friend safe
for the canebrake, the sugar mill, and the riding boss, and his island a
safe place for decent American citizens to do business in."[62] This cyni-
cal view of U.S. intervention was common enough, but Agee's criticism
could also pass easily for secondhand Beals. There is the same mix of
anti-imperialist sentiment and strong paternal perspective for this land
that "lies spread before heaven in her wealth." As Agee attacks the values of "decent American citizens," he is simultaneously trying to convey
an experience in Cuba to his decent American readers. This conflicted
gesture lies at the heart of documentary, which endeavors to make the
foreign legible even as it participates in constructing its subjects as different from its audience. But this conflict is also central to the Pan American project, which attempted to represent the hemisphere as a knowable,
unified whole but which simultaneously stressed the crucial economic
differences.

Through these representations of Pan American progress, and in the
work of Beals and Evans in particular, I have attempted to trace the
complicated, and often contradictory, politics of representing poverty
in Latin America and the U.S. South. What makes a figure like Beals so

intriguing is that, at first blush, he appears to be an enlightened soul from North America, a champion of those who are trampled under the forward march of industrialization. Of course, as I have shown, such advocacy is complicated by latent patriotism and by a U.S.-centered concept of modernity that is difficult to slough off. Beals's writing should prove a cautionary tale not to take the northern critiques of industrialization at face value, no matter how decidedly anti-imperialist the authors may insist that they are. But more important this posture of indignation in the face of U.S. imperialism masks the narrative of underdevelopment at work in even the most radical texts. Ideas about "Pan American progress" were persistently championed by the PAU's *Bulletin*, but they were also reinforced through these supposedly critical representations of poverty in the Americas.

Women, Migration, and
Memories of Pan Americanism

5 Pan Americanism Revisited

Hemispheric Feminism and Ana Castillo's *The Mixquiahuala Letters*

As a woman I have no country. As a woman I want no country. As a woman my country is the whole world.
—Virginia Woolf, *Three Guineas*

I cannot say I am a citizen of the world as Virginia Woolf, speaking as an Anglo woman born to economic means, declared herself. . . . As a mestiza born to the lower strata, I am treated at best as a second class citizen, at worst, as a non-entity.
—Ana Castillo, "A Countryless Woman," in *Massacre of the Dreamers*

PAN AMERICANISM WAS AN IDEA brimming with the promise of hemispheric unity, but it was a promise that rang hollow for women and for people of color. In Carleton Beals's racist link between the U.S. South and Cuba and in the Pan American Union's eugenics conference in Havana, it was clear that transnational cooperation was hardly an all-inclusive vision. What's more, the concerns of women during this period were neglected, and women were largely denied the means to represent themselves on the Pan American stage. To be sure, women were active both as artists and intellectuals during the early twentieth century, and scholars have shown the importance of Latin American writers such as Gabriela Mistral and Victoria Ocampo, and more recently Rachel Adams has illuminated the transnational network of U.S. and European women working in Mexico in the 1920s.[1] These studies have been important in rethinking our understanding of the intellectual contributions made by women in the Americas, but I want to turn instead to women's travel writing and its attempt to forge explicitly hemispheric bonds within the rhetoric of Pan Americanism I have been exploring. In an era when national laws withheld basic equality from women, the idea of Pan America provided a landscape of alternative, though still limited possibilities.

There is a need, then, to return to the Pan American era in order to look for acts of self-representation. Many of them are difficult to locate since they were marginalized during their time and it is only upon revisiting them from a historical distance that we realize how significant they were. This action of intellectual recovery is precisely the critical endeavor Ana Castillo engages in with her first novel, *The Mixquiahuala Letters* (1986), which is a central focus of this chapter. While Castillo's novel takes place decades after the Pan American era, it is a work invested in looking back at previous generations of women. It is only in the "revisiting" (an important word in *The Mixquiahuala Letters*) that the original act attains its significance. For this reason Castillo's example also provides the methodology for this chapter. By revisiting the forgotten works of women like Muna Lee and Erna Fergusson, I hope to reveal a genealogy of Pan American feminism that challenged some of the patriarchal discourse coming out of the PAU. However, this movement mirrored in many ways the dynamics of male-dominated Pan Americanism since the agenda was typically set by white U.S. women, who presented themselves as the "natural" center of feminist progress that the rest of the Americas should emulate.

Megan Threlkeld, who has done work on the early Pan American women's movements of the 1920s, observes, "These women internationalists saw themselves as citizens of an international community long before they were full citizens of their own countries."[2] However, she also points out the continuing condescension of U.S. women as they worked with their counterparts from other nations. At the 1922 Pan American Conference of Women in Baltimore, not only did women from the United States set the agenda of the meeting, but their rhetoric clearly marked a colonial difference within the group. As an example of this mind-set, Threlkeld presents a letter from Carrie Chapman Catt, who proposed that a Pan American women's organization should include delegates from all member nations, but in addition "it might have a meeting or two during the convention which would give the Pans the sense that they were still in it."[3] The notion that there would be "Pans" and "Americans" at this conference speaks volumes about the perception of Latin America and the Caribbean. Even when the stated goal was hemispheric solidarity, the term *Pans* marks the inhabitants of these regions as somehow "extra-American," part of the periphery whose center was in the United States. And so, while Pan American women's movements were frequently in opposition to the male-dominated institutions of the PAU, they echoed the thinking of those same institutions in their refusal to include non-U.S. women as equal partners.

Castillo's remark on Virginia Woolf in the epigraph is in many ways a response to a history of division within feminist thought. Her belief that the experience of being racially and economically subaltern sets her apart from Woolf's "Anglo" feminism reflects the critique of mainstream feminism put forward in the 1980s by Chicana intellectuals and decolonial thinkers from across the globe. The important collection *This Bridge Called My Back* (1981) was motivated by the desire, as Cherríe Moraga and Gloria Anzaldúa explained it, "to express to all women—especially to white middle-class women—the experiences which divide us as feminists."[4] The contributors to the volume went on to offer their own vision of feminism understood through their experiences as women of color. Chela Sandoval later framed this epistemic position as U.S. Third World feminism, which, when compared with the priorities of the dominant feminist theory of the 1980s, revealed "two different understandings of domination, subordination, and the nature of effective resistance."[5] Sandoval goes on to discuss U.S. Third World feminism as "sets of imaginary spaces" and as a "topography of consciousness" that remaps feminist consciousness in opposition to the dominant discourse.[6] It is the metaphor of space that is most relevant to Castillo's critique and to any notion of Pan American feminism since all of these oppositional epistemes begin with the premise that challenging the dominant discourse and reimagining one's relationship to the nation are part of the same project.

Within this context any claim to internationalism, such as Woolf's, comes from a position of privilege. Thus Castillo's formulation of the "countryless woman" suggests an inversion of Woolf, whereby the premise "As a woman I have no country" does not lead to the conclusion that "as a woman my country is the whole world." Instead Castillo evokes the condition of statelessness and invisibility. Despite the seemingly clear-cut denunciation of what she terms "Anglo feminism," Castillo's work demonstrates a much more complicated relationship with writing by white women and by women of color. She frequently returns to both sets of texts, mining them for what is useful, pointing out the gaps in their universalist assumptions but also filling in such gaps with her imaginative supplements to an earlier generation of women's writing.

The tensions within Pan American women's movements in the early twentieth century are the same ones Castillo tries to negotiate in her writing. Her novel *The Mixquiahuala Letters* centers on the relationship between a white woman, Alicia, and a Chicana, Teresa, and the way their multiple journeys through Mexico by turns strengthen and unravel their sense of solidarity. By reading Castillo's novel as a meditation on an earlier generation of women writers in the Americas, I consider the divergent visions of what women's liberation in the Americas looked like in these texts. While at the height of the Pan American era such writing was marginalized and ignored, a second visit demonstrates how these writers articulated the goal of Pan Americanism and made it their own.

The Early Days of Pan American Feminism

A group of fifteen hundred women gathered in Havana in 1928. Outside the official proceedings of the Sixth Conference of American States, where Machado was welcoming President Coolidge and where the findings of the previous month's eugenics conference were being discussed, the First Pan American Women's Auxiliary Conference met to discuss the status of women in the Americas. Excluded from the main proceedings, these women organized a kind of *salon des refusées*, composed of leading feminists from the Americas, female scientists, and wives of diplomats attending the conference.

The most important accomplishment of the Women's Auxiliary Conference, as Francesca Miller has pointed out, was the decision to organize "a Pan American Union of Women."[7] By basing their organization on the model of the U.S.-centered PAU, there was always the danger that the agenda of the North American women would dominate the movement. However, the platform that was adopted in Havana managed to articulate a set of objectives on which the women of all twenty-one member nations could agree. The nascent movement would aim

> to promote the general education of women and to secure for them higher standards of education; to secure the rights of married women to control their own property and earnings; to secure equal guardianship; to encourage organizations, discussion, and public speaking among women and freedom of opportunity for women to cultivate and use their talents; to educate public opinion in favor of granting the vote to women, to secure their political rights and finally to promote friendliness and understanding among all Pan American countries, with the aim of maintaining perpetual peace in the hemisphere.[8]

The goals of suffrage, equal access to education, and property rights were shared by contemporary women's movements within the various member nations of the PAU. What is different about the Women's Auxiliary Conference is the hemispheric stage on which its members advanced their cause. Feeling stymied by the intransigent governments of their home nations, they saw the Pan American conference as a way to make an end run around such barriers since, if they could succeed in introducing a measure on the floor of the conference, it would have to be voted on by the legislatures of each member nation. Although they were excluded from the main proceedings of the conference, at the end of the five-week program delegates from the Women's Auxiliary stormed the plenary session of the larger Pan American conference and presented an Equal Rights Amendment to be applied throughout the hemisphere. Reporting on the Havana conference for the *Nation*, Muna Lee began her article defiantly and suggested that her fellow delegates were even more determined than Nicaragua's anti-U.S. guerrilla leader: "Sandino was kept out of the Sixth Pan-American Conference at Havana, but the Women's Party of the United States got in."[9]

Muna Lee de Muñoz Marín was herself emblematic of the transnational feminist movement of her day. Born in the United States but living her adult life in Puerto Rico, she was a poet, translator, and cultural ambassador for over four decades. For much of that time, if a U.S. reader encountered a poem by a Latin American author, odds were that it had been translated by Lee. This included the bulk of *Poetry*'s 1925 Spanish American number as well as the New Directions *Anthology of Contemporary Latin-American Poetry* (1941), which was the first collection of its kind to appear in the United States.[10] When the New Directions volume was published, Lee made clear how important she believed translation was, telling an interviewer that there was "no better way to develop friendship between the United States and Latin America than to translate and publish the literature of each region for the other."[11] Her literary career was centered on cultural exchange between the Americas, and in many essays she endeavored to make the culture and history of Latin America known to her mostly U.S. readers. As the editor of her work, Jonathan Cohen, has described it, she led a "Pan-American Life."[12]

But Lee was also a champion of women's causes throughout the hemisphere. She devoted much of her writing to the history of women such as Anne Bradstreet and Sor Juana Inés de la Cruz and to portraits of contemporary women from around the globe, which she published as "Notes from a Feminist's Travel Diary" in the important journal *Equal Rights*. It was as a public speaker, though, that she was most poignant on the subject of women's rights, promoting universal suffrage and the protection of married women's property rights, among other issues. Speaking to the delegates of the Women's Auxiliary in 1928, Lee addressed the gender inequalities of the hemisphere with a crucial simile: "Our position as women, amongst you free citizens of Pan America, is like the position of my Porto Rico in the community of American States. We have everything done for us and given us but sovereignty. We are treated with every consideration of being regarded as responsible beings. We, like Porto Rico, are dependents. We are anomalies before the law."[13]

Lee's invocation of Puerto Rico redeploys the well-worn analogy of women and land as a critique of patriarchy in the Americas. While many oppressed groups in the hemisphere have invoked the history of colonialism in their struggles for equality, the status of women in the early twentieth century is more aptly reflected in Puerto Rico's ambiguous status as a dependent state having everything "but sovereignty." Amy Kaplan has discussed at great length the status of Puerto Rico during this period and the way efforts to define the island's status also shaped the nature of the U.S. Empire. She cites the U.S. Supreme Court's conclusion in *Downes v. Bidwell* (1901) that Puerto Rico was "foreign to the United States in a domestic sense."[14] This paradoxical phrase is at the core of Kaplan's study of the role that domesticity itself played in the idea of a U.S. Empire. Lee's simile then returns us to the contradictions of U.S. foreign policy and the doublespeak of Pan Americanism.

Lee also identifies the general ambiguities of the nation-state at this time. As women's suffrage movements met with firm oppositions in most Latin American nations, formations other than the nation-state inspired the thinking of feminists in the Americas and allowed them to articulate alternative structures of solidarity. If a dependent, quasi-state such as Puerto Rico represented the reality for women, the international stage of the Pan American Union held the alluring if hollow promise of overcoming the gender inequality cemented in national laws. In her study of women's movements in Latin America, Miller explains why this transnational forum was so appealing: "By the 1920s and 1930s, the international forums seemed to offer activist women the opportunity to effect reform through the passage of resolutions that would oblige signatory governments to raise the issues within their domestic arena."[15] While the conferences and meetings held by the Pan American Union were for most of the delegates acts of diplomacy and international courtesy, Lee and other leading women attended these meetings out of tactical necessity.

These early feminists were seen by most of their male contemporaries as distractions from the central business of the PAU, yet many women saw their movement as a return to the more fundamental Pan American dream of Simón Bolívar. Their idealism, their desire for a new social order in the Americas as well as their desire for transnational laws governing their rights led these Pan American feminists to compare themselves with Bolívar and a forgotten nineteenth-century ideal of hemispheric unity.[16] In concluding her report to the *Nation* on the Women's Auxiliary Conference, Lee invoked the old dream of transnational unity: "The women of no country will look upon the cause as won until it is won for all. Here at last is a unity of ideal and effort which establishes a real, a spontaneous, a spiritual commonwealth of Pan-America."[17] The implication here is that the male delegates of the PAU have squandered the hopes of Pan Americanism (spending their time at eugenics conferences, trade meetings, and other dubious affairs) and that it will have to be the women who will "at last" realize the old ideals.

In her speech to the auxiliary conference, Lee highlighted the historical ties of the two Americas, the cultural unity brought about by the hemisphere's women:

> The woman of colonial times displayed the same splendid traits in Latin America and in Saxon America. She worked and fought beside her men; gaily and gallantly she dedicated her strength of body and spirit to building the Americas. And now, with one impulse of the heart, though in the ringing accents of four languages, she reminds you of this, of which you should never force her to remind you. She asks that the countries she has helped to create recognize in her the powers by which they have benefited during four centuries.[18]

In this evocation of the Pan American woman, whose "strength of body and spirit" built the Americas, Lee places her on equal footing with the Founding Fathers of North and South America. Lee's rhetoric also strives for equality in terms of the hegemony implicit in her portrait of the Americas. Like the hemispheric mythologies we saw in chapter 2, Lee's vision of a shared colonial past in North and South America conceals the material realities of the continents' histories. In stressing the similarities among the women of the Americas, she naturalizes the experiences of white bourgeois women as the default subject position for the hemisphere. Not only does the image of the mythical Pan American woman who "worked and fought beside her men" occlude the experiences of indigenous women (who were often fought *against* by the colonial cultures Lee celebrates), but it also ignores the history of enslaved women in the Americas.

Lee and other U.S. women at the conference would never have stated explicitly that the twentieth-century concerns of indigenous women,

women of color, and the poor and working classes were not theirs, but her vision of American history reveals the particular kind of women they were there to defend. What's more, by linking the movement to the past in this way, Lee's vision of the hemisphere is not presented as something radically new but rather as something the so-called Pan American woman must "remind you of." In many ways it is this historical loop, this returning to the past in order to move forward, that defines Lee's Pan American feminism.

While Lee's migration from the United States to Puerto Rico informed her attitudes toward women's rights, the exile of Luisa Capetillo in the United States provides an interesting counterpoint for considering feminist thought in the Americas. The Puerto Rican writer, labor leader, anarchist, and feminist made a name for herself in union politics, first in her native Puerto Rico from 1905 to 1912, and then among workers in the United States.[19] Her political actions, and the scrutiny she received from police, led to her migration in 1912 to New York and eventually to the Tampa–Ybor City region of Florida, where she joined the diasporic community of Cubans and Puerto Ricans who worked in the local tobacco industry. But she also published experimental literary texts that combined essays, short stories, and plays, all of which were inflected with her political ideals and involve characters coming to consciousness and challenging both capitalism and patriarchy. Of special relevance is Capetillo's *Influencias de las ideas modernas* (1916), which was composed largely in the United States. Here she articulates a vision of women's freedom that extends beyond borders, but rather than looking to any sort of Pan American diplomacy, her argument for challenging patriarchy is rooted in her experience as a worker and as a labor organizer.

Over the past several decades scholars have recovered Capetillo's work, beginning with Norma Valle Ferrer's biography in 1990 and Julio Ramos's selection of her work in *Amor y anarquía* (1992) and leading up to the reissue and translation of her writing by Arte Público Press. This scholarly fascination has had to do as much with her biography as her writing. Born to working-class, autodidact parents, Capetillo was encouraged to challenge the conventional expectations for women in Puerto Rico, in terms of both education and marriage. Her parents took charge of her education at home, teaching her French and encouraging her to read Tolstoy, Hugo, and George Sand, among other writers and political thinkers. Capetillo's parents also served as a model for her own critique of marriage. Her mother and father never married, a fact

Capetillo spoke of with pride throughout her life, and provided her with an alternative to the institution she would later describe as a condition of slavery for women of all classes.

In her break with the conventional gender roles of her time, Capetillo made clear that for her the liberation of the worker and the liberation of working women were both part of the same anarchist future. This correlation has come to be symbolized by her transgressive use of fashion; she often wore pant-skirts (or harem skirts) to labor meetings and is considered the first Puerto Rican woman to wear a suit. She observed in her essay "Vestimenta de la anarquista" ("Attire of the Anarchist"), "This practice of wearing pants is perfectly suited to the era of women's progress. And this practice will necessarily continue to vary the fabrics from the thinnest to the finest and most delicate and we will end up wearing only a veil or chiffon to cover ourselves."[20] She goes on to write that this new epoch will soon be upon us and that these changes in fashion are needed since "it is the sociological, communist, anarchist progress which is asserting itself."[21] This era had not yet arrived at the beginning of the twentieth century, though. In 1915, while in Havana, she was arrested for wearing men's attire, and a photo of her in a Cuban newspaper caused a scandal at the time and has since become an iconic image of her defiance.

As provocative as these actions were, it is important to remember that Capetillo's challenge to patriarchy was interwoven with her challenge to the exploitation of labor under the current structures of transnational capitalism. Ramos has argued for understanding her intellectual trajectory within the context of the tobacco factories of Florida, where she held the traditional job of factory reader. The role of the *lector* was to read aloud and lead discussions on the factory floor while the tobacco workers rolled cigars. This practice usually put the tobacco industry at the vanguard of union activity in Cuba, Puerto Rico, and Florida. In addition to being a focal point for labor organizing and revolutionary activity among the diaspora community as well as playing a formative role in Capetillo's development as a labor leader, the tobacco factories, Ramos argues, even shaped the hybrid form of Capetillo's literary work through the variety of texts she would have read there. He writes, "It was foreseeable that the emergent labor discourse would be heterogeneous, 'undisciplined,' and that it would exceed the limits of specialization, contrasting, precisely, the ideals of 'purity' and discipline." It is this same heterogeneity he finds in Capetillo's four published works.[22]

Lisa Sánchez González, who has repositioned Capetillo as a foundational writer of the Puerto Rican diaspora, has noted Ramos's emphasis on her background in "labor discourse" and asked the very pertinent question, "But what are we to make of Capetillo's specific role as an anarcho-*feminist*, as a working-class woman vying for a position as a 'new discursant' in this transnational context, and in what she and her anarchist colleagues considered a *supra*national movement?"[23] In answer to this, Sánchez González suggests that Capetillo's work must be understood outside of a national context, as part of a transnational struggle for women's liberation. With the nationalist movements in Puerto Rico having no role for a transgressive thinker like Capetillo, her migration to the United States, both physically and intellectually signaled an expansion of her thinking. Thus her particular brand of feminist thought, dependent as it is on the locations of Puerto Rico and Tampa and of the labor conditions in both those places, provides another way of understanding Sandoval's topography of consciousness. It is precisely her relation to the material conditions around her that shape Capetillo's thought as well as the coming to consciousness of the characters in her writing.

At the root of Capetillo's analysis is the premise that the "current social system, with all its errors, is sustained by the ignorance and slavery of women."[24] Therefore her anarchist critique is predicated upon rethinking the history and current condition of women. This serves as the important first step toward revolution since, she argues, the ideology of patriarchy is imbedded even within her own community of radicals. In "Some Interesting Letters from a Panamanian Anarchist," she reveals that a male friend who has been able to thoroughly unthink the presumptions of bourgeois capitalism is nevertheless bound to certain ideas concerning women. In Capetillo's literary texts, letters serve an important role, and in *Influencias de las ideas modernas* they stand alongside her essays and plays as part of the same artistic project. While most of the letters in the volume are written by Capetillo and explicitly advance her views to friends and associates, "Some Interesting Letters from a Panamanian Anarchist" is the exception since it includes only letters that Capetillo received and none of her responses.

In this selection of letters, received while Capetillo was living and organizing in Tampa, the unnamed "Panamanian anarchist" writes to her of their common struggle and simultaneously works to persuade her (unsuccessfully) to give up her activism and move into his home, where they might rely on his salary alone. Rather than point out the subtext of domination that pervades the letters, Capetillo's arrangement allows the anarchist to expose these views himself. In addition to trying to persuade her to move in with him, he also reveals his notion of women's biological frailty even in the midst of declaring his own feminist ideals. He writes:

> Humanity cannot enjoy freedom while women are not free. A woman who gives her body over to the spasms of an enslaved pleasure will never bring forth healthy, strong children. Maternal bosoms that dilate in the pleasure of coitus, under the pressure of pain and fear that reign in today's marriages will not produce the fruit with all its liberty, because the muscles of life don't take pleasure in its dominion and recreation of maternal functions . . . .
>
> Fight with valor in the field of women's liberty. Woman is the one who gives humanity its life and direction. Without free women, man cannot be free.[25]

This letter articulates decidedly unmodern notions about women's physiology that historically had been used to argue for "protecting" them from the stress of physical or intellectual labor. The writer makes the case for equitable marriage between men and women, and yet his rationale is that the pressures of marriage in its current state will constrict a woman's chest muscles and prevent her from nursing "the fruit with all its liberty." Even so, the anarchist seems unaware of the contradictions since his letter ends with triumphant declarations about the "field of women's liberty." Such statements, republished in the context of *Influencias*, intentionally ring hollow in the ears of Capetillo's reader.

Capetillo's brilliance is in the arrangement of these letters. Her text calls for a careful and resistant reading of the "Panamanian anarchist" that challenges common sense, and her other writing applies a similar methodology to the history of women. She begins one of her short essays in *Influencias* by asking, "Why call George Sand *indecent* in the publicity for her books?"[26] She then looks back on centuries of women who have been disparaged by generations of male historians: "I see queens, empresses, intelligent women who ask for vindication because their conduct and behavior have been exaggerated in an abusive matter. Why accuse a free woman like Ann Boleyn of being a prostitute . . . ?"[27] Instead Capetillo offers a resistant history, which challenges the accounts of these women's lives and elevates them from the rungs of inferiority where historians have placed them. "I refuse," she writes, "to accept as depraved or perverse any woman conceptualized as such by any historian who erroneously believes that women do not have the right to use their complete freedom without being perceived as depraved, frivolous, etc., while men have been able to do and attain whatever they want."[28] The "vindication" of Sand and Boleyn is consistent with Capetillo's larger project of reimagining the status of women across the globe. Just as she worked to advance the cause of laborers in Puerto Rico and the United States without regard to national borders, so too was her retelling of history decidedly international, drawing in so-called indecent women from all classes and backgrounds.

While Lee and Capetillo present different versions of feminism in the Americas, both look back to some retelling of history in order to create their own particular narrative of women's progress. Lee is also a reader of history, situating contemporary women's struggle for equality within the larger context of liberty in the Americas, even though she neglects important differences between the women of North and South America. It is this historical approach of these writers that will allow us to understand Ana Castillo's method in *The Mixquiahuala Letters*. In the case of each of these writers, the events of the past are not merely to be retold; rather they must be reexamined for new meaning. Indeed for Lee and Capetillo this is a crucial part of their methodology. Thus, as we move through an analysis of Castillo's novel, it will also offer an occasion to revisit the history of women in the Americas more critically.

Rereading History: Ana Castillo and Her Sources

Although written long after the Pan American era, Castillo's work is deeply invested in the politics of transnational feminism as well as the experience of women travel writers in the early and late twentieth century, and her novel thus affords an opportunity to reappraise the earlier period. She engages the writings of women in the early twentieth century, but she does so cautiously since she continues to be skeptical of the overwhelming Anglocentrism of those movements. In her essay "Transcontinental Affinities," Castillo represents her own intellectual development as growing out of an identification with Third World feminism:

> Although born and raised in the United States, I feel more affinity with the feminist writings of Egyptian Nawal el Saadawi than white American feminists, such as the famous American radical, Kate Millett. I find more in common with post-revolutionary Algerian women than the women who were part of the sexual revolution of the 1960s in the United States and Northern Europe. Spanish culture and my indigenous blood are at the root of my empathy. The immediate reasons for my connections are racism and classism. Due to my mestizaje I descend from a labor force long exploited by

Anglo capitalism; therefore, it is true that I have certain social bonds with women of "third world" countries.[29]

While Castillo sees herself as a Chicana intellectual, part of a specific movement that was still defining itself in the 1970s and 1980s, she also situates herself within a larger historical and geographical context as a woman of color. This, in part, grows out of the internationalist outlook of the early *movimiento*, which positioned the struggles of Chicano nationalism as parallel with the decolonial struggles in Africa and other revolutionary movements of the 1960s, as well as the Third World feminist discourse of the 1980s. However, in claiming a "common" experience among women from different parts of the globe, Castillo in many ways recapitulates the rhetoric of the Anglo women she criticizes. Just as Muna Lee's invocation of a universal experience of women in the Americas erases important differences, so too does Castillo's appeal to "affinities" position her own experience as the zero point of feminist critique.

Despite her stated differences with them, in *The Mixquiahuala Letters* Castillo insists upon returning to the work of earlier Anglo women, such as Erna Fergusson and Emma-Lindsey Squier, in order to find some sort of usable past but also to reconsider the silences of these early texts in which the experiences of women of color are present. Castillo's is an act of recovery that locates the women of color in these early texts and attempts to understand them within the larger history of colonialism.

What results from Castillo's intellectual inquiries is an alternative hemispheric community that replaces the exclusions of the Pan American era with the inclusiveness that has resulted from her formulation of Chicana feminism. Her application of these ideas extends beyond traditional notions of Chicana identity and toward a transnational identity, as she explains in *Massacre of the Dreamers: Essays on Xicanisma* (1994): "If Xicanisma is not a nationalist politic, then what is it? Xicanisma is an ever present consciousness of our interdependency specifically rooted in our culture and history. Although Xicanisma is a way to understand ourselves in the world, it may also help others who are not necessarily of Mexican background and/or women. It is yielding, never resistant to change, one based on wholeness not dualisms" (226). In its quest for transnational community, Castillo's Xicanisma shares some of its goals with Pan Americanism. However, her emphasis on the "yielding" quality of Xicanisma sets it apart from the Pan American project, which sought to understand all of the Americas within the narrow bounds of U.S-defined modernity. This is in essence an effort to take up the subject position of "the Pans," both in the sense of being marginalized from mainstream "America" and in the sense of embracing the totality. Flexibility and the acceptance of change are qualities that Castillo draws from specific examples of women of color and applies to a broader transnational context. Elsewhere in *Massacre of the Dreamers* she further defines her idea of Xicanisma: "On a pragmatic level, the basic premise of Xicanisma is to reconsider behavior long seen as inherent in the Mexic Amerindian woman's character, such as, patience, perseverance, industriousness, loyalty to one's clan, and commitment to our children. Contrary to how those incognizant of what feminism is, we do not reject these virtues" (40). This idea of transnational Xicanisma grows out of the condition of being marginalized from both patriarchal society and Anglocentric feminism, which, Castillo argues, has dismissed core elements of Mexic Amerindian womanhood. In addition to her declarations in her essays, though, *The Mixquiahuala Letters* reinforces this ideal of a transnational Chicana identity.

Throughout *The Mixquiahuala Letters*, Castillo understands the position of women of color within a transnational frame. Her characters are bound less by the nation-state than by a global economy that either exploits them for the cheapest of labor or confines them to the domestic sphere. Her analysis is at once transnational and deeply historical, since the history of colonialism in the Americas and the meeting of European and indigenous cultures lie at the root of the present-day problems she critiques. In *Letters* the adventures and obstacles that the two female characters face are inflected with historical significance. They represent the struggle of Chicana feminists in the late 1970s and early 1980s, but Teresa and Alicia are also occasions to reflect on the history of women in the Americas.

One of the central concerns in *The Mixquiahuala Letters* is the recovery of lost stories and silenced voices. Though the novel can be read in any order, in Letter One we are introduced to Teresa's Aunt Filomena, whose name suggests Philomela. Thus Ovid's story, in which Philomela is raped and has her tongue cut out, silencing her song, is an important tonic note for Castillo's novel, in which male violence is always a threat. But just as important is Philomela's alternative means of communication, her weaving of a tapestry that will eventually tell her story. Teresa describes the life of her aunt: "She took in laundry, children of working-out-of-the-home-mothers and whipped out some mean drapes on an old pedal Singer."[30] Filomena's sewing reinforces the allusion to the Greek myth (she even works on a Singer), but it also situates her character at the center of a very real labor economy, one that places women of color at the bottom. For Castillo, labor and family obligation are the ties that united women around the globe.

Tía Filomena, living in the San Fernando Valley, is not merely representative of Mexican American women. Instead Castillo positions her within a larger community of "countryless" women of color. In her essay "A Countryless Woman: The Early Feminista" Castillo declares, "Ours is a world imbued with nationalism, real for some, yet tenuous as paper for others. A world in which from the day of our births, we are either granted citizenship or relegated to the netherstate of serving as mass production drones. Non-white women—Mexicans/Chicanas, Filipinas, Malaysians, and others—who comprise eighty percent of the global factory work force, are the greatest dispensable resource that multinational interests own. The women are in effect, represented by no country" (*Massacre* 24). Much of Castillo's writing is devoted to representing these women of the "global factory work force" who have gone unrepresented. By beginning one path of *The Mixquiahuala Letters* with Tía Filomena, who like so many women of color lacks a country to represent her, Castillo establishes a tone for her novel and even a methodology.

As we read the *Letters*, untold stories from the lives of Alicia and Teresa (from troubled marriages to artistic aspirations to abortions) surface, as do the stories of past women of the Americas. For Castillo politically engaged reading is fundamental to recovering these untold stories, and recovering these stories from the void of history is necessary to formulate a present-day Chicana identity. She elaborates on this method, which is so much a combination of research, knowledge, and identity: "As Mexic Amerindians we must, to find a clue as to who we are and from whom we descend, become akin to archaeologists" (6). Like William Carlos Williams's, Castillo's invocation of archaeology is meant to challenge traditional history. Whereas women's voices have been excluded from that dominant narrative, Castillo's writing, both her fiction and nonfiction, digs down to find these voices. Significantly she distinguishes herself from "Eurocentric intellectuals" whose work has excluded the study of women of color both in the academy and in publishing, but throughout her work she maintains an uneasy relationship with such intellectual traditions.

Castillo herself is an academic and has had a vexed relationship with the scholarly tradition to which she belongs. *In Massacre of the Dreamers*, she recounts the way her early feelings of being alienated from her indigenous heritage led her to graduate school and a master's degree in Latin American and Caribbean studies from the University of Chicago.

She remembers this as a simultaneously personal and political act of inquiry: "In 1979 the first generation of college educated Chicanas was in the making and their investigations and publications were also difficult to come by. It was indeed a question of each one becoming a *re-conquistadora*, exploring herself as subject through scholarship" (9). In becoming a "re-conquistadora" of the history of the Americas, Castillo sought to challenge the traditional source materials on which history is based. She describes the source material for her master's thesis, "The Idealization and Reality of the Mexican Indian Woman," as deriving from two fields: "imaginative literatures and anthropology" (7). However, her early scholarship also challenged the methods of history writing by insisting on an act of overreading, the method of archaeology recovery and self-definition she would later explore in her fiction. She writes of her early, frustrated attempts to locate women's voices, "Unfortunately the writings of mestizos, criollos, Spaniards, and Anglos from the nineteenth century up to that time (1979) did not reveal anything more than stereotypes. At best I found ethnographic data that ultimately did not bring me closer to understanding how the Mexic Amerindian woman truly perceives herself since anthropology is traditionally based on the objectification of its subjects. . . . In neither the creative literature nor the ethnographic documentation, did I hear her speak for herself" (7). In *The Mixquiahuala Letters*, she also negotiates these same two modes of writing—the creative and the ethnographic—in order to reformulate representations of women in the Americas. Again we see the use of formal hybridity to challenge established ways of knowing. Castillo, like the other Pan American modernists I have considered in this book, uses mixed-genre writing to challenge the disciplinary boundaries that constructed Latin America as an object of study. More specifically she is interested in the way Chicanas and other women of color have been made the subjects of anthropological study. In her blend of academic writing and epistolary fiction, Castillo has raided the archive and reframed the ethnographic writing about women of color through the narration of her character Teresa.

Alvina Quintana has referred to Castillo's novel as "a parody of modern ethnographic and travel writing."[31] She compares the novel's representation of Chicanas with the discourse of ethnographic fieldwork and suggests that Teresa functions as a native informant for Castillo, giving voice to an authentically Chicana experience of trying to forge an independent, empowered identity in the United States and Mexico. However, Castillo disrupts the conventions of academic ethnography through the open form of her novel (which I will explore in a moment), thereby decentering the authoritative voice of the anthropologist. It is in this manner, Quintana explains, that *The Mixquiahuala Letters* "functions as an oppositional feminist discourse," engaging and disrupting traditional modes of representing women.[32]

Reflecting back on this book's larger concern with knowledge production, we can understand Castillo's position both inside and outside the academy as creating an ambiguous relationship with the logic of Pan Americanism. She approaches the history of the Western Hemisphere much in the way a conventional scholar would, carefully researching her source material. However, her work is markedly unconventional since the subjects of her research—women of color—have largely been excluded from Pan American knowledge production (or at least excluded from any position that would control representations of themselves) and because her methods of writing about these subjects take less "official" routes. It is the break with the conventional form of the novel that allows her this epistemic disobedience. Just as the other subjects of this book, such as Carpentier, reorganized disciplinary knowledge into forms that were neither recognizable as novel nor academic studies, so too does Castillo challenge traditional structures of knowledge. If the structures of history and indeed the conventional novel have not allowed women a voice, then Castillo finds an alternative tradition of expression in the epistolary form.

The Mixquiahuala Letters is structured as a series of letters written by one of the protagonists, Teresa, to the other, Alicia, recounting their travels through Mexico and the history of their relationship. While the epistolary structure engages with a long tradition of English novels, Castillo's work is indebted to two more recent examples: *The Color Purple* (1982) by Alice Walker and *The Three Marias: New Portuguese Letters* (1973) by Maria Isabel Barreno, Maria Teresa Horta, and Maria Velho da Costa. Walker's novel, which achieved notoriety just as Castillo was beginning to compose her novel, was certainly a model for the way letters could strengthen bonds between women separated by great physical distance (one in the United States, one in Africa) and allow for an escape from the domestic sphere and its patriarchal abuses. The notion of the "dead letter" is something Castillo also takes from Walker since all of the Mixquiahuala letters are written by Teresa with no reply. For most of *The Color Purple* the letters do not reach their intended addressee, but this discourages neither Celie nor Nettie from writing them.[33] It is the act of writing that strengthens these bonds, and Teresa's letter writing makes Alicia present in the novel by revisiting and reinterpreting their numerous shared experiences.

The Three Marias provides a different kind of model in which exchanged letters offer an occasion to make the private public. It was an important book for Castillo, which she had been reading as early as 1978 and which she frequently taught in her class Feminist Journal Writing.[34] The book is a compilation of letters exchanged by three Portuguese women—Maria Isabel Barreno, Maria Teresa Horta, and Maria Velho da Costa—in which they express their mutual struggles to evade the social constrictions placed on women in 1970s Portugal. What is particularly interesting for thinking about Castillo is that these letters are proposed not just as a conduit for understanding women in Portugal but also for understanding literature more generally. The "three Marias" begin their volume, "Granted, then, that all of literature is a long letter to an invisible other, a present, a possible, or a future passion that we rid ourselves of, feed, or seek."[35] As with *The Color Purple* and ultimately *The Mixquiahuala Letters*, the addressee need not write back; she is "an invisible other." The letters is this volume are indeed composed by three women, but none of them is signed, thereby making each letter a more "open" text.

Each letter in *The Three Marias* recalls a shared memory or shared experience. Therefore the letters do not add new information but instead return again and again to past events in order to strengthen the bonds forged by those shared memories. At the beginning of these letters, which will often loop back upon themselves, the authors explain their discursive strategy:

> Hence it will not be necessary to ask ourselves whether what brings us together is a common passion for different exercises, or the common exercise of different passions. The only question we need ask ourselves is what form our exercise will take—nostalgia or revenge. Yes, it is doubtless quite true that nostalgia is a form of revenge, and revenge a form of nostalgia; in both cases we are searching for something that will not force us to retreat, for something that will keep us from destroying. Nonetheless, passion is still the motive force and its exercise its meaning.[36]

Even the syntax of this statement enacts the method of the book, looping back upon itself and returning to the same idea. The importance of the return is clear from the beginning of *The Three Marias*, yet the manner of the return, whether out of "nostalgia or revenge," is still contested. These terms clearly influenced Castillo since they are also competing forces in her novel and, as she suggests, the competing forces in modern feminism. For instance, she offers nostalgia for domesticity in the figure of Tía Filomena, who longs for a simpler era, "back in the days when marriages were meaningful" (*Letters* 16). Castillo's own return to past events is alternately nostalgic and vengeful. The manner of this interpretive return is ultimately up to the reader since the novel presents a malleable, open form.

In addition to drawing upon an alternative epistolary tradition, Castillo's novel also employs an open structure with no definitive organization for her group of letters. The open structure of *The Mixquiahuala Letters* is indebted to the novel *Rayuela* (*Hopscotch*, 1963) by Julio Cortázar, to whom Castillo has dedicated her book. In her note to the reader, Castillo states, "It is the author's duty to alert the reader that this is not a book to be read in the usual sequence. All letters are numbered to aid in following any one of the author's proposed options" (n.p.). She offers three different sequences, "For the Conformist," "For the Cynic," and "For the Quixotic," after which she adds the final note: "For the reader committed to nothing but short fiction, all the letters read as separate entities. Good luck whichever journey you choose!" (n.p.). The open structure offers the reader a good deal of freedom, which has been noted by nearly every critical reading of the work.[37] However, by suggesting multiple paths in the table of contents, *The Mixquiahuala Letters* instantly begs for multiple readings. What reader would be content with the "Conformist" narrative? And a truly "Quixotic" reader, for that matter, could hardly be expected to follow Castillo's prescribed sequence. A careful reader of the table of contents also notices that some letters are included in some sequences and excluded from others, making just one reading of the novel inherently incomplete.

By encouraging repeated readings at the outset, Castillo introduces the idea of narrative revisiting, which, I argue, is crucial to our understanding of the *Letters* as well as our understanding of transnational feminism in the Americas. Castillo's formal experiment also performs the kind of conceptual disruption that is the hallmark of Pan American modernism. As I have shown in the previous chapters, writers of that era challenged the hegemonic structures of knowledge that defined Latin America by creating texts that were themselves boundary-crossing, hybrid forms. Similarly Castillo disrupts the traditional structures of narrative and the Eurocentric presumptions of progress that go with them. She instead presents what we might term a Chicana approach to narrativity, which, as she has written of Xicanisma itself, is more "yielding" and allows for ways of knowing that do not follow linear models of progress.

While some critics have noted Castillo's dialogue with other authors (Cortázar, Walker, the "three Marias"), no one has commented on her explicit reference to Erna Fergusson's travelogue, *Mexico Revisited* (1955). In Letter Fifteen, Teresa remarks, "When i stopped to see you [Alicia] for a few days on my way from one place to another, you mentioned *Mexico Revisited*. Wearily, you muttered, never having been able to pull apart its entanglement in your memory. You sensed, in the end, it all had to have meant something, that, if we were able to analyze, it would be pertinent, not just to benefit our lives, but womanhood" (47). I take seriously Alicia's suggestions that Fergusson's book is "pertinent" not just to an understanding of *The Mixquiahuala Letters* but also to the legacy of transnational feminism in the Americas. Even though Castillo's novel is set in the 1980s, it offers the occasion to loop back on a previous text, one that is already a "revisit." It is because of this that my own argument must move back chronologically, to a previous generation of women writers. The analysis of Fergusson's work that follows is intended not only to illuminate Pan American "womanhood" but also to help theorize the act of revisiting as fundamental to the methodology of Castillo's writing as well as to the methodology of my own book.

Travel Writing Revisited: Erna Fergusson in Mexico

Fergusson was a prolific travel writer and amateur anthropologist whose studies of New Mexico and the Southwest laid a significant foundation for students of the region. She also traveled extensively throughout Latin America and, along with two books on Mexico, published several monograph studies of American nations: *Guatemala* (1937), *Venezuela* (1939), *Chile* (1943), and *Cuba* (1946). Though she often focused on the present-day, "modernizing" aspects of each country, her writing always provided a longer historical context for understanding twentieth-century Latin America. Much of this involved rewriting the history of women in the Americas. Although she was an Anglo-American woman from a wealthy background, her frustration with the male-dominated literary scene of her day led her to seek out alternative social formations from across the hemisphere and thereby find different models for the "new woman" she sought to define.[38]

Fergusson's *Mexico Revisited* is one of her last books, and she brings to it the reflection and self-awareness of an experienced traveler. It is also, I want to stress, an occasion to reconsider her status as a woman in the Americas. Fergusson begins her narrative at the U.S-Mexico border and stresses the fact that she is traveling in a foreign country, alone: "On the bridge, the last lanky Yankee drawled his 'So long' and the first Mexican smiled his welcome. Immediately I heard the word that was to greet me every day. '*Sola?*' Was I alone? It might be disapproving, but it always resulted in friendly offers of service. A kind man directed me to a parking-place, and another walked a block out of his way to show me the post office."[39] As she continues her drive south, the incredulous questioning continues for this brazen North American woman traveling *sola* through Mexico. Behind this one word, Fergusson's interlocutors are questioning her unorthodox decision to travel without a man—whether her father, brother, or husband—and what this signals about her character and about her sexual behavior. This is an issue central to Castillo's novel, and the significance of traveling *sola* will resonate throughout the *Letters*. As the manner in which they are viewed by Mexican society becomes clear to the two characters, Teresa observes, "Clearly, we were no ladies. / What was our greatest transgression? We traveled alone. (The assumption here is that neither served as a legitimate companion for the other)" (59–60).

In addition to passing a moral judgment on Fergusson and on Castillo's characters, the question also raises some genuine concerns about the safety of women travelers. In *Mexico Revisited*, police and border guards regularly point out to Fergusson the dangers inherent in traveling alone, but, at least in the text, she is able to diffuse these concerns with humor: "Was I not afraid? I soon developed a standard reply. How could I be afraid in a country whose police were so courteous and efficient?"[40] However, by beginning her book in this way and continually returning to the issue of traveling *sola*, Fergusson highlights much more important themes: her defiant independence and the constant threat of male violence, both of which also recur in Castillo's novel.

Fergusson's book, as the title indicates, is already an act of revisiting. She had recounted her earlier travel through Mexico in the book *Fiesta in Mexico* (1934) and now covers some of the same geographic terrain. But whereas her first book was a study of fiestas, her later work concerns itself with the much more serious matter of the status of women in Mexico. The occasion to revisit Mexico—which goes unstated in Fergusson's narrative—was that two years earlier, in 1953, Mexican women had gained the right to vote. However, such important social issues remain in the background of *Mexico Revisited*, as Fergusson chooses to articulate them through old stories and personal narrative. With political and personal events closely interwoven, the book is as much a reappraisal of Mexican society as it is a reappraisal of her earlier life. This is true of the significance of being *sola*. In *Fiesta in Mexico*, there is a similar instance in which Fergusson is questioned about going to a party *sola*. In this case, though, she explains the locals' incredulity as some sort of embarrassment that she has no friends. As the party goes on, those who question her become less subtle. In a barrage of questions, one woman asks Fergusson, "'*Sola*? Alone? You came alone? I saw you, and I wondered. I looked all around to see your husband or your son or your guide, and I saw nobody and I thought how sad if the Señorita came alone. You had, then, no friend to come with you?'"[41] While the woman points out her social transgression through false courtesy, Fergusson seems unable to read between the lines and misses the suggestion of what traveling *sola* really means. In beginning her second book on Mexico with a reflection on this term, Fergusson seems to have in mind this previous moment from *Fiesta in Mexico*. Here, then, we have the first instance of Fergusson rereading herself. In doing so she is able to decode the signs of patriarchy that she did not fully understand two decades before.

By stressing the connection between *Mexico Revisited* and *The Mixquiahuala Letters*, I hope to make clear that this methodology of revisiting, of reconsidering an experience, is crucial for understanding Castillo's novel, but it also tells us something about how women in the Americas reimagined their own experience within a transnational context. Aside from being travel narratives, the two books share an interest in interpretation and reinterpretation. Even though Fergusson's journey as a white woman from the United States is different from Teresa's experience as a Chicana traveling through Mexico, Castillo seems to find Fergusson's rereading to be a productive methodology. Throughout *The Mixquiahuala Letters*, she similarly excavates episodes from Mexico's past and present and brings the stories of independent women to the surface. But again hers is a method not just of uncovering but of reinterpretation, and she routinely relies on the reader to infer her subtle social critique.

Despite Fergusson's being, as Castillo dismissively labels Woolf, an "Anglo woman born to economic means," she demonstrates an awareness of class in her portrait of Mexican women. In the marketplace at Pátzcuaro she listens to a speech delivered by a woman from the right-wing *sinarquista* movement. Fergusson paints a striking portrait of this strong, well-spoken woman—"Beautiful and beautifully dressed, she spoke with ease, grace, and a voice that carried without strain"—but she undercuts this speaker's politics with narrative cutaways to the working women of the market:

> Her theme was that Mexico, the beloved *patria*, must return to the old virtues of the home with woman in it. As the dark drew in, the market women hefting their heavy burdens for the long trot to the dugout canoes on the lake lingered a moment, listening. The speaker was warming up. True Mexican women, she was saying, did not spend their mornings in the beauty parlors and their afternoons playing canasta; they dedicated their lives to their children, their charities, and their church. Few market women remained; only those who were still packing and roping their wares, but they did not seem to listen as the speaker reached her peroration. The true *mexicana* asks no vote, no part in politics; she asks only to remain in her home, to support her husband as the true Veronica did. The last market women slowly trotted off.[42]

In the background of this *sinarquista*'s speech Fergusson places the market women, "hefting their heavy burdens," for whom the world of beauty parlors and canasta seems far removed. The dilemma of either voting or staying home invokes a false nostalgia for a lost era of domesticity, not unlike Lee's colonial women or Tía Filomena's "back in the days when marriages were meaningful." Fergusson frames the *sinarquista*'s perspective as a product of the speaker's class position since the market women, as Fergusson demonstrates, are already outside their homes. As women of color, they are defined primarily by their labor and only secondarily by their sex. As readers, we are obviously meant to reject the *sinarquista*'s idea of the "true *mexicana*" and look instead to Fergusson for a definition. For her the answer lies in industrialization and the emergence of women as a middle-class labor force.

A mica factory in Querétaro, staffed entirely by women, offers Fergusson's vision of the new working woman. While the technology at the factory is evidence of Mexico's industrial advance, its "human aspects," Fergusson writes, "are even more suggestive of what is happening in Mexico."[43] Between the two poles of the *sinarquista*'s aristocratic domesticity and work of the *indígenas* in the marketplace, Fergusson imagines industrial labor as an ennobling act that will pull Mexico's poor indigenous women into "modernity": "Most of these girls come from what Mexicans call their 'humble class.' Many of them when hired are unshod, uncombed, poorly dressed, and quite without address or apparent sense, though they must have had at least two years of schooling." However, the factory transforms these women into petit-bourgeois subjects, patterned after the growing postwar middle class that Fergusson is familiar with in the United States. Their journey toward respectability is swift: "The manager said it took about three weeks to turn a spiritless creature into a brisk and efficient young woman. This factory is making not only mica for precision instruments, but new women for the middle class."[44] The image of a factory turning out middle-class women reflects the optimism that those on the U.S. left felt toward industry. As we saw with Carleton Beals and Stuart Chase, the encroachment of transnational capitalism promised the "uplift" of the impoverished classes of Latin America at the same time that it brought the "loss" of indigenous cultures that the left so cherished. Fergusson, despite her advocacy for the advancement of women in Mexico, clearly understands white, middle-class women in the United States to be the model for that advancement.

For Fergusson the women who are left out of the industrial labor force are also excluded from the forward march of history. Women from this "humble class" who "have not had the advantages of factory training and union protection work as a rule as maids, which means that they belong to a past age."[45] This vision of modernity is one that Castillo critiques in her writing. Indeed the twentieth century did bring many working-class women into factories on both sides of the U.S.-Mexico border, but Fergusson and Castillo differ on their analysis of this historical shift. Fergusson, from her position as a white woman writing from the 1950s, sees the factory as a path to the middle class, while Castillo, from her position as a Chicana in the 1980s, sees the mestiza factory worker becoming a "countryless woman," whose position in the labor economy makes her a second-class citizen.

This attitude toward the past is what characterizes Castillo's relationship with women travel writers of the Pan American era. She returns to their work not simply to denounce it as the work of out-of-touch white women or to repeat its sentiments but rather, as Fergusson herself terms it, to "revisit" these texts from the past. This is a key term in two senses. In addition to the literal act of visiting again (as in Fergusson's or Teresa and Alicia's multiple visits to Mexico), there is also the interpretive sense of *revisit*, which the *OED* defines as "revise, reinspect, re-examine." For Castillo travel and interpretation are inextricable; as we shall see, each time her characters return to the same location or remember the same event, it is not an instance of repetition but rather one of revisiting.

The Mixquiahuala Letters: Revisiting and Revising Pan American Feminism

The fictional events of Castillo's novel are structured around a series of trips that Teresa and Alicia make through Mexico and the United States. They seek out the same destinations and relive previous experiences, but just as important to the novel is that Teresa returns to these places through the act of remembering them and writing them down in her letters. The redundancy of these journeys is something that Castillo plots out self-consciously, and Teresa too is aware of the need to explain these "returns." She writes to Alicia of her return to Yucatán: "You may wonder why, of all places to vacation, i chose that one. It wouldn't let me rest. In all honesty, the men, the bitter resignation, hold no significance and didn't hinder the beauty of the place" (*Letters* 124).[46] There is a way in which "place" marks for Teresa both geographical locations and memories, and thus she must explain to Alicia the reason for her second trip as well as the reason for revisiting it in her letters.

The motive for such revisiting, as I have suggested with regard to Fergusson, is to reinterpret the original event and make new meaning. In this case, as the two women travel *sola* along a southern route taken by travel writers and anthropologists, Castillo searches for a way of understanding their journey as neither deviant nor an object of study. Castillo returns to each narrative moment in order to make revisions, and thus she distances the structure of her work from that of pure repetition, which lends itself to nostalgia or melancholy. In Letter Two, written in verse, Teresa makes clear to Alicia that their experiences do not belong in a blues song:

> Our
> art is not a hankerchief [*sic*] to wring out with sobs of
> *my man done gone and left me* over and again
> like a warped Billie Holiday record. (17)

Pure repetition has its place in the blues lyric, but the methodology of *The Mixquiahuala Letters*, as Teresa suggests, is that of revisiting, of returning with a different perspective. Castillo makes clear references to this not only in the passage directly referring to Fergusson's book but also in Teresa's descriptions of their travels, "vagabonding throughout the Southwest and Mexico revisited" (42) and arriving in "Mexico City, revisited time and again" (92). In addition to the direct allusions to Fergusson (who, after all, spent much of her life traveling in the Southwest and Mexico), Castillo suggests that there is an interpretive component to this revisiting that distinguishes it from repetition. Long after their second trip to Mexico ("Five years since our return"), the two characters still go back to these memories, working to make new meaning. Teresa begins Letter Nineteen:

> You wanted to decipher one day,
> you said,
> as we stirred our stoneware cups with star of anis and earl grey, what it
> could've meant. (59)

The moment in which Teresa and Alicia sit together over their tea is one act of revisiting, but the narrative moment in which Teresa writes her letter revisits the material once again, adding another interpretive layer. While Alicia's scope of vision allows her to reappraise the fictional events of the novel, Teresa's position as narrator and sometime stand-in for Castillo allows her to also double back on the history of women's travel writing in the Americas. As she continues to write the letter, recounting Alicia's desire to figure out "what it could've meant," Teresa offers her own interpretive conclusion, capturing the conflicting relationship between their Chicana identity and Mexican culture: "Mexico. Melancholy, profoundly right and wrong, it embraces as it strangulates" (59).

This duality, "it embraces as it strangulates," echoes yet another of Castillo's sources, Emma-Lindsay Squier's *Gringa: An American Woman in Mexico* (1934). Like Fergusson, Squier was an upper-middle-class Anglo woman who published a number of travelogues telling of her adventures in Mexico. Her tone, though, is more flippant than reflective, and she tends to come to quick conclusions, such as this one about Mexico's contradictory nature:

> Ask yourself rather if you do not know some strange, glamorous character who intrigues, stimulates—and exasperates you; whom you alternatively want to kiss—and spank; yet whom you go on loving because you can't help yourself; regardless of faults and blemishes—regardless of anything at all!
> Mexico is like that.[47]

As Castillo appropriates this anthropomorphization of Mexico, she inverts the direction of the action. Squier, the eponymous "Gringa," sits in judgment of the country, alternately kissing and spanking her troublesome friend. For Castillo's Teresa, however, the journey to Mexico is a complicated reappraisal of her Chicana identity, and it is her submission to Mexico's social expectations that allows the country to embrace and strangle her.

Castillo is certainly in dialogue with previous generations of Pan American travel writers, but even as she revisits their work she complicates women's travel writing by narrating *The Mixquiahuala Letters* through the voice of a woman of color. In order to appreciate the complexity of this Chicana travelogue and its pattern of returns, we must ourselves return to Teresa and Alicia's first trip to Mexico. In Letter Three Teresa recounts how they met during their first summer in Mexico, two women in their early twenties, one from Chicago and the other New York. Both found themselves "enrolled at a North American institution in Mexico City for a summer to study its culture and language" (18). And, of course, the "North American institution" turns out to be a terrible disappointment. "i had worked at odd jobs for the tuition and boarding expenses," Teresa writes, "only to find the school with the heavy Aztec name just a notch above fraudulent status" (18). Teresa's quest for self-identity has led her to a school where she is surrounded by "California blonds and eastern WASPS" and where the instructors reinstitute the racial hierarchies that Teresa and Alicia thought they had left behind in the United States. The male instructors flagrantly give preference to the blond women in their classes, cherishing the proximity to true *norteamericanas*. Teresa, despite her U.S. passport, does not count because of her dark skin and indigenous features. The other students are not there to clarify their sense of Chicana identity, or, as Teresa puts it, none of them "had any objective but to undergo an existential summer of exotic experiences" (18). Her derision of this kind of tourism as well as her disappointment with this "North American institution" echo the frustration with the U.S. academy that Castillo expresses in *Massacre of the Dreamers*.

Teresa finds some comfort, though, in a weekend excursion to Mixquiahuala, "a pre-Columbian village of obscurity, neglectful of progress, electricity notwithstanding" (19). Mixquiahuala offers her another "place" from which to understand her identity, but again this has as much to do with a place of memory as with the geographic location. The village, then, serves as an example of Sandoval's "topography of consciousness," allowing Teresa a retreat where her quest for identity can be understood outside of conventional modes of representation. However, in describing it as a place "neglectful of progress," Castillo also reflects a tradition of North American nostalgia about rural Mexico. Mixquiahuala is removed from the transnational labor economy that was driving Fergusson's young women toward middle-class respectability and removed from conventional institutions of knowledge. On the one hand, this seems to be part of the same fantasy about pre-industrial lands that Stuart Chase and other U.S. travelers indulged in. However, there might be something transgressive in Castillo's description of Mixquiahuala. It is, after all, not *neglected by* progress but rather "*neglectful of* progress," suggesting that the town has willfully opted out of the modern economy. The crucial point, though, is that Castillo's text is continually in dialogue with previous generations of travel writing, and it is the tension between recapitulating the representations of U.S. travelers in Mexico and forging an new ethos of travel that is at the core of Teresa's letters.

It is on their second journey through Mexico that Teresa and Alicia depart from the path of U.S. visitors and decide to be "travelers rather than tourists" (65). While this journey leads them away from the leering instructors, they must now face the glares of local inhabitants as well as the dangers of traveling *sola*. Hoping to leave patriarchal expectations behind in the United States, they find new cultural expectations that ensnare them. They are caught between two cultures, neither of which is willing to accept the two women on their own terms. Teresa remembers of this second trip: "Society has knit its pattern so tight that a confrontation with it is inevitable" (59). Largely because they travel without a male escort, because of the way they dress and their level of education, she and Alicia disrupt social norms: "We had abruptly appeared in Mexico as two snags in its pattern. Society could do no more than snip us out" (59). This metaphor returns us to the novel's textile imagery and Tía Filomena laboring at her Singer. Not only are these characters deviating from social norms; they are also deviating from the expectations of the labor system. In contrast to the tightly knit fabric of mainstream society, they are defective merchandise and unsalable on market. This transgression has social consequences: throughout this second trip, Teresa and Alicia are made the objects of catcalls, subtly veiled threats, and attempted rape. "Suffice to say," Teresa writes, echoing Fergusson, "women traveling alone were vulnerable to harassment from all sorts" (85).

In many ways the travels of Castillo's two characters form an effort to redefine *sola*. They are, unlike Fergusson, each traveling with a companion, and, even though the society around them assumes that another woman does not qualify as a legitimate traveling companion, the letters serve as an act of legitimation. *The Mixquiahuala Letters* revisits the bond between Teresa and Alicia, and each act of return imbues that bond with new meaning that redefines the social mores of both the United States and Mexico. Their connection, outside the tightly knit pattern of

society, is a network of dreaming that harkens back to Castillo's opening invocation to *Massacre of the Dreamers*. There she quotes a passage
from Laurette Séjourné's *Burning Water* (1956), in which she recounts
the last days of the Aztec Empire and how anyone dreaming anything
about the empire was to report to the palace to share the dream. Upon
hearing all of the dreams and finding no salvation for his empire, Moct-
ezuma ordered the massacre of the dreamers, and "from that day there
were no more forecasts, no more dreams, terror weighed upon the spirit
world" (*Massacre* n.p.). In her nonfiction and in the fictional relationship of Teresa and Alicia, Castillo attempts to resuscitate the tradition
of dreaming as a politically vital act. In *Letters*, Teresa recounts that
by the second trip she and Alicia connected: "Like delicate creatures
of an alien world we balled up immersed in networks of dreams" (*Letters* 121). What Castillo suggests here, and what Teresa and Alicia strive
for, is a transnational connection that allows a common "Mexic Amerindian" ancestry to create a form of Pan American unity that could not
have been conceived of either by the PAU or by the Pan American feminists who lobbied for women's rights earlier in the century.

Beyond the binary of being *sola* or with a man, Teresa and Alicia
forge a spiritual unity through which they are solitary but certainly not
sola: "For the first half of the decade we were an objective one, a single
entity, nondiscriminate of the other's being" (*Letters* 122). As evidence of
this Teresa's letters mostly narrate the story of "i" and "you." However,
she occasionally diverges into a distant third person, which pushes this
"objective one" into a larger context so that it stands in for all women of
color and therefore articulates a unifying transnational feminism.[48] In one
of several instances of this, Teresa narrates her experiences as having happened to some unnamed character ("a woman"). The narrative traces the
woman's path of prescribed heteronormativity, leading her from court-
ship, straight on through to marriage. But then Teresa interrupts this with
a direct address to Alicia, stressing "i" and "you":

> She makes decisions, takes her life back into her own hands. If loving a man,
> loving men who run cities, states, countries establish organizations, head
> schools, manage and own businesses is surrendering oneself to a level of
> inferiority simply because—
> *No! i lied.* . . . Oh, Alicia, if i were back in that miserable hotel in the
> ancient city where gods, warriors, and women all fell beneath the blows
> of imposing invaders but what killed them was their disparate energies, i
> wouldn't deny to you again that i understand why you hated yourself. (113)

Two important factors work to break the trance of Teresa's third-person narrative. First, the bond with Alicia (the "you") allows her to assert more forcefully the "i" of her narrative, with all its inherent doubts and regrets. Second, the tense changes between these two paragraphs, moving from the vague present to a past that returns Teresa to her past moments with Alicia and even extends back to a mythologized version of the Conquest, when "gods, warriors, and women all fell beneath the blows of imposing invaders." This one moment exhibits all the interpretive work of revisiting I have explored in this chapter. It is the return to the past that allows Teresa to disrupt the dominant metanarratives that surround her as a mestiza woman. She claims a hemispheric femininity by stressing her history with Alicia, and she simultaneously claims an indigenous heritage that links her to the Aztecs. Thus the colonial wound is made immediately relevant to the characters' lives as Teresa identifies the "imperial invaders" at the root of twentieth-century patriarchal structures. As she makes these historical juxtapositions, what she ultimately offers Alicia is a path toward self-identification that resists the easy categories of nationalism. Teresa finds neither "American" nor "Mexican" as appropriate communities to contain her identity and instead turns to Alicia and to the history of colonialism as a means of identity formation.

The epigraphs that began this chapter, in which Castillo differentiates herself from Woolf, address the central concerns of Teresa, who attempts to build upon a legacy of twentieth-century Anglo feminism in order to articulate her identity as a mestiza. Many of the early figures of Pan American feminism, such as Muna Lee, operated on the assumption that the same feminist movement that was gaining ground in the United States could simply be transposed onto the women of Latin America. Such a position, though, ignores the complexities of race in the Americas and the reality that many women of color remain, to use Castillo's phrase, second-class citizens in the hemisphere.

The distinction here is one of agency, of the mestiza's ability to assert her status to the same degree that *norteamericanas* have been able to in the twentieth century. Teresa clearly articulates the differences between earlier Pan American feminists and her own quest for a hemispheric feminism:

> Women in the United States could rally around government buildings, flash placards at media cameras, write letters of complaint to their congressmen (or congresswomen if that were the case) but in the ancient land where

villages still remained unchanged since the sixteenth century, two foreign women with more book knowledge that the average local official, wearing faded blue jeans of the day, bandannas tied brusquely around their heads and casually dropping socialist terms in conversation, stood little chance of gaining favorable odds. (86)

For Castillo's characters there is no plenary session of the Pan American Union to storm with an Equal Rights Amendment. Nor are their travels through the hemisphere made at the service of the U.S. State Department or the Carnegie Institution. Teresa and Alicia seek to assert themselves, but it is not at a conference; they seek knowledge, but their introspections are not the kind of disciplinary knowledge that will reinforce the logic of Pan Americanism. Instead Castillo offers the vision of a hemispheric community apart from state sponsorship, one that retrieves silenced voices from the past in order to form an alternative hemispheric identity.

This method of revisiting the past is not just some quirk of Fergusson's or Castillo's but is instead a fundamental part of Chicana internationalist thought. In *This Bridge Called My Back*, Norma Alarcón's essay offers what she terms a "re-vision though Malintzin," in which she rereads the mythologies of the Conquest and challenges the male-dominated histories that have placed Malintzin (or Malinche/Doña Marina) in the role of betrayer or prostitute.[49] Malintzin has been, in Luisa Capetillo's terms, the ultimate "indecent" woman of the Americas. Therefore the reclamation that Alarcón argued for became central to the decolonial project of Chicana feminism in the 1980s, and Castillo's early writing was certainly a product of this desire to rewrite the histories of Chicana women. However, *The Mixquiahuala Letters* also presents a re-vision of twentieth-century women's travel writing. Contrary to her statements in *Massacre of the Dreamers* and elsewhere, the writings of Anglo women in the Americas are an indispensible part of Castillo's method. This level of engagement is subtle, but it adds a crucial layer of meaning to Castillo's work and to any understanding of feminism in the Americas.

6 Decolonizing the Dance

Katherine Dunham's Transnational Approach to Anthropology and Performance in Haiti

> When people ask me, as they do now, what of those mystic or occult experiences I believe in, or why I spend so much time in their search and research, I find myself answering . . . that I honestly do not know. I am there to believe or not believe, but willing to understand and to believe in the sincerity of other people in their beliefs, willing to be shown, to participate, and where the participant begins and the scientist ends, I surely could not say.
>
> —Katherine Dunham, *Island Possessed*

IT HAD BEEN THREE DAYS since Katherine Dunham left behind Port-au-Prince and journeyed to the countryside, where she now found herself lying on the floor of a small hut along with eight strangers, all packed closely against one another. As part of the Vodou initiation ritual, they had not been allowed to move from the floor save to turn over in unison every few hours. Through the hut's only window came the smells of rich and spicy foods (the floor-bound initiates would be allowed none of this), yet this was barely discernible to Dunham as the sweat from the other bodies filled her nostrils. Beyond anything she might have read about Haitian folk culture or observed from a distance, her participation in this ritual gave her a different understanding of the culture and provided her with corporeal details she would remember for decades.

A young graduate student from the United States, Dunham had been awarded a Rosenwald Fellowship to conduct anthropological research in Haiti in the summer of 1936. For most anthropologists of the era, merely observing Haitian folk dances and Vodou rituals would have been sufficient and an opportunity all too hard to come by.[1] For the intrepid Dunham, however, participation was the key to her methodology, and in this case it required her initiation into Haitian Vodou. Her academic advisor, the noted anthropologist of African cultures in the Americas Melville Herskovits, had dissuaded her from attempting the *canzo*, or trial by fire, and so Dunham had settled for the *lave-tête* initiation rite instead.

(This too gave Herskovits pause, but he was not insistent.) Literally a head washing, the ceremony entailed marrying oneself to a *loa*, or spirit. Beyond experiencing this initiation rite for the sake of her research, Dunham approached it as a serious spiritual commitment and even decades later made regular offerings to her *loa*, Dambala, the serpent.

This is hardly the manner in which anthropologists of the 1930s, or any time for that matter, were expected to work, but from the beginning of her academic career, Dunham had challenged convention. As an African American woman, she immediately stood out as an undergraduate in the University of Chicago's Anthropology Department, but even more surprising to some was that she was a trained dancer who still performed on stage. As Dunham recalled later, some of her professors insisted that she had to choose between being a scholar or a dancer. However, it was her ability to inhabit both roles that made her uniquely qualified to promote dance anthropology and among the first to insist that dance could be the subject of serious academic inquiry. As she freely admits in the epigraph above, in her work it is never easy to tell "where the participant begins and the scientist ends," yet she did not merge the worlds of anthropology and dance merely for the sake of novelty but rather as a form of intellectual resistance.[2] By refocusing attention on Afro-Caribbean dance and religious practice and by bringing these cultures to the U.S. stage, Dunham situated this knowledge outside the anthropologist's gaze and redefined it as a vibrant form of Pan-African cultural production.

As much as mainstream Pan Americanism relied on the stated belief that this was a hemisphere of equal nations, working in cooperation toward shared goals, I have shown in the previous chapters that this was rarely the case. Beneath the rhetoric of the PAU there was a clear division between the peoples of the Americas, marking off those who controlled and produced knowledge about the hemisphere from those who were studied. In the case of Haiti, as we shall see, Pan American representations of the island were often primitivist, and they framed the U.S. occupation as an opportunity for Haiti, which would benefit from its inclusion in the developed world. It was to be, no doubt, another example of "Pan American progress." This political and economic relationship ran parallel to—and was indeed sustained by—certain academic relationships with Haiti, especially the work produced by U.S. anthropologists. During the occupation the production of academic studies on Vodou and other aspects of Haitian culture increased dramatically, making this "magic island," as William Seabrook would call it, legible to U.S. readers. However, Dunham's approach to Haiti was decidedly different. I argue that her rethinking of anthropological practices was part of her larger challenge to the power dynamics between the United States and Haiti. She simultaneously reimagined an alternative kind of Pan Americanism, one that created networks of cooperation and understanding among peoples of the African Diaspora.

Dunham's methods were transformative and exhibited much of the transdisciplinary knowledge production I have been exploring in this book. In previous chapters I have endeavored to show how artists appropriated disciplinary knowledge about the hemisphere and repurposed it for their own ends. With Dunham, though, we see a U.S. academic who challenges the discipline from within. A dancer herself as well as an anthropologist, from the start she disrupts the neat categories of observer and participant. Ultimately her work enacts a performance epistemology and proposes a resistant "repertoire," as Diana Taylor would have it, as an alternative to the dominant forms of knowledge production of the Pan American archive.[3] What's more, her travels throughout the hemisphere, both as a researcher and a performer, allowed for an alternative means of cultural exchange as she incorporated folk dances from a variety of cultures into her performance, a method that would come to be known as the Dunham Technique.

The process meant that her knowledge about the dances of Haiti would not just show up in her master's thesis but would also be translated to the stage. To return to Walter Mignolo's argument about decolonial thinking, Dunham's work reflects his idea that "changing the terms of the conversation implies epistemic disobedience and delinking from disciplinary or interdisciplinary controversies and the conflict of interpretations."[4] Dunham's fusion of anthropology and performance enacts just this kind of "epistemic disobedience." It is this means of knowledge transmission, of combining folk culture and modern dance, of blurring the distinction between *anthropos* and *humanitas*, that allowed Dunham to articulate a common cultural identity among the peoples of the African Diaspora.

Millery Polyné has suggested that we understand this period of relations between African Americans and Haitians in terms of what he calls Black Pan Americanism. Arguing that neither black nationalism nor Pan Africanism is a sufficient lens for understanding this solidarity, he shows how "U.S. African Americans used the idealized tenets of Pan Americanism—mutual cooperation, egalitarianism and nonintervention between nation-states in the Americas—to strengthen

Haiti's social, economic and political growth and stability."⁵ This was an alternative vision of Pan Americanism to the one being articulated by the PAU, and it co-opted the egalitarian ideals of a hemispheric community in order to promote a common cause among African peoples throughout the Americas. By traveling throughout the Caribbean to conduct research and then taking her dance troupe on tour in the United States and the rest of the hemisphere, Dunham was able to promote a vision of Black Pan Americanism, creating a transnational community that did not divide its people along the same racial and economic lines of U.S.-defined modernity.

While Dunham's performance career enacts a compelling means of transnational knowledge production, I am interested in her textual production as well. Her book, *Island Possessed* (1969), recounts her early experiences in Haiti, but it was written over thirty years later and from the vantage point of Dakar, where Dunham lived for a number of years and where she was active in the cultural life of Senegal. Because of this geographic and temporal distance, the text is a combination of memoir and anthropological account, as well as a conversation between the two Katherine Dunhams: the young graduate student in Haiti and the accomplished, world-renowned performer in postcolonial Senegal. As I will demonstrate, Dunham views her experience in Haiti in 1936 through the lens of the decolonial movements of the 1950s and 1960s and thereby emphasizes the politically resistant potential of the Afro-Caribbean cultures. While the younger Dunham was certainly aware of the politics of colonialism at work in Haiti, arriving as she did only a year after the end of U.S. occupation, Dunham the author of *Island Possessed* is in a better position to understand the role that art, and more particularly dance, can play in the movement to decolonize a culture. Having moved to the newly independent Senegal in 1965 and taken an active role in President Léopold Sédar Senghor's Black Arts Movement, Dunham was aware of the transformative political potential that performance could have. Looking back at postoccupation Haiti, she revisits a moment typically understood as the beginning of the Good Neighbor Policy and therefore an important step in the narrative of Pan American progress.⁶ However, her text subtly reframes 1936 Haiti as a moment of possibility when careful attention to the embodied knowledge of Haitian dance and Vodou ritual offers the basis of a transnational consciousness and an alternative to the logic of Pan Americanism.

The Early Years of Katherine Dunham
and the Anthropology of the Dance

As a reviewer for the *New York Times* put it midway through Dunham's career, there were two ways of thinking about her. "One group," he explains, "recognizes in her a woman of fine intellect, a sincere student of anthropology and its broader and more practical implications. The other group sees her as a beautiful, highly sexed theatrical entertainer, with surprisingly few inhibitions in the material she puts on the stage."[7] Ultimately the reviewer decides that she is both "Schoolmarm" and "Siren," which he offers as a compliment of sorts for her ability to embody multiple male fantasies. The tension between her identities as an anthropologist and a dancer would be a consistent preoccupation for reviewers, for more traditional academics, and for Dunham herself.

In the numerous articles and autobiographical reflections she produced during her lifetime, she frequently brought up reviewers' inability to categorize her. During her company's tour of *Cabin in the Sky* (1940–41; fig. 22), which was eventually made into a film for which Dunham would do the choreography, she could not help but notice the reviewers of her day struggle to write about someone who was both a performer and a scholar. She noted in her essay "Thesis Turned Broadway," "I find myself referred to, and on the very same day, both as 'the hottest thing on Broadway' and 'an intelligent, sensitive you woman . . . an anthropologist of note.' Personally, I do not think of myself as either one of these extreme phenomena. But eager reporters, confronted by the simultaneous presence of two such diverse elements, have often failed to grasp the synthesis between them."[8] In the same essay Dunham goes on to justify her dual role as artist and student, explaining that all artists strive to capture something of universal human experience, and so the study of anthropology would be a natural asset. Rather than being a scholar and coincidentally a performer, Dunham worked to synthesize these two fields from the very beginning of her career.

Since her early childhood she had been a dance enthusiast, performing locally in the Chicago area. She later moved to Hyde Park to begin her undergraduate studies at the University of Chicago, where her older brother was then completing his doctorate and where he would become the first black instructor in the Psychology Department.[9] As she began to pursue these studies in her early twenties, Dunham was unwilling to give up her life as a performer. This was due in part to financial need. (In later years, when she ran the Dunham School of Dance, timely

Figure 22. Katherine Dunham in *Cabin in the Sky*,
1940–41. (Katherine Dunham Papers, Special Collections Research Center, Southern Illinois University,
Carbondale)

performances would help to keep the school running.) However, the
confluence between these two identities, even early in her career, was
central to her methodology and is ultimately what enabled her to break
new ground both in the field of anthropology and in modern dance.

Her travels and anthropological work in the Caribbean in the
1930s provided Dunham with a repertoire of dance styles which she

incorporated into her choreography throughout her career. It was in this way that she was able to bring the performance cultures of Haiti, Martinique, Jamaica, and Trinidad to stages in the United States and eventually to the movie screen. Her first full-length ballet, *L'Ag'ya* (1938), was named after a traditional dance she had observed and filmed while in Martinique in 1936. The dance is thought to mimic a cockfight and usually involves two male participants competing with one another in aggressive, confrontational choreography. In adapting the dance to the modern dance stage, Dunham incorporated many of the movements, and she also developed the dance's premise into an adversarial plot for her ballet, in which, at the climax, two men compete over the female character Loulouse, played by Dunham herself.[10] In other productions her choreography was less indebted to a single dance form and instead blended several styles. For instance, beginning in 1939 the Dunham Company performed *Tropics* and *Le Jazz Hot: From Haiti to Harlem*, both of which offered review-style performances that fused several dances from the Caribbean with modern European forms. Dunham's choreography was also featured in a number of Hollywood films in which she and her company performed, including *Carnival of Rhythm* (1941), *Pardon My Sarong* (1942), and *Stormy Weather* (1943). Throughout this period her previous anthropological work continued to inform her career as a performer, and her choreography has had a lasting impact on modern dance.[11]

But this dual identity also informed Dunham's fieldwork, and her experience as a dancer is what allowed her to participate in the rituals of the communities she observed in the 1930s. Dunham was not the only U.S. anthropologist interested in Haiti and Vodou culture in particular; this work was pioneered by her academic advisor, Herskovits. Nor was she the only African American woman to conduct fieldwork in Haiti since she was followed by Zora Neale Hurston, whose study of Haiti in 1937 was ultimately published in her anthropological travelogue, *Tell My Horse: Voodoo and Life in Haiti and Jamaica* (1938).[12] Even these studies, though, as focused as they were on Haitian folk culture, paid little scholarly attention to the study of dance. Some previous observers of dance in the Caribbean (to the extent that U.S. anthropologists were interested in dance at all) had observed and photographed the dances, attempting to chart every step and movement, but Dunham endeavored to understand the performance as a dancer and choreographer, and she therefore brought a different, participatory knowledge system to the practice of ethnography.

This duality provided Dunham a new way of conducting anthropological research, and it also led her to infuse her choreography with the knowledge she had gained by researching the folkways of various communities of the Americas. Beyond any academic thesis, this method of researched performance, the Dunham Technique, was her means of bringing the folk knowledge of the Americas into the mainstream of U.S. culture. Throughout her long life Dunham continued to advocate and teach the integration of anthropology and dance, giving her first classes in Chicago and establishing in 1944 the Dunham School of Dance and Theater in New York. She would later lead classes in East St. Louis and Carbondale, which brought professional dance instruction to many poor communities for the first time and also provided a grounding in African diasporic culture. As Ojeya Cruz Banks has argued, Dunham's teaching was part of her larger decolonial project since "her educational philosophy and curriculum decolonized the Black body through using African-derived dances as primary educational content, thereby challenging Eurocentric models of education and countering the psychology of racism and colonialism."[13]

Dunham wrote numerous articles and gave many lectures espousing her revolutionary technique for modern dance, but perhaps no document is more telling than her 1963 prospectus for a book never written, titled simply "Dunham Technique." In it she outlines the essential methods of her technique and stresses the importance of studying what she refers to as "primitive societies" both as a way to innovate in modern dance and as a way to legitimize other cultures. The prospectus recounts that she had been "disturbed in [her] early years of social anthropology at the lack of emphasis on the complex of the dance in primitive society" and that her own research in the Caribbean had aimed to fill this gap. "Also involved" in this early research "was an element of rebellion against the often condescending attitudes toward not only Negro performing arts but those of all deprived, minority, 'exotic' folk."[14] Especially interesting here is that, looking back on her work from 1963, Dunham understands that work as having global implications beyond the particular focus of her research and performance. At various points in the 1930s her study of dance centered on Martinique, Cuba, Jamaica, and, most profoundly, Haiti, but she now sees her work as defending more than just one particular culture against condescension. She understands her early work as championing "all deprived, minority, 'exotic' folk" in a way that unites them beyond the confines of national borders.

In the process of conducting her work in the 1930s and 1940s she encountered the reality of what it meant to be black in the United States and the rest of the Americas, being one of the few women of color in her discipline and having to battle segregation almost daily as she toured the United States with her interracial dance troupe. Yet later, from the vantage of midlife and the decolonial movements of the 1960s, Dunham understood her work as a larger "rebellion" against the status quo and the implied dominance of European cultures. This is why her trip to Haiti in 1936 serves as such an important moment for understanding Dunham's work as well as her vision of Black Pan Americanism, a focus that, thus far, Dunham scholars have not emphasized. At the moment when postoccupation Haiti was attempting to articulate the path of its "second independence," Dunham was there attempting to resolve her university training in anthropological observation with the embodied experience of African diasporic culture. The memoir she wrote thirty years later recounts a time of personal struggle in which she was pulled between two career paths, but, looking back on her experiences from Senegal in 1969, she also frames her trip as an early venture toward the decolonization of knowledge.

Pan American Progress: The Good Neighbor Policy in the Shadow of Occupation

Dunham arrived in a newly independent Haiti when the U.S. occupation was still a fresh memory in the national consciousness. The departure of marines from the island was in many ways the signature gesture of Franklin Roosevelt's Good Neighbor Policy. When Haiti's president Sténio Vincent visited the United States in the spring of 1934, he laid the groundwork for the new diplomatic relations that would begin when U.S. forces left in August of that year. Vincent received an official reception at the White House, and while in Washington he was also fêted with a luncheon held by the Pan American Union. There Secretary of State Cordell Hull formally welcomed Vincent and stressed the historical role Haiti had played in the formation of the Pan American idea: "It was in Haiti that the Great Liberator, Bolívar, found constant encouragement as well as valuable material assistance. Your great [predecessor], Pétion, was one of the first to uphold the sanctity of human rights and of individual freedom. The principles for which he stood are now coming to fruition in this organization of American republics dedicated to inter-American cooperation and good will."[15] This rhetorical move of grounding twentieth-century politics in the liberation movements of the nineteenth century was a convention of the Pan American Union, as we have seen in previous chapters. However, this "cooperation and good will" also appealed to Roosevelt's new Good Neighbor posture. Indeed not only was Vincent received at the White House, but when Roosevelt embarked on his multinational diplomatic tour later that year, Vincent had the opportunity to return the favor as the first stop on the U.S. president's itinerary. By all appearances the beginning of the Good Neighbor era marks an apparent shift from the overtly imperialist policies of earlier in the century. U.S. troops were no longer occupying Haiti or Nicaragua, and the "gunboat diplomacy" of the previous decades was left behind. However, the logic of Pan Americanism persisted into the 1930s and 1940s through the narratives of progress and development which continued to dominate how North Americans understood the hemisphere.

The years Haiti spent under U.S. occupation had occasioned an intense interest on the part of U.S. writers, academics, and tourists, all of whom found an exotic and premodern land that had been tamed and made accessible by the marines. J. Michael Dash has revealed the way these literary depictions of barbarism and savagery convinced their U.S. readership of the necessity—indeed the civilizing mission—of the occupation.[16] Among the numerous books produced by U.S. authors during this period, many quickly faded into obscurity, but others, like William Seabrook's sensational tale of primitivism and sorcery, *The Magic Island* (1929), were still cited as definitive sources on Haitian culture even at the time of Dunham's visit.[17] However, in the years just after the United States left, a new narrative about Haiti emerged, which focused on its independence and its path toward U.S.-style development.

In the mid-1930s Haiti still made regular appearances in the *Bulletin of the Pan American Union*'s "Pan American Progress" section, and the advances it made in education, health, and infrastructure were noted with paternal pride. For instance, the article "The Haitian Rural School at Work" (1937) traces current progress in education back to the benefits of U.S. occupation. It begins with the premise that Haiti is experiencing a kind of second revolution; in the first sentence the author immediately draws a contrast with the island's original independence from France: "Although the independence wars were class wars intended to free the slaves from the exploitation of their masters, the idea of public education was too far removed to become a set goal of the newly found Republic."[18] The article then reflects on the persistent problem of education in Haiti, namely that it centers on an urban elite imitating European classical education and leaves the rural poor to their own devices. However, we then learn about examples of U.S. largesse that have advanced the cause of vocational education in the countryside. "In 1925," for instance, "in connection with the Technical Agricultural Service, the American Occupation opened a certain number of farm schools. These, for the first time, attempted to give a more practical education."[19] Though the article focuses largely on the actions of Haitian officials, by setting up this contrast with French colonialism the author positions the United States as a good steward of Haiti and attempts to rewrite the occupation as a form of relief work rather than colonization. While providing rural Haitians with schools and literacy education is laudable on its surface, the emphasis on "practical" education says a good deal about the goal of creating more useful, technically skilled workers throughout the hemisphere. The period of U.S. military interventions and that of the Good Neighbor Policy may have had markedly different appearances, but the Pan American project of spreading U.S. notions of economic development was a consistent structural objective throughout both eras.

Well into the 1940s Haiti was still dealing with a colossal amount of U.S. debt which kept its economy bound to the interests of foreign creditors and maintained an economic occupation of the country. When the U.S.-backed president Élie Lescot was overthrown in 1946 and Dumarsais Estimé was elected, the hollow nature of Haitian independence was brought into the center of public debate. Coming from Haiti's black peasant class and espousing a *noirist* form of nationalism, Estimé troubled the elite,[20] but beyond these internal politics his presidency also destabilized the dependent economic relationship between Haiti and the United States. Soon after taking office he began a campaign to renegotiate Haiti's debt, traveling to Chase Manhattan Bank in New York and sending numerous diplomatic missions to Washington. Although these trips met with little success, they made Estimé a cause célèbre among both Haitians and African Americans, who viewed him as fighting a larger battle for racial and economic equality in the hemisphere. Numerous black newspapers in the United States followed the developments in Haiti closely and often framed the news within a broader postcolonial struggle. For instance, a 1948 article in the *Chicago Defender* marked the anniversary of Haitian independence by noting, "On January 1, 1948, Haiti observed her 144th independence day. Haiti is, of course free—in the word's broad sense. She was the first free republic in the Latin Americas. But even now, after 144 years, the people are battling to throw off a yoke of economic slavery held tightly in place by the

United States."[21] Over a decade after the United States had left Haiti, the long shadow of occupation still limited the economic and political freedom of the nation. Despite the rhetoric of neighborliness advanced by Washington, these economic policies were clearly understood, both in Haiti and within the African American community, as extensions of U.S. domination.

Mary A. Renda and others have remarked on African Africans' focus on Haiti during this period and its symbolic role as the inspiration for a new generation of political change. They were concerned with the contemporary U.S. occupation, and also, as the *Defender* article makes clear, with the Haitian Revolution. In this political climate and amid numerous representations of the revolution, including Arna Bontemps's historical novels *Black Thunder* (1936) and *Drums at Dusk* (1939), Renda argues, the "Haitian Revolution offered a useful point of departure for elaborating" a "new vision of African American life."[22] The period during and after the U.S. occupation was also a crucial time for African Americans to rethink their relationship with the imperial state, and this tension in "American" identity was part of Dunham's experience in the 1930s.

In recounting in her memoir her own time in Haiti, Dunham is extremely conscious of the legacy of U.S. occupation as well as the possible reception she might receive as a U.S. citizen. Tellingly the first sentence of *Island Possessed* frames her arrival as a second "invasion" of the island: "It was with letters from Melville Herskovits, head of the Department of Anthropology at Northwestern University, that I invaded the Caribbean—Haiti, Jamaica, Martinique, Trinidad, passing lightly over the other islands, then Haiti again for the final stand for the real study" (*Possessed* 3). While the analogy is a playful one, there is a more serious implication here, of which Dunham, the 1969 author, must have been aware. With the letters that she names, the young graduate student brings with her the authority of the U.S. university and the structures of Western knowledge through which she intends to understand Haiti and its people. The rest of *Island Possessed*, however, will unravel these structures of knowledge as Dunham moves from observer to participant, so that this opening passage serves to establish all that must be unlearned and this tongue-in-cheek moment of recolonization will lead in the text to the decolonization of Dunham's understanding of Haiti.

This opening passage also alludes to the manner in which the U.S. presence forced underground the Vodou culture of Haiti's countryside, where hidden instruments symbolized the resistance to the material as well as cultural invasion of U.S. forces. One of the central tensions throughout *Island Possessed* is the uneasy relationship between Vodou knowledge and the U.S. culture of progress shared by the former occupiers as well as the Haitian elite:

> When I arrived in Haiti, not long after the exodus of the Marines, there were still baptized drums hidden in hollow tree trunks and behind waterfalls. President Sténio Vincent paid deference to "folklore" for the sake of the growing interests of tourists in the island, but an air of secrecy clothed all the serious ceremonies and it was not the policy of the first government after the Occupation to sponsor young women visitors in investigations that might verify to the world outside what has been a crucial problem to Haitian statesmen since the independence: the irreconcilable breach between the thin upper crust of the Haitian élite . . . and the bubbling, churning ferment of the black peasant, who really were by numbers and by historical content and character and humanness, I was to find, the true Haitian people. (*Possessed* 3)

When in Washington, President Vincent had to walk the fine line between asserting his nation's new independence and accepting the Pan American rhetoric that kept Haiti tied to U.S. interests. But this was also the president who at home had to negotiate the centuries-old tension between the Haitian elite's aspirations toward European modernity and the vital culture of the "black peasants" Dunham describes.

The ambiguous status of the folk culture Dunham intended to study was a problem for Haitian politicians and intellectuals as they wrestled with the legacy of European cultural dominance and the historic demonization of Vodou. The most important work on Vodou culture at the time was done by the Haitian scholar and activist Jean Price-Mars, whose groundbreaking work *Ainsi parla l'oncle* (*So Spoke the Uncle*, 1928) argued that Haitians draw their national identity from African cultures rather than the French establishment. The first serious consideration of Haitian Vodou by a Haitian, *Ainsi parla l'oncle* was significant in establishing folk culture as an object worthy of study. However, writing during the U.S. occupation, Price-Mars intended his book to have a political valence as well. His work was an act of academic recategorization, of reevaluating the role of folklore in Haitian society, but the stakes were also much higher since the occupation government had established a Code Pénal for prosecuting Vodou practices.[23]

This legacy of criminalization was something that Dunham too had to deal with as she negotiated the Haitian state's contradictory practice of policing and promoting rural folk culture. The rise of U.S. tourists during the occupation had increased interest in Vodou culture, but it also predetermined the dances and cultural practices those visitors would see since the Haitian state sanitized these performances in order to make them ready for foreign consumption. Many early anthropologists, even Herskovits, based their research on performances that were specifically choreographed for tourists.

From Evanston to Port-au-Prince: Dunham's Evolving Ethnographic Practice

While she was clearly indebted to the work of Herskovits and others, Dunham's evolving methodology in the 1930s not only signaled a transformation in the study of Haiti but also marked the birth of dance anthropology. As we shall see, she was ultimately able to transcend the boundary between "folklore" produced for outsiders and the Vodou practices of the Haitian countryside. This was due to her ability to blend her roles as scholar and performer, but it was also due to her ability to defy the racial categories of Haitian society. Previous U.S. visitors had all been white and male, but Dunham points out that she was a first: a light-skinned African American woman who was, as she put it, "easy to place in the clean-cut American dichotomy of color, [but] harder to place in the complexity of Caribbean color classifications" (*Possessed* 4). The supposed difficulty in categorizing Dunham left many of her acquaintances among Haiti's elite bewildered, but it also allowed her to pass more freely through Haitian society. The Vodou practitioners knew that she was from the United States, but perhaps they did not close off their lives in the way they would have to white scholars; nor did they recognize her light skin color as a mark of the Haitian elite. Instead Dunham was apparently outside these categories, and she believed that many of the Haitians she encountered recognized her purely as a fellow descendent of the African Diaspora.

However, U.S. racial categories were never too far away, and their importation to Haiti worked hand-in-hand with the military occupation and the previous wave of U.S. writers who inscribed Haiti within these familiar categories. In her own account of the U.S. occupation, Dunham points out that the U.S. forces were "unfortunately made up mostly of Marines from the southern United States" who brought with them their own notion of racial hierarchy (*Possessed* 25). These U.S.-centered ideas about race also informed the occupation government's criminalization of folk practices. We have already seen in previous chapters that U.S. scientists and travel writers imported racial hierarchies to Cuba and the effects this had on the way the black population was controlled through state policy. In Haiti, however, this phenomenon was far more prolonged and shaped the day-to-day existence of those living under occupation. Even by the time Dunham arrived in Haiti, the meaning of Haitian Vodou and the issue of who had the authority to represent Vodou were very much in flux among the county's Christian elites.

In the 1920s and 1930s the Haitian government outlawed the practice of Vodou rituals and dances, which were then linked with one another in a very fundamental way. These collective practices were criminalized in much the same way that *brujería* had been criminalized in Cuba as a means of state control over its black peasant class. However, Vodou practices were allowed by the state under very specific circumstances, as Kate Ramsey has shown in *The Spirits and the Law: Vodou and Power in Haiti*. Foreign tourists and, more recently, foreign anthropologists demanded an "authentic voodoo experience," and so the Haitian government occasionally authorized performances of some folk dances, stripped as much as possible of any spiritual meaning.[24]

Herskovits was one of the consumers of these productions; many of the ethnographic descriptions that appear in his *Life in a Haitian Valley* (1937) were based on such state-sponsored dances. Ramsey has argued convincingly that this academic demand effectively changed the understanding of Vodou folk rituals: "The cycle of ceremonies on behalf of which Herskovits intervened seems to have been officially permitted by occupation and local authorities only because the visiting American researchers wished to attend them. In some sense, then, they were authorized because they had been officially reframed as ethnographic performances that were of scientific interest to these foreign visitors."[25] Once again state control and academic study worked hand-in-hand to neutralize the cultural meaning of this practice. As soon as these dances could be observed, described, and categorized within the archive, they were also more easily "disciplined," in terms of both Western knowledge production and state control. Much of Herskovits's scholarship, from his work in Haiti to his book *The Myth of the Negro Past* (1941), focused on defending African Diasporic culture from the racist science of his day.[26] However, in his methodology Herskovits was still operating from the mode of outside observer and thereby reinforced the dominant mode of documenting and archiving Haitian folk culture.

Herskovits often expressed frustration with the lack of anthropological work being done on dance, but he saw this as a largely methodological problem since dance seemed to resist standard modes of ethnographic observation. Elsewhere Ramsey has explored Herskovits's methodology in relation to that of Dunham and the means by which she moved away from the positivist approach of her advisor.[27] This is not to say that Herskovits did not want to pursue anthropological studies of Haitian dances himself; rather a scientific description of dance simply did not seem possible to him without sliding into the "literary" accounts of travel writers, leaving the decidedly objective Herskovits at what Ramsey has described as a "disciplinary impasse" in his work.[28] She goes on to explain that Herskovits believed this impasse would be overcome with the greater use of film recording in anthropology, a key premise that would be taken up by a future generation of anthropologists but a method Dunham ultimately rejected.[29]

As part of her Rosenwald Fellowship she had been loaned a film camera, which she took with her as she conducted research around the Caribbean. Ramsey offers a fascinating account of Dunham's correspondence with Herskovits during this period, as she mailed reels of film back to Northwestern, where Herskovits was the first to view the completed footage.[30] This model of research quite aptly enacts the power dynamics of the archive that I have been exploring in my larger argument about U.S. knowledge production. Haitian dancers are recorded on celluloid by the "objective" Dunham, who, even though it is her gaze and her technology that make the performance legible, must wait to see the results of her work. The footage was not developed in Haiti and thus this cultural knowledge could not be understood from the periphery but only from the zero point of the U.S. university. Herskovits encouraged Dunham to pursue this mode of research, and as a result "her early research in Jamaica, Martinique, and Trinidad was oriented around, even dominated by, the demands of filmic documentation."[31] However, this method began to wear on Dunham. Not only was it a burden to transport and set up the 16mm camera without the help of any assistants, but it also kept her separated from the performers she was studying. By the time she arrived in Haiti, she was beginning to rethink her ethnographic approach and frequently left behind the camera, as she recalled later: "I had had little use for it, being busy with my vaudun activities" (*Possessed* 218).

Indeed, as Dunham had learned in earlier research, there were many cultural practices that could not be filmed. While state-sanctioned Vodou rituals could be recorded, there were secret and even illegal performances at which her camera would not have been permitted. She recalled an earlier experience with her camera in Trinidad that left her "traumatized":

> A Shango priest heard the clicking of the camera from the cabin where I was supposed to have been in sanctified seclusion before entering the ceremony. Shango dances were fairly common in Trinidad, but not the ceremonies, and this one had been arranged in strict secrecy. I have a few feet of film of a desperate white rooster, head down, wings flapping, beak open in a last gasp for air as the priest's knife descends to cut its throat. Then there is the surprised face of the priest turned toward the cabin door and, after that, kaleidoscopic disorder, part of which is the priest catapulting toward the door, flinging chicken and knife into the air in his anger. My camera was snatched away from me in an embarrassing episode from which only the intervention of the friend who had arranged things saved me. (*Possessed* 218)

As the camera records this brief moment of "kaleidoscopic disorder," Dunham is faced with the object of study asserting his subjectivity by ending both the Shango ceremony and her recording of it. More than just an embarrassment, this moment served to teach her the barriers that the camera created and led her toward the conscious choice to become a participant. While Herskovits dismissed the notion of the participant observer and actively discouraged Dunham from stepping out of her traditional role as observer, this disobedience was ultimately what allowed her access to what could not be filmed, what could not be archived. In moving away from the state-authorized performances as well as the established anthropological methods of observations, Dunham enacted a new form of dance scholarship in Haiti.

This is the participatory method she describes in *Island Possessed*. Though this is a written account of her experience in Haiti and therefore cannot fully capture her physical engagement with her informants, the text offers us a window into what made Dunham's methodology so revolutionary. When she emerges from the *lave-tête* initial rite I referred to at the outset of the chapter, the nine initiates are invited to dance with the gods who await them outside. Dunham, her muscles tight from her days lying on the cramped floor, lightheaded from fasting, joins in the dance. While she clearly observes the other dancers, the fact that she has participated in the preparatory rituals for this dance allows her to fully experience its hallucinatory potential:

> The joy of dancing overwhelmed me and I found myself sometimes in front of Doc, at other times in front of Téoline or La place or Georgina in the ruptured movements of the feints, then gasping, stumbling, teetering on the verge of rhythm- and fasting-induced hypnosis, returning to the sheer joy of motion in concert, of harmony with self and others and the houngfor and Damballa and

with all friends and enemies past, present, and future, with the wonders of the Haitian countryside and with whatever god whose name we were venerating, because by then a number had been honored and I had lost track. It was so good in every sense of the word to dance to the drums of the gods that Sunday in the Cul-de-Sac, and this feeling of the rightness of these cult dances has never left me. (*Possessed* 131–32)

This is not the objective ethnography of a traditional social scientist; the passage does not even fully describe the choreography of this dance. However, Dunham's method offers us other important knowledge about the *lave-tête* ceremony—the confusion, the exhaustion, the joy—which cannot be accessed through mere observation. Stephanie Leigh Batiste has rightly observed that "Dunham's work positions ethnography itself as performance, recognizing studied cultures and her own activity as continually in process."[32] It is just this fluidity between observer and participant, between study and artistic creation that allows Dunham to disrupt the traditional hegemonic relationship of ethnography. Once the performative elements within ethnography itself are exposed, formerly stable academic conclusions about Afro-Caribbean cultures are opened up to new ways of understanding.

From Archive to Repertoire: Dunham's Performance Epistemology

Beyond just formulating an alternative, participatory anthropology, Dunham established new methods for transmitting the knowledge she gained in the Caribbean. While she did write up her work in Haiti as a formal master's thesis, which was later published,[33] her performances with the Dunham Company were the primary means by which she sought to communicate her work throughout the Americas. More specifically by reproducing the cultural knowledge of Haiti for African American audiences, Dunham saw her work as creating a transnational network of understanding for the cultures of the African Diaspora. She recalls in *Island Possessed* that even for the Vodou practitioners in Haiti it was important that she transmit what she had learned to the other "children of Guinée" since, according to her, they understood this transmission as central to maintaining the diasporic community:

That I would come into their midst, able to worship these gods in dance, and knowing, if fragmentarily, the essences of the religion which had meant for them spiritual and, in periods of their history, physical survival, confirming to them that segments of family, relatives known to have been separated from them and carried to some land vaguely north, others vaguely south, seemed to be of utmost importance to the cult itself—as it was important that I carry the meaning of the true vaudun to my people in that other country. I made no effort to disillusion these well-meaning informants about what might be expected of the children of Guinée dispersed to the north, but listened, repeating as I could the songs and litanies and instructions. (*Possessed* 106–7)

This is yet another instance of Dunham's changing the terms of anthropology and moving beyond the role of observer. Her informants do not merely occupy the role of *anthropos*, remaining static and unaware as the North American scholar traces the history of their migration. Instead Dunham imagines them to be people who are aware of the history of migration from Africa, and in her presentation of them they see themselves as part of a larger community spread throughout the Americas. In her writing Dunham offers the reader the perspective of her informants and, in presenting their view of her, suggests that the terms of transcultural exchange have shifted. While these particular Haitians may be useful to Dunham's research, providing her with material for her thesis as well as a broader cultural understanding of the Americas, this traveling graduate student in turn sees herself as useful to them since she serves as a potential messenger who can carry word back to their long-lost brothers and sisters in the North. Dunham is aware, both in the text and seemingly in this moment in 1935, of the role that she is taking on since she endeavors to "[listen] and [repeat] as I could the songs and litanies and instructions." Throughout the rest of her career she would take this role very seriously, constructing through her writing, lectures, and most of all her performances a transnational network for transmitting African cultural knowledge.

Dunham's most important method by which to "carry the meaning of the true vaudun" was through her performance. These were not exotic embellishments simply aimed at pleasing audiences; instead Dunham's work constituted a performance epistemology, through which both the performers and their audience could understand the cultures of the Americas. This method challenges the logic of Pan Americanism through dance and allows her a way to disrupt the primacy of the written archive and assert an alternative way of understanding one's identity and locating oneself within the hemisphere.

Diana Taylor's work in *The Archive and the Repertoire* has made important strides in legitimizing performance as knowledge production, and her ideas have no better illustration than the work of Katherine

Dunham. Taylor claims that "we learn and transmit knowledge through embodied action, through cultural agency, and by making choices." It is in this way that Dunham's work would clearly exemplify Taylor's claim that "performance . . . functions as an episteme, a way of knowing, not simply an object of analysis."[34] In her critique of the writing-centered knowledge production that the archive enforces, Taylor, channeling de Certeau, points out that the archive works to separate "the source of 'knowledge' from the knower."[35] In this way social scientists from North America might write *about* the performance cultures of Haiti or Jamaica and thereby relocate that knowledge to books, audio recordings, and film reels that will reside in U.S. libraries rather than in the bodies of the practitioners of Vodou. One of the myths surrounding the archive that Taylor tries to dispel is that "it is unmediated, that objects located there might mean something outside the framing of the archival impetus itself. What makes an object archival is the process whereby it is selected, classified, and presented for analysis."[36] If we look back to Dunham's ethnographic practice, this archival power structure is what she resists as she moves away from film—which is easily classified and presented for analysis—and toward an engagement with a Vodou "repertoire," to use Taylor's term. As Taylor defines it, the "repertoire requires presence: people participate in the production and reproduction of knowledge by 'being there,' being part of the transmission."[37] By participating in performances herself and then reproducing those performances on stages throughout the Americas, Dunham disrupts the traditionally hierarchical knowledge structures of the hemisphere.

Dunham's Pan American Politics of Race: Performing *Southland*

Perhaps the best illustration of the rebellion and critique inherent in the Dunham Technique is her company's short-lived performance of her original ballet, *Southland* (1950–51). I will return to Dunham's anthropological work later in order to discuss her evolving attitudes about race and about Pan African culture, but an important step in this evolution is her confrontational depiction of lynching in this performance, which provoked a standoff with the U.S. State Department and nearly ended the Dunham Company. First performed in Santiago, Chile, in 1951, this powerful critique of U.S. racial violence was enacted on an international stage, articulating a critique of race and power that would not have been tolerated at home. (It was in fact never performed in the United States.) The performances, first in Santiago and later in Buenos Aires, did come under attack from the U.S. State Department, and it is worth exploring both *Southland* the performance and its reception to understand the politically volatile expression of dance that Dunham used to destabilize the racial hierarchies of the Americas. For a performer who was by then famous for bringing Caribbean and South American dance forms to the U.S. stage, in this case Dunham's method works in the opposite direction as she turns her anthropologist's gaze back on the United States and attempts to make the roots of its racial violence legible to the rest of the Americas. This is an inversion of the Pan American project and ultimately an alternative form of transnational knowledge production.

Southland was very much a product of South America. As Constance Hill notes, it was commissioned by the Symphony of Chile and "researched, composed, choreographed, designed and rehearsed in the last months of 1950 in Buenos Aires."[38] Even though Dunham admitted in the prologue to *Southland* that she "[had] not smelled the smell of burning flesh, and [had] never seen a black body swaying from a Southern tree,"[39] the ballet was, like her other works, well researched and she incorporated details from her study of lynching records at the Tuskegee Institute.[40] While official censorship and the ever-present threat of violence would have made a U.S. performance of *Southland* unthinkable, exploring this provocative subject matter on a foreign stage just as inevitably ran up against cold war policies of discretion. As Penny Von Eschen has shown, the State Department closely monitored U.S. performers abroad, actively supporting and funding artists who might show U.S. culture in a positive light and censoring any inconvenient discussions of racial inequality.[41] That a woman of color would air the nation's dirty laundry on a stage in Santiago was a brazen affront to this policy and testifies to the potential for political and social action Dunham saw in performance.

The ballet begins with an acknowledgment of this political climate and the expectation that *Southland* will be received as un-American. In a prologue read by Dunham herself before the first performance, she declares, "The man who truly loves his country is the man who is able to see in it the bad as well as the good, and seeing the bad, declaim it at the cost of liberty or life."[42] She goes on to assure her Chilean audience that the United States is a "great and wonderful country" but that racial violence is a persistent part of that society and needs to be addressed. The ballet program also stresses that the performance is not meant to single out the United States but is rather a more universal appeal, "directed, insofar as its intentions surpass purely theatrical and artistic aspirations, toward the conscience not of one nation but of all human beings who are not yet aware of the destructive dangers of hatred."[43] Despite these attempts to inoculate her ballet against accusations of un-Americanness by making it universal, *Southland* is immersed in the specific cultural context of the U.S. South. For instance, during the performance Dunham has members of her troupe sing a number of distinctly African American songs, from spirituals to blues standards and even Billie Holiday's 1939 antilynching anthem, "Strange Fruit."

The action of the ballet is meant to be archetypal, as Dunham points out: "This is the story of no actual lynching in the Southern states of America, and still it is the story of every one of them."[44] The story involves four main characters, a young black couple (Lucille and Richard) and a white couple (Julie and Lenwood), whose lives become intertwined in a series of events that lead to Richard's death at the hands of an angry mob. After the ballet's opening, we see an argument between Julie and Lenwood turn violent, and then, after beating her severely, Lenwood flees the scene, leaving the young woman lying on the ground unconscious. Richard enters the scene and, after pausing to consider the social taboo of touching a white woman, bends down to help Julie. Upon regaining consciousness, Julie is startled by Richard and screams out, "Nigger!"—the only spoken word of the ballet. From there the violence quickly escalates as a white mob appears and summarily lynches Richard on stage. The remainder of the ballet involves a meditation on the consequences of this violence as Julie must deal with the guilt of her false accusation and Lucille and the rest of the black community mourn their most recent loss.

The State Department's efforts to silence the Dunham Company's message were swift and effective. Constance Hill has thoroughly recounted this strategy, which began by pressuring newspapers in Santiago not to run a review of *Southland*. Since, as Hill notes, every paper at that time was dependent upon the United States for its supply of newsprint, editors were simply informed that if they ran reviews of Dunham's ballet, their supply would be cut off. Thus, with the exception of a single communist paper, all the papers of Santiago were silenced.[45] This episode is a remarkable literal demonstration of the way the United States could control the flow of knowledge in the Americas. Dunham's performance so disrupts the U.S. narrative of freedom and equality that any record of *Southland* must be stricken from the archive. After further pressure from the U.S. ambassador, production of the ballet was quickly shut down and the Dunham Company was forced to leave Santiago a few days later. The company would eventually revive the ballet in Paris for a short run in 1953, but the emotional toll of enacting a lynching on stage as well as the political and financial costs of performing the ballet led to its being permanently cut from the repertoire. From then on funding from the U.S. government, which the Dunham Company relied on for its international tours, was withheld.

In later years many of Dunham's dancers resented the production of *Southland* for having marginalized and nearly bankrupt the company and for racializing and politicizing what the dancers had seen as an international troupe that transcended U.S. racism.[46] Despite the hesitancy of her performers, Dunham herself always viewed the issues confronted in the ballet as central to her goals as a performer. She believed that if dance could not be used as a means of social inquiry and education, then there was no point to it. It is in *Southland* that Dunham attacks most explicitly the racial categories of the United States, but this was an issue she would return to throughout her career in her written work and performances. Just as the racial injustices of the U.S. South are more obvious when staged in Santiago, so too do the Haitian class divisions between mulatto elites and black peasants become more absurd when Dunham writes about them from Dakar and places them in the context of the African Diaspora.

This is not to say that racial identity did not factor into Dunham's thinking, but she resisted an identity based on skin color and other positivist information that could be easily categorized. Instead she invoked something less tangible—a feeling of community. Reflecting on her own interracial marriage, how little her husband thinks about "blackness" and how little she thinks about "whiteness," Dunham nevertheless articulates a black sensibility: "I am, however, sensitive to 'kind,' to blackness in the sense of spirit, a charismatic intangible, and this is what the Haitians and Brazilians and Malaysians and Chinese and those Africans with whom I have had time really to discuss things must have felt, must feel. I am inclined to think that the real creative work of mankind is the discovery and good treatment and nourishment of these things, with no guiding handbooks that teach in the intellectual sense, just as I feel that this is no way to teach choreography" (*Possessed* 74). The analogy here between racial identity and choreography is significant: it makes racial identity less stable and more fluid, and it simultaneously denies an "intellectual" understanding of race. It is difficult to know how conscious Dunham may have been of the implications of her analogy, but by keeping race out of "guiding handbooks" the student of anthropology may very well have had in mind the history of positivist science that had turned out book after book on the phenotypic distinctions between the races. Instead Dunham locates racial knowledge within the body. It is passed along like choreography from one participant dancer to another without passing through the formalized categories of race science.

Dunham's preference for a "blackness in the sense of spirit" also allows for a transnational understanding of racial identity. As she explored the different but equally arbitrary racial categories of Haiti and other Caribbean islands, her intention was to illustrate not only that such categories place unnecessary limits on the individual but that they also prevent the formation of solidarity among the African Diasporic community. While *Southland* is significant for Dunham's work as a resistant ambassador, opposing U.S. social issues on a South American stage, perhaps her most important role in creating a Black Pan American racial identity was forging the conceptual connections between postoccupation Haiti and postcolonial Africa. Her career as a dance anthropologist did not have the ultimate aim of transporting knowledge about Caribbean peoples to the elite knowledge centers of the U.S. academy. Rather she took on the burden of being an ambassador between the cultures she observed in Haiti and other African Diasporic communities.

Island Possessed: Decolonizing Memory and Ethnography

It becomes increasingly evident that Dunham's transnational thinking on race and her transdisciplinary approach to anthropology are part of the same resistant thinking that challenges not just the borders of academic disciplines but the borders of coloniality as well. Although anthropology in the 1930s was still dominated by the model of European observer and colonial subject, Dunham's participation in the dances and rituals of African Diasporic communities signals a shift in the power relations of anthropology.

In addition to being epistemologically transgressive, Dunham's writing is formally transgressive, and it is the genre of memoir that allows her to connect disparate kinds of knowledge. Just as the texts I have examined in previous chapters represent hybrid genres, so too does Dunham's *Island Possessed* merge ethnography and memoir. And so, as much as Dunham's performance career is important for thinking about ways to challenge the archive, her writing also enacts its own challenge to academic structures of knowledge. Her book defies easy categorization since it is at once a memoir and an ethnographic study, but it is this fusion of genres that allows Dunham to disrupt the conventional representations of Vodou. Just as her performance epistemology reflects the move from observer to participant, the inclusion of her own experiences in Haiti allows for a kind of textual participation, which gives *Island Possessed* a geographic and temporal mobility. Throughout the text Dunham moves between 1936 Haiti and 1969 Dakar, stopping along the way at a number of locations and memories that have personal as well as global significance. As she looks back at her lifelong relationship with Haiti's president Dumarsais Estimé, she reflects, "One of my consistent peculiarities has always been my attitude toward the present moment. The moment without my feeling it or being aware of it may be taking some monumental place in some center of consciousness, and the anticipation of it or the memory of it may be exquisite or painful or both. But like Alice in *Through the Looking-Glass* the present diffused in the roundness of time is the way I see time and events" (*Possessed* 46). In her recounting of her experiences in Haiti in 1936, the present certainly loses focus from time to time, but I would argue that, unlike Dunham's own comparison with Alice's "diffused" perspective, her memoir is instead *infused* with decades of memories and historical events that occurred before and after the textual present. In her writing about Estimé, for instance, she does not just represent the young government minister attempting to court this visiting American graduate student. Her textual portrayal is also imbued with Estimé's later term as president as well as his exile in Jamaica, and she even finds in him an echo of Toussaint L'Ouverture and the beginnings of the *négritude* movement she would later experience in Senghor's Senegal.

Dunham the writer consciously places these layers of meaning onto her younger self so that the textual present is enriched by her perspective from thirty years later and from the other side of the Atlantic. She admits that, at the time, she "did not realize that my friend [Estimé] was the first in defining the concept of negritude, the placing of the black race in its proper perspective and accord with the rest of the world, a prise de conscience" (*Possessed* 46). Her thoughts then turn from this very particular and local moment in the present to the spread of *négritude* and then to transnational celebrations of African Diasporic culture, which in her view were intimately related to Estimé accomplishments:

> Negritude, as nationalism, swept Africans in Paris from the 1940s on and flourishes now as a plea for humanism though so easily bordering on

nationalism. During the summer of 1965, at [a preview of] the World Festival of Negro Arts in Dakar, I saw Jean Price-Mars, frail, almost blind, but still the father of so many of our efforts. I wondered if he thought of Estimé and the Bicentenary Exposition of December 1949, commemorating the 1749 founding of Port-au-Prince by the French. It seemed hardly the place or time to ask him. (46–47)

Dunham seems quite consciously to play on the meaning of her last sentence as though, within the world of this text, 1936 Haiti actually is the place and time to ask all of these questions. I want to devote some time to exploring the rich topography Dunham lays out in this important passage in order to examine how the work of Price-Mars and the Dakar World Festival of Black Arts in 1965 add meaning to her understanding of Haiti and her understanding of Vodou.

While much of Dunham's writing over the years offers a sympathetic depiction of Haitian culture and a counterpoint to the narratives of savagery seen in works like Seabrook's *The Magic Island*, this is due in large part to her mature, unromantic view of Haiti, which is the product of the decades she spent thinking about the country after her initial research trip. For instance, in *Island Possessed* she devotes a good deal of space to recounting her visit to the exiled Estimé in Jamaica in the early 1950s. As she reflects on Estimé's exile and the threats to his life, she writes, "I knew how Estimé had been loved, was still loved, and the fact that his life would be in danger even outside the country turned all the years that I had known Haiti into a mockery. I had dreamed of, written about, acquired property in, spread the good word far and wide about a country of which I really knew nothing" (53). While at that moment she is disillusioned with the Haitian elite, she still thinks of herself as an ambassador for Vodou culture. She still advocates the cultural knowledge that can be transmitted through performance, but what she sees in Estimé's exile is the extent to which the economic policies of the United States and the Pan American Union could still dominate Haitian politics nearly twenty years after the occupation ended.

As she recounts the stress and sense of failure during Estimé's Jamaican exile, her narrative shifts once again, this time to an earlier memory of flying to Haiti in July 1949 to be made a Chevalier in the Haitian Legion of Honor by then-president Estimé. He was a much different man from the one she had met during her 1936 trip, now worn down by political opposition at home and demoralized by his inability to relieve Haiti's debt burden and thus advance its position in the hemisphere.

The continued subaltern status of the black republic was mirrored by the treatment Estimé received on his diplomatic missions to the United States. Dunham recalls, "I knew of some of his trials, but not all. I knew that he had gone to Washington for a Pan American Union conference, been refused expected hotel accommodations because of color, stayed in a Negro hotel, I am told, separated from the other chiefs of state—those classified as non-Negro—and had left vowing never again to set foot on American soil, though in the end he did" (*Possessed* 51). This was not Estimé's only encounter with U.S. segregation. As Dunham notes, he did return after being deposed from the presidency in May 1950, as he and his family wandered the globe in search of asylum.

In 1952 they arrived in New York, which Estimé's wife later remembered in her memoir as a "monstrous, multi-tentacled city."[47] The family attempted to find a hotel that would take them but were told repeatedly that there were no vacancies. Lucienne Estimé recalled, "At the beginning of the '50s, racial segregation was alive and well, a reality in New York as it was in any other U.S. city. Nothing else mattered to these ruthless owners: it did not matter the least bit in their eyes that one was from a French culture or that one had been the President of a nation."[48] Clearly such discrimination was humiliating for Estimé, a current and former president, and it also suggests that the racial hierarchies that played out on the personal and political levels were interconnected. Dunham re-creates the conditions of Estimé's exile by anchoring her narrative to the moment of this Pan American Union conference when he was denied access to the conference hotel and his nation was simultaneously denied a restructuring of its U.S. debt. While his ouster from the presidency was ostensibly due to internal Haitian politics, the narrative linkages of *Island Possessed* make clear that the power structures of the hemisphere ensured that the first black president after occupation would not be able to achieve his goal of economic independence for his nation.

However, on the other side of the Atlantic, Dunham found a counterexample of how transnationalism might work. From 1965 to 1969 she lived and worked in Senegal and took an active role in the political and cultural revolutions taking place in Africa during those years. While in *Island Possessed* the memories of Estimé's decline become a parable of Haitian politics and the disappointment of independence movements, Dunham's text is equally informed by her time in Senegal, where she influenced and was influenced by the Black Arts Movement of President Léopold Senghor. Dunham had become acquainted with Senghor in Paris, where he saw her company perform, and this led to a working relationship when she moved

Figure 23. Katherine Dunham with President Léopold Senghor in Dakar, May 1962. (Missouri History Museum, St. Louis)

to Dakar (fig. 23). According to Ruth Beckford, at Dunham's first formal audience with the president in 1962, he told her that "when her company first opened in Europe, it had caused a cultural revolution that paralleled their political and economic revolutions. Different people's chiefs-of-state in sub-Sahara Africa had been encouraged and inspired by her formula" of arts education.[49] This praise from Senghor was more than just flattery since for the past three decades both he and Dunham had been on the forefront of advancing Pan-African culture and arts.

Senghor himself had been one of the twentieth century's early proponents of a transnational Black Arts Movement, promoting the artistic ethos of *négritude* for most of his artistic and political career. The concept of *négritude* had emerged among francophone intellectuals as a response to the European discourse of primitivism and its history of locating African culture and art within the natural history museum rather than the art gallery. Black artists and writers living in Paris in the 1920s and 1930s, such as Aimé Césaire and Senghor himself, were among the first to formulate the ethos of *négritude* as a means of empowering colonial subjects to stop emulating the European models they aspired to and instead to embrace an artistic mode rooted in the cultures of Africa. While many black intellectuals moved away from the ideas of *négritude* in later years, denouncing them as universalist and as recapitulating the primitivism of the European perspective, Senghor remained a lifelong advocate well into the 1960s, when, as independent Senegal's first president, he put his ideas into action through a state-sponsored arts program. What came to be known as the École de Dakar served to promote the arts not just in Senegal but throughout the nations of the African Diaspora.[50]

It was this cultural project that Senghor had in mind when he organized the Premier Festival Mondial des Arts Nègres (First World Festival of Black Arts) in 1966. In presenting Dakar as the center for Pan-African arts, Senghor was in part burnishing his own political image in order to maintain his tenuous control over Senegal. However, this festival was a signature moment for asserting a Black Arts Movement on an international stage. At the height of the decolonial movement in Africa, the festival attracted revolutionary artists from across the continent, such as Wole Soyinka, as well as black luminaries from the rest of the world, such as Langston Hughes. As important as the Black Arts Festival was for the political and cultural advancement of newly independent African nations, it was also a formative moment in the intellectual life of Katherine Dunham. Senghor had invited her to serve as an unofficial U.S. ambassador at the festival, and after the event was over she remained in Dakar to head the new National Ballet. These years spent living in Africa enabled Dunham to fully synthesize many of the ideas about African Diasporic culture she had been dealing with throughout her career.

Dunham's lecture at the World Festival of Black Arts offers a window into her thinking at this time. While most of the talk focuses on the role the arts should play in postcolonial Africa, she argues that performance is ultimately the key to a transnational network for the African Diasporic community to exchange knowledge about its culture. Again for Dunham performance is always a means of cultural transmission, which she emphasizes as she explains the need for these "new" African nations to consult their elders: "The Old Ones, the Wise Ones who know the form of dance not only in its externals, but in its fundamental meaning to the society, in its social organization, its historical importance and in its function, would be the professionals, the Masters. Without this knowledge of the ethos and mores, we are apt to present only entertainment, or at most a superficial view of a trait of the culture of a people deserving far more attention."[51] Maintaining the important social function of African dance required not only this generational transmission of knowledge but also a persistent effort to educate performers and audiences about the cultural contexts that made these dances more than entertainment. Describing the multilevel education she provided her dancers as part of the Dunham Schools in New York and Chicago, she advises modern-day African dancers to pursue learning in the "historic, socio-economic, religious, aesthetic, organizational and traditional values of the performing art technique of his own country" in order to understand performance "from an intellectual or 'knowledge' point of view as much as physical."[52] With this advice she is clearly promoting her Dunham Technique to the performers of these newly independent nations and making the same point that she made throughout her career, namely that dance is a means for understanding and transmitting vital cultural knowledge.

And of course dance is also a means of creating community. At the Dakar festival Dunham could explicitly articulate this concept since Senghor's chief goal was to foster a political and cultural sense of Pan-African unity. Yet this had long been a practice of Dunham's as she used her anthropological fieldwork and her dance company's performances to transmit cultural knowledge between various points in the Americas and reveal a Black Pan American identity that lay occluded behind national borders. This effort at forging a sense of transnational community can be traced back to her work in Haiti in 1936. I have traced the evolution of her methods from observation to participation, but this was not merely an innovation in scientific technique. It also allowed Dunham to straddle the border between science and folk wisdom and to commune with the people who embodied these cultural practices. Just a few years after the Dakar festival, when she was composing *Island Possessed*, Dunham recalled this sense of community she felt in Haiti:

> I was beginning to feel at home with them, to sense the tie of kinship that must hold together secret societies the world over. We were associates in things not common to all men, and still, this should be a reason why I would have no place here other than scientific investigation, and I was not at all certain that this was true. In all my adult school years, I had rigidly avoided sororities and club memberships of all sorts, secret or otherwise—all forms of belonging that required an etiquette or process to achieve a belonging. I had always prided myself on thinking only of "man" in the broadest, most inclusive usage of the term. Here, three thousand miles from my center of learning, either for my own awakened and undefined needs, or under pretext of fulfilling a mission, or a mixture of both, I was deep in the most banal and, at the same time, most esoteric of secret society inductions, that into

ceremony, ritual, secret pact, blood sacrifice, into the vaudun or voodoo of Haiti. (79)

Vodou is, in and of itself, a transnational phenomenon of the African Diaspora. Yet it also serves as a metaphor for the alternative communities and networks of knowledge transmission that are possible. Far from her "center of learning" at Northwestern University, Dunham finds that by participating in this Vodou ritual she is able to arrive at a different sort of learning, one that is not removed and housed in academic institutions but rather a kind of knowledge that resides inextricably in the knower.

Throughout her long career Dunham's writing and performance served as a mode of decolonizing knowledge. To return to the language of Mignolo, it is Dunham's "epistemic disobedience," her refusal to be bound by the traditional disciplinary structures of knowledge, that allows her to formulate an alternative hemispheric community. This Black Pan Americanism is rooted in a shared history, but it is a sense of community that would not necessarily emerge from traditional ethnographic practices. Dunham's method, her performance epistemology, is the key strategy for thinking beyond the logic of U.S.-centered Pan Americanism and revealing these alternative transnational networks. However, one needn't dance to resist this logic. Dunham's performance epistemology is but one form of intellectual resistance. Throughout this book I have shown how various writers and artists challenged the dominant narrative of Pan Americanism and offered alternative ways of understanding the hemisphere. There are numerous possibilities and numerous avenues of resistance, but each one requires that the borders of disciplinary knowledge be transgressed along with the borders of the nation-state.

Epilogue

Singularity, Multiplicity, and *Pan American Unity*

THE IDEOLOGICAL PROJECT OF PAN AMERICANISM was to convince the varied peoples of the Americas that there was one, singular vision of the hemisphere. This, of course, would be the vision of Pan America as viewed from U.S. centers of power such as the Pan American Union. Its aim, as I have endeavored to make clear, was to normalize the values and objectives of U.S.-defined modernity as the ideal for all the peoples of the hemisphere. Such a singular vision of the hemisphere was, however, challenged from the beginning. Not only were the PAU's opponents critical of its latent imperialism; they also challenged the idea of a totalizing vision of the Americas and the presumption that it could all be seen and understood from Washington, D.C.

Certain Pan American modernists engaged and challenged this U.S.-centric vision in order to reveal the fractured reality of life in the Americas. As we have seen, there was certainly not a singular view of the hemisphere on which everyone could agree. I have selected writers and artists who challenged and complicated a unified vision of the hemisphere. To be sure, each one was to varying degrees interpolated into this totalizing conception of the hemisphere, but their work also challenged U.S.-centered knowledge production and offered an alternative, hybrid understanding of Pan Americanism. William Carlos Williams, for instance, shared his contemporaries' fascination with Mesoamerican archaeology and to a great extent reinforced the idea of Latin America as an archaeologized region, but he also used these Mesoamerican themes to criticize the consumerism of U.S. modernity. In doing so he articulated an alternative Pan Americanism, one in which workers and artists were united in their opposition to Doheny, Morgan, and the capitalists of the hemisphere. Likewise Ana Castillo's notion of Xicanisma articulated a transnational connection among women of color throughout the

Americas. Each of these Pan American modernists has suggested alternative hemispheric communities. These may be idiosyncratic notions of Pan Americanism, and many of them have their own shortcomings, but their plurality of perspectives offers a new way to think outside the dominant logic of U.S.-defined modernity and envision alternative landscapes we might call "Pan America."

One way of understanding Pan America is to consider how the hemisphere was represented in maps of the period, and in this epilogue I will focus on the conceptual mapping of Pan America as a way to understand Pan Americanism both in its own time and in terms of what it might mean today. Walter Mignolo has demonstrated how the ideological work of cartography has defined the Americas, especially in *Local Histories / Global Designs*. While much of Mignolo's work focuses on colonial systems, in particular the way European geography and organizations of knowledge reformulated indigenous American cultures in the fifteenth and sixteenth centuries, his later work has also observed the subsequent remapping of the globe in the twentieth century. As the concepts of First and Second World nations took hold, Latin America became increasingly marginalized, relegated to the Third World.[1] Between the colonial maps of the Western Hemisphere that the Spanish and Portuguese first made and the cold war divisions of the twentieth century, the idea of a Pan America serves as a kind of way point. It is a hybrid moment in which the Americas are viewed as a singular, coherent place even as the cultural, political, and artistic differences fracture that unified ideal. If Pan America was never a reality, the idea of mapping out this imaginary place is an important moment in the intellectual history of the Americas.

The practice of mapping both literal and conceptual space is also a useful way to approach the current state of Hemispheric American studies. As scholars redraw the borders of their disciplines, trading one set of boundaries (the nation-state) for another (the hemisphere), it is important to reflect on the motives for and consequences of these new borders. Donald Pease has observed, "Globalization reawakened the geographical imagination that flourished during the epoch of discovery when Euro-Atlantic imperial adventurers deployed maps to exercise cartographical dominion over the so-called New World. Transnational Americanist geographers have set about remapping the United States' relationship both to its own regions and to its direct or indirect imperial territorializations."[2] Thus the politics of the transnational turn are invested in a corrective to the enduring colonial power structures in the Americas, and certainly much of the scholarship in American studies to come out in the past two decades has successfully worked toward this remapping of the U.S. role in the hemisphere. However, thinking about the transnational turn by the light of the Pan American era leads to some more complicated conclusions. The rhetoric of Pan Americanism was, on its surface, inclusive, and it too attempted to redraw the history of colonialism in the Americas. As I have shown, though, this reimagining of geographic space simultaneously reinforced a U.S.-centered narrative of modernity. Writers and scholars of the Pan American era argued for the "newly imagined terrains" Pease refers to, but they used these new maps to repackage old power structures. So too might the transnational turn be silently reinforcing a U.S.-centered model of American studies. For this reason, the Pan American era provides valuable lessons for scholars working in the twenty-first century since hindsight allows us to see the underlying motives of Pan Americanism laid bare. While both of these historical moments entail a conceptual remapping of the Americas, we might look to some literal attempts to map Pan America in order to illuminate the promises and pitfalls of a Hemispheric American studies.

To understand this era—and what twenty-first-century scholars of American studies can take away from it—I will consider two works from 1940, a moment that might be understood as the last gasp of Pan Americanism. The first is Carleton Beals's book *Pan America: A Program for the Western Hemisphere*, and the second is Diego Rivera's mural painted for the Golden Gate International Exposition, *Pan American Unity*. Beyond the oft-repeated ideals of Pan Americanism, they both attempt to articulate what a place called Pan America might look like. By locating this aspiration in a place, as Beals and Rivera do in quite different ways, we can get a sense of the competing values of that Pan America and how its meaning was contingent upon the perspective from which it was understood.

Beals's *Pan America*: The Archive and the Storehouse

Writing just before the U.S. entry into World War II became inevitable, Beals begins *Pan America* with the twin premises of U.S. isolation and the eventual victory of the Axis powers. Consequently the Western Hemisphere would need to cope with the reality of an Axis-controlled Europe that would deny the United States some of its longest and most reliable trading partners. In anticipation of this, Beals articulates his plan for a fully autonomous Western Hemisphere. In its detailed economic analysis and proposed trade arrangements, *Pan America* envisions a cooperative system in which each nation of the Americas would offers its economic strengths to benefit the hemisphere. This book is an important capstone to the period, marking the last point at which Pan Americanism, in the way that I have been defining it as an archival project, was still viable.

From the vantage of 1940, Beals presents a succinct history of inter-American relations in the previous decades. Beginning his history in 1914, when the United States "had new responsibilities thrust upon it" by the previous war in Europe, Beals highlights the changes that the United States has made in terms of "our information, our diplomacy, our banking services, [and] our commercial relationships."[3] He correctly observes the interrelation between these institutions, and it becomes clear that the control of information about the hemisphere is what enables all the other forms of control. While recounting the "improvements" in hemispheric relations Beals devotes a good deal of space to advances in material development and transportation infrastructure. (Pan-American Airways receives special praise.) The key development, however, has been made within the sphere of knowledge production as the regions of Latin America have become more frequently the objects of study for students in North American universities:

> One of the really great assets of the new situation is our wider knowledge of and interest in our southern neighbors. In 1914 few courses in Latin-American subjects were given in our universities. Today the vogue for such courses is spreading even to our smallest institutions. Students are thus provided with a lifelong interest. Cultural intercourse is not easily directed in new channels, but the United States has responded to the new developments with remarkable alertness. . . . This is also the most constructive side of the work of the Pan-American Union. (399–400)

Thus Beals imagines a hemisphere based on mutual understanding, but this is a far cry from the understanding that José Martí called for in "Nuestra América," which urged the nations of the Americas to become acquainted with one other (*conocer*). Beals's hemisphere, on the other hand, is predicated upon acquiring knowledge (*saber*) about one's neighbor. While learning about the other culture is an admirable goal, I have shown throughout this book the consequences (sometimes intended, sometimes unintended) of constructing Latin America as an object of study. When one side sets the terms of the relationship, establishing beforehand both the definition of *modernity* and who qualifies as modern, any attempt at Martí's acquaintance is already undermined by these structures of knowledge.

One of the motivating forces behind the study of Latin America, and certainly a central motivation for the Pan American Union, was the desire to locate and control the hemisphere's natural resources. A knowable Latin America was consequently a more exploitable one, and, as I have stressed, commercial motives went hand-in-hand with academic study. Indeed the study of Latin America enabled a U.S.-centric vision of modernity in which the hemisphere was divided into a northern archive and a southern storehouse, one producing and organizing knowledge and the other providing the raw materials for a modern Pan America.

As Beals sets out to define the Pan America of the future, he reinforces these divided roles for the two Americas but insists that this should not make one region superior to the other. Instead this would be a relationship of equals and would move North Americans beyond what Beals sees as the prevailing attitude of U.S. neocolonialism: "Many Americans dyed with a sense of Anglo-Saxon superiority look upon the southern countries merely as our oyster to be devoured, or as shock troops for our safety, or as pawns in the game of world power. We think of Latin America as a storehouse of natural wealth that Americans, by some divine right, should possess and exploit; as a sort of unhappy hunting ground for adventurous concessionaries, unregulated American investment, or colonial exploitation dressed in a garb of benevolence" (429). However, as enlightened as this anti-imperialist rhetoric may sound, I have shown that Beals is perfectly capable of advancing two contradictory arguments at once and that his denials of "Anglo-Saxon superiority" do not mean that his own work is free from it. In *Pan America*, his contradictory attitudes persist. He devotes much of his book to reinforcing the idea of "Latin America as a storehouse," having recommended earlier in the volume that "we devote our national energies to making completely secure the materials not found in the United States, but vital for our industry and protection" (132). Beals imagined a hemisphere in which the nations of Latin America would trade with the United States as equals, and he attacked promoters of neocolonialism who would take materials by force, as Hitler was presently doing to expand the German *Lebensraum*. But even though Beals denounces the violent seizure of Latin America's resources, his plan still commits the necessary first step of *understanding* the region as a storehouse. His method of conceptualizing Latin America—even as he professes to defend it—demonstrates the colonizing work that can be done simply by organizing knowledge about the region.

Beals's map of the hemisphere most clearly articulates his vision of Latin America as a storehouse for an isolationist United States. In devising this "South American storehouse," as he calls it, he lists the commodities the United States currently imports from Latin America and then locates potential resources that might fill gaps left by the end of European trade. While Cuba, for instance, was at that time a source for sugar, manganese, chromium, and tobacco, it would also need to produce iron and barium for the U.S. marketplace (n.p.). As practical as this plan may be to deal with the alternative reality of an isolated Western Hemisphere, Beals's act of remapping Latin America according to its natural wealth recapitulates the familiar narrative of U.S.-defined modernity, in which the "unified" nations of the Americas are separated into an industrial North and an underdeveloped South.

In addition to presenting the nations of the Americas as the source of raw materials that could be put to use in the more "developed" United States, such a map articulates a vision of the hemisphere as seen from the hegemonic position of the United States. This clearly represents the singular, unified vision of a Pan America. It is the vision articulated by the Pan American Union throughout the early twentieth century, one in which all of the regions, cultures, languages, and peoples of the Americas merge into one body of knowledge. That archive is located geographically and epistemically in the developed center of the hemisphere, in the centers of power in Washington, D.C., and in the logic of modernity which positions the United States as that center. This center, of course, does not appear in Beals's map of the "South American storehouse." It is instead the point from which the storehouse is viewed, understood, and mapped.

In Beals's plan for the hemisphere, we see the homogenizing force of Pan Americanism. This discourse, which emanated from centers of institutional power such as the Pan American Union, solidified the idea of a single, knowable hemisphere that must be viewed from the north. However, he does attempt to give his readers the "view from below." Given that the opinion of Latin Americans was "rightly prejudiced" against U.S. policy, he suggests that we look to another measure of hemispheric unity, "not the tophat [sic] statements put forth at official Pan-American reunions for American consumption, but certain attitudes often displayed within southern borders, in the press, at public gatherings, or by their intellectual leaders" (430). Now, regardless of the attitudes toward Latin America that Beals espoused, he did so from a consistently North American perspective. Yet by pointing his reader away from "tophat" Pan Americanism and toward intellectual leaders, he recognizes the use of an alternative Pan Americanism composed of multiple intellectual centers. This promise of a multiperspectival view of the hemisphere is not actually fulfilled in his text, but it is perhaps the most usable element for a Hemispheric American studies.

Rivera's *Pan American Unity*: Two Americas in One City

One way to understand this pluralistic vision of Pan America is through another example from 1940, Rivera's *Pan American Unity* (fig. 24). The mural was created for the Golden Gate Exposition of 1940–41, one of many Pan American cultural conferences of the era, and the movable panels were later relocated to City College of San Francisco, where the mural currently resides. This was the last mural that Rivera would paint in the United States, and it portrays a far less confrontational stance toward contemporary U.S. culture than did some of his previous work. The key to this is Rivera's vision of Pan America, which he maps out not in terms of an entire hemisphere but rather in a utopian version of San Francisco. By presenting a local understanding of Pan America and multiple perspectives from which to view it, Rivera offers a more usable template for Hemispheric American studies than the unified vision of mainstream Pan Americanism.

Pan American Unity (or, as it's formally known, *The Marriage of the Artistic Expression of the North and of the South on This Continent*) sets out to create a harmonious, utopian vision of hemispheric cooperation by tracing the parallel histories of Anglo America and Latin America and joining the efforts of their artists and workers into a common goal. The mural makes use of some familiar Rivera iconography: the harmonious pre-Columbian cultures on the left-hand panel echo his depictions of Tenochtitlan at the Palacio Nacional (1935); the workers that appear in each of the panels are positioned as the celebrated heroes of tomorrow; and Frida Kahlo makes yet another appearance in the center panel. However, there are important differences in the details and the perspective that mark *Pan American Unity* as unique. The mural is as much a product of 1940 as Beals's *Pan America*, and in the lower right we can see the figures of European fascism threatening Rivera's hemispheric utopia. There the faces of Hitler, Mussolini, and Stalin appear in a spectral cloud, whose pale and vacant palette sets it off from the rich colors of the rest of the mural. As a counter to this political evil, Rivera positions democratic artistic expression, including images from Edward G. Robinson's *Confession of a Nazi Spy* (1939) and Charlie Chaplin's *The Great Dictator* (1940), which had been screened at the Golden Gate

Exposition. As Rivera explained in his artist's statement for the exhibition, "Both [films] dramatized the fight between the democracies and the totalitarian powers. A hand rose up out of a machine as if to ward off the forces of aggression, symbolizing the American conscience reacting to the threat against freedom, in the love of which the history of Mexico and the United States were united."[4] As with Beals's *Pan America*, threats from outside the Western Hemisphere are the occasion to unite across national borders, but rather than focus on natural resources, Rivera appeals to a common history of democracy.

Rivera's most unique contribution to this hemispheric union is his refusal of a totalizing view of Pan America. While *Pan American Unity* insists upon its specific location—San Francisco—in a way that Rivera's other murals had not, the composition simultaneously fractures that specificity by including Tenochtitlan, the Rocky Mountains, and several unlocatable settings in the lower panels. Anthony Lee has also observed this aspect of *Pan American Unity*: "What is more notable . . . because it is new to Rivera's work, is the emphasis on *place*—on the exposition itself as a space for a unifying vision."[5] Rather than mapping the hemisphere,

Figure 24. Diego Rivera, *Pan American Unity,* 1940. City College of San Francisco. (© 2014 Banco de México Diego Rivera Frida Kahlo Museums Trust, Mexico, D.F. / Artists Rights Society, New York)

Rivera chooses to locate its rich array of cultures in a single city. His aim is to include the disparate parts of the Americas without simplifying their cultures into knowable categories. While maps like those of the PAU or Beals's "South American storehouse" organize knowledge about Latin America in order to categorize and control that knowledge within the bounds of U.S.-defined modernity, Rivera presents us with multiple views of both the city and the hemisphere that resist an easy synthesis.

It is important to note, however, that Rivera's vision of the hemisphere was still rooted in an idea of northern industry and southern spirituality. He described this unity in a letter: "For years I have felt that the real art of the Americas mostly came as a result of the fusion of the machinism and new creative power of the north with the tradition rooted in the soil of the south, the Toltecs, Tarascans, Mayas, Incas, etc., and would like to choose that as the subject of my mural."[6] However, the pre-Columbian history and religiosity Rivera presents is not resigned to the object of study but is incorporated into modernity in a way they had not been in previous murals. For instance, his murals in Detroit depicted Coatlicue side by side with deified machines, but, as Antonio Rodríguez notes, in *Pan American Unity* Rivera synthesizes the two worlds (fig. 25).[7] With this central image, the mural makes the indigenous a part of modernity in a way that makes the division between industrial center and subaltern storehouse obsolete.

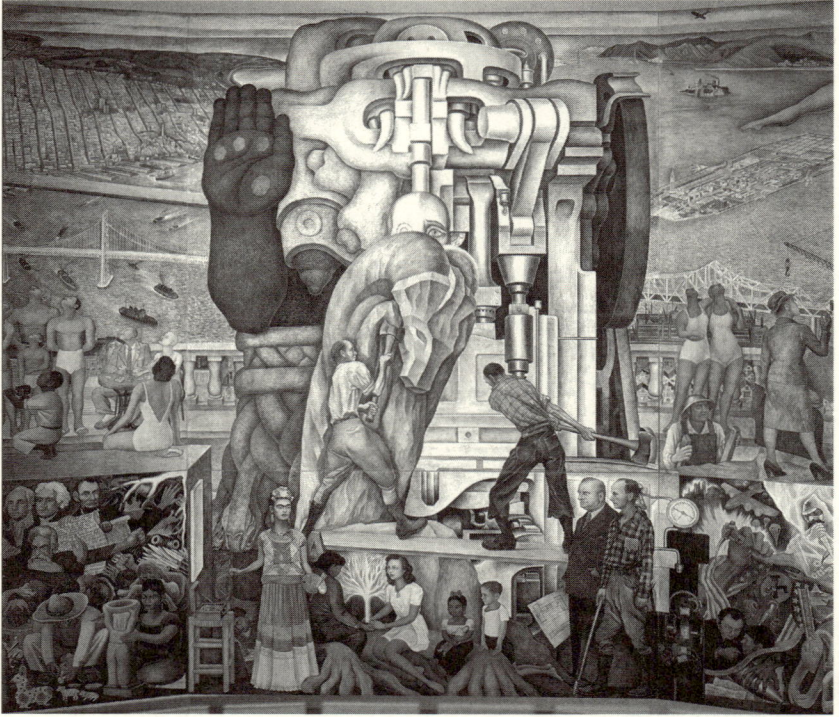

Figure 25. Diego Rivera, *Pan American Unity*, detail. (© 2014 Banco de México Diego Rivera Frida Kahlo Museums Trust, Mexico, D.F. / Artists Rights Society, New York)

Therefore we can also understand the mural as an alternate way of knowing, a different understanding of space that might counter maps like those of Beals and the PAU. This is in many ways a de-centered archive that presents a view of the hemisphere that cannot be broken down and categorized along disciplinary lines. The setting of the mural tempts the viewer into resolving all of its elements into one realistic depiction of San Francisco Bay, but there is a multiplying effect at work in *Pan American Unity* that denies the viewer a singular understanding of the image.

While I want to think about the mural as an alternative to mainstream Pan Americanism, it is certainly not oppositional. Rodríguez has suggested that, "after the rebelliousness shown in the murals at Radio City and the New Workers School, these movable frescoes are a compromise, or, to put it bluntly, an opportunist retreat."[8] *Pan American*

Unity's depiction of a harmonious, cooperative hemispheric community is certainly different in tone from Rivera's other U.S. murals and avoids the confrontational Marxist politics of *Man at the Crossroads* (1933). While Rivera's politics may have shifted by 1940, this mural is not merely a "compromise" or "retreat" but instead a multiperspectival view of the hemisphere. Rather than an imperialist understanding of Pan Americanism, which provoked a backlash from Julio Antonio Mella and others, Rivera selects part of North American culture with which to identify and unite. He acknowledges that there are resistant and even dissident elements in the United States and that a hemispheric community need not be dictated by government institutions. Instead he portrays cooperation among workers, artists, and intellectuals of the Americas. By shifting and multiplying the gaze within the mural, he also breaks the relationship of subject and object, of the northern scholar and the southern "culture." *Pan American Unity* depicts a network of cooperation that is selective. Again it does not attempt to map an entire Pan America but instead depicts specific loci of collaboration.

Rivera's vision of solidarity is not rooted in the arbitrary geography of the nation-state or even the hemisphere. These kinds of boundaries Martí dismissed long ago: "The geographical situation of our coexistence in America does not forcibly entrain, except to the mind of some degree candidate or recent graduate, a political union."[9] Nor is this solidarity limited by language or the reductive binary of "Saxon" and "Latin" cultures, which Martí in fact reinforced with his articulation of "Nuestra América." The collaboration that Rivera depicts goes beyond these divisions. As Mignolo observes, "Alliances, in the last analysis, are not established by languages or traditions only, but by common goals and interests in the field of forces established by and in the coloniality of power."[10] Cultural exchange, acquaintance, and a set of common goals are all at work in Rivera's *Pan American Unity*, and so the mural might serve as a productive model for hemispheric scholarship.

As I have made clear in this study, there were different versions of Pan Americanism, and we can see this divergence even in the examples of Beals and Rivera. While the dominant version of Pan Americanism, as well as the resistant examples I have considered, had numerous cultural, political, and economic effects, I have focused on Pan Americanism's organization of knowledge in part because I believe it is most applicable to the state of transnational scholarship today. In offering suggestions for *how* to do Hemispheric American studies, I have suggested that including a multiplicity of voices and scholars is a fundamental step toward thinking outside the logic of U.S.-centered modernity at work during the Pan American era. I have tried to do so by including the critiques made by Martí, Mella, Carpentier, Capetillo, and others, but even in this regard I have not gone as far as I might have to include the multiplicity of perspectives that would allow us an understanding of Pan Americanism. To strive for a "complete" picture of Pan Americanism, though, perhaps misses the point. The greater imperative is that Hemispheric American studies avoid the totalizing narratives that we have seen in the idea of Pan Americanism. Even in critiques of the U.S. imperialism at work within Pan Americanism, a master narrative is reinforced that does not accommodate divergent work of the period. We should instead think in terms of a multitude of Pan Americas, which differ based on the position from which they are viewed—from within and without, from above and below—and the values they are said to entail: indigeneity, artistic collaboration, the common cause of workers. It is this kind of shared goal, or set of goals, that should be a premise of any act of hemispheric scholarship. What's more, such studies should eschew easy resolutions or claims that reinforce the notion of a single, knowable Western Hemisphere. Martí warned that the "disdain of the formidable neighbor who does not know her is our America's greatest danger," but the greater danger might be neighbors who *believe* they know something that is universally applicable to all of the Americas.

Notes

Introduction

1. "Laying of the Corner Stone of the International Bureau of the American Republics," xv.

2. At the turn of the twentieth century the Bureau of the American Republics (as the Pan American Union was originally known) typically hyphenated the term *Pan-American*. However, around 1910, when the agency restructured itself as the Pan American Union, it began to print the term without the hyphen and continued to do so throughout the life of the agency. While certain authors and corporations used the hyphenated term (Pan-American Airways, for instance), I use the unhyphenated spelling in this book since it was the most common form used during the period.

3. "Laying of the Corner Stone of the International Bureau of the American Republics," xvi.

4. My use of "informational empire" borrows from Ricardo D. Salvatore, discussed later in this introduction.

5. Césaire, "Poetry and Knowledge," 134.

6. Here I am thinking particularly of Kaplan and Pease, *Cultures of United States Imperialism*; Rowe, *Literary Culture and U.S. Imperialism*; Kaplan, *The Anarchy of Empire in the Making of U.S. Culture*; as well as more recent studies by Ana Brickhouse and Kirsten Silva Gruesz. For surveys of and reflections on the hemispheric turn, see Bauer, "Hemispheric Studies"; Levander and Levine, "Introduction"; Fox, "Commentary"; McClennen, "Area Studies beyond Ontology."

7. Fishkin, "Crossroads of Cultures," 25.

8. Sommer, *Proceed with Caution*, x.

9. Gruesz, "The Occluded History of Transamerican Literature." The most notable example of this kind of scholarship is Brickhouse's landmark *Transamerican Literary Relations and the Nineteenth-Century Public Sphere*, which has greatly influenced my own work.

10. For a sample of this argument, see Barrenechea, "Good Neighbor/ Bad Neighbor"; McClennen, "Inter-American Studies or Imperial American

234 Notes to Introduction

Studies?" Perhaps the harshest accusation of "intellectual tourism" comes from Saldaña-Portillo, *The Revolutionary Imagination in the Americas,* 262. We should also keep in mind the critique from within Native American studies, which, in the words of Philip J. Deloria, finds in Hemispheric American studies a "whiff of intellectual imperialism" ("American Indians, American Studies, and the ASA," 679). Furthermore, as Huang et al., "Charting Transnational Native American Studies" point out, Native American scholars are often wary of the transnational turn in American studies since they see the occlusion of national borders as undermining the political and intellectual autonomy at the core of tribal nations.

11. Brickhouse, "Scholarship and the State," 717.

12. See Brickhouse's discussion of this episode in *Transamerican Literary Relations and the Nineteenth-Century Public Sphere,* 1–2, 265n2, as well as her reference to Johnson, *Simón Bolívar and Spanish American Independence, 1783–1830.* For more on the Congress of 1826 and Pan American appropriations of Bolívar, see chapter 2.

13. Gruesz, "The Occluded History of Transamerican Literature," 123.

14. Martí, "The Washington Pan-American Congress," 340.

15. Ibid., 345, 367.

16. Berger, *Under Northern Eyes,* 18.

17. Darío, *Songs of Life and Hope / Cantos de la vida y esperanza,* 85.

18. Ibid., 85. For a thorough discussion of Darío's poetry and its relation to Pan Americanism, see Prieto-Calixto, "Rubén Darío and Literary Anti-Americanism/Anti-Imperialism."

19. Mella, "Hacia la internacional americana" (1925), in *J. A. Mella,* 211–12. My translation.

20. Martí, "Our America," 295.

21. For examples of this work, see Oles, *South of the Border*; Delpar, *The Enormous Vogue of Things Mexican.*

22. While my use of "modernity" does involve standard notions of industrialization and technological advancement, I also understand modernity in the way Mignolo deploys it, as a much longer process that is intertwined with coloniality. Although the Pan American era did not entail colonialism in the conventional sense, I argue that its control of knowledge about the hemisphere reflects the evolving relationship between modernity and coloniality in the early twentieth century.

23. Salvatore, "Libraries and Legibility of Hispanic America," 191–92.

24. Barrett, *Annual Report of the Director,* 3–4.

25. Foucault, *The Archaeology of Knowledge,* 129.

26. Mignolo, *The Darker Side of Western Modernity,* 10.

27. Salvatore, "Local versus Imperial Knowledge" 78n2.

28. Luis-Brown, *Waves of Decolonization,* 7.

29. González, *Designing Pan-America,* xii. Within this growing field, Claire F. Fox's *Making Art Panamerican: Cultural Policy and the Cold War* should

also be singled out for the important work it does to highlight the PAU's crucial role at the intersection of culture and foreign policy. However, Fox's argument is concerned with the post–World War II period, when agendas of the PAU and Organization of American States were quite different from the period I am thinking about here.

30. Meanwhile the PAU shifted its focus as well. No longer as central to State Department interests, the Organization of American States as well as its cultural branches became less U.S.-centered as they included more and more delegates from other nations in key roles, a process Fox has described as the "Latinization" of these institutions. Important publications also shifted their focus. The *Bulletin of the Pan American Union* didn't disappear but was instead rebranded as *Américas* in 1949, and it largely abandoned its previous mercantile interests in favor of documenting cultural and artistic exchange.

31. Pérez, *Cuba in the American Imagination*, 1.

1. Mesoamerican Modernism

1. *Broom* 4, no. 1 (1922): n.p.

2. Williams, "Prologue" to *Kora in Hell: Improvisations*, in *Imaginations*, 24, hereafter cited parenthetically.

3. I am indebted to Jesse Lerner for identifying these Aztec-themed works. See Lerner, "A Fevered Dream of Maya."

4. His father, William George Williams, collaborated on translations for the Spanish American number of *Others* (1916). His mother, Raquel Hélène Williams, collaborated with Williams on several projects later in her life, including a translation of Pedro Espinosa's *El perro y el calentura* (1625), recently reissued as *The Dog and the Fever*, edited by Jonathan Cohen.

5. Marzán, *The Spanish American Roots of William Carlos Williams*.

6. Mariani, *William Carlos Williams*, 9–10.

7. Sánchez González, "Modernism and Boricua Literature," 243. See also Sánchez González, *Boricua Literature*.

8. Delpar, *The Enormous Vogue of Things Mexican*, 92.

9. In *Paterson* I (1946), Williams writes, "I remember / a *Geographic* picture, the 9 women / of some African chief semi-naked / astraddle a log, an official log to / be presumed, heads left" (*Paterson* 13). Mike Weaver has traced this reference to a 1926 issue of *National Geographic*, which Williams still remembered (or misremembered) twenty years later. See Weaver, *William Carlos Williams*, 202. See also Christopher MacGowan's note (*Paterson* 257).

10. Letter to Marianne Moore, April 14, 1924, in Williams, *Selected Letters*, 63.

11. Williams, *Something to Say*, 179, from an unpublished review of John Ciardi's *Mid-Century American Poets* (1950).

12. Williams, *The Autobiography of William Carlos Williams*, 183.

13. Williams, "The American Background," in *Selected Essays*, 142–43.

14. On the primacy of the Pan American Union Building, see Ingle, *Mayan Revival Style*; Totten, *Maya Architecture*.

15. For a description of the grounds, see Ingle, *Mayan Revival Style*, 7.

16. "The International Bureau and Its Building,"725.

17. Ibid., 725–26.

18. Ibid., 729–30.

19. Lerner's *The Maya of Modernism* examines the cultural exchanges among Yucatán Maya, U.S. travelers, and the Mexican state in the twentieth century. He also traces the way modern-day Maya were constructed as "living fossils" (17).

20. González, *Designing Pan-America*, 83. González's rich analysis of the House of the Americas is especially useful for understanding the tropical themes of the building. He remarks that these details in the interior design of the building work to suggest the "homogeneity among the southern races as well as a reference to a negative stereotype of the concept of time in Latin cultures that implicitly treats it as the opposite of the progressive concept of time associated with the United States" (69).

21. Salvatore, "Libraries and Legibility of Hispanic America," 191–92.

22. Ibid., 198.

23. "Maize or Indian Corn," 993–94.

24. Ibid., 994.

25. Morley, "The Foremost Intellectual Achievement of Ancient America," 110.

26. Ibid., 110.

27. For a fascinating account of Morley's work monitoring German agents at work in Mexico, see Harris and Sadler, *The Archaeologist Was a Spy*. See also Boas, "Scientists as Spies."

28. For an account of this era in archaeology, see Evans, *Romancing the Maya*.

29. See Ortega y Medina, "Monroísmo arqueológico," 37–86. See also the discussion in Delpar, *The Enormous Vogue of Things Mexican*, 93–94.

30. Totten, *Maya Architecture*, 5.

31. Wright, *A Testament*, 111.

32. For a more detailed discussion of the influence of the World's Fair on Wright's work, see Alofsin, *Frank Lloyd Wright*, 222–23. For more general discussions of Wright's interest in Mayan architecture, see Braun, *Pre-Columbian Art and the Post-Columbian World*.

33. Wright, *Modern Architecture*, 4, cited in Braun, *Pre-Columbian Art and the Post-Columbian World*, 138.

34. The most comprehensive work on Stacy-Judd has been done by Jesse Lerner, first in his 2001 article, "A Fevered Dream of Maya: Robert Stacy-Judd," and more recently in *The Maya of Modernism*. Much of background on Stacy-Judd here draws upon Lerner.

35. Hampton, "Creating a New World Architecture," cited in Lerner, "A Fevered Dream of Maya."

36. Stacy-Judd, *The Ancient Mayas*, 9–10.

37. Ibid., 116.

38. Ibid., 116–17.

39. Pratt, *Imperial Eyes*, 134.

40. *Broom* 4, no.1 (1922): n.p.

41. Letter from Matthew Josephson to Lola Ridge, October 1922, Princeton University Library, cited in Kondritzer, "*Broom*," 63.

42. Letter from Williams to Harold Loeb, February 1922, Princeton University Library, cited in Mariani, *William Carlos Williams*, 195.

43. Sacken, "Maya Art," 88.

44. See Loevy, "William Carlos Williams' *Rome*."

45. Williams, "Rome," 45, hereafter cited parenthetically.

46. Williams owned a 1917 edition of the book, which is now at Fairleigh Dickinson University in Rutherford, New Jersey. See Schmidt, "Descriptive List of Works from the Library of William Carlos Williams at Fairleigh Dickinson University," 45.

47. Hudson, *Idle Days in Patagonia*, 42.

48. Ibid., 40, 44.

49. Colby, *Stratified Modernism*, 3.

50. Schnapp et al., "Archaeology, Modernism, Modernity," 4.

51. Ibid., 7–8.

52. Conrad, *Reconfiguring America*, 17.

53. Letter to Horace Gregory, July 22, 1939, in Williams, *Selected Letters*, 185, cited in Conrad, *Reconfiguring America*.

54. Rodríguez García, "The Culture of Conversation and the Voice of the Indian in Williams Carlos Williams's 'Père Sebastian Rasles,'" 489.

55. Williams, *I Wanted to Write a Poem*, 42–43.

56. See Conrad, *Reconfiguring America*, 156–71, especially 171n13.

57. Ibid., 87.

58. Cohen, introduction to Williams, *By Word of Mouth*, xxxvi.

59. The poems included were "All the Fancy Things," "Brilliant Sad Sun," "Adam," "Eve," "The Flower," "Cancion," and "To Elsie."

60. Williams, "An Informal Discussion of Poetic Form," 43.

61. Ibid., 44.

62. See Cohen, introduction to Williams, *By Word of Mouth*, xxxvi.

63. Kutzinski, *Against the American Grain*, 18.

64. Ibid., 41.

65. Williams, *Paterson*, Book III (1949), 101, hereafter cited parenthetically.

2. Hemispheric Mythologies

1. For further discussion of Gamio's work in this context, see Brading, "Manuel Gamio and Official Indigenismo in Mexico"; Zermeño, "Between Anthropology and History."

2. Coffey, *How a Revolutionary Art Became Official Culture.*

3. Bolívar, "The Jamaica Letter," 28.

4. Ibid., 29.

5. Orozco, "A Note from the Artist."

6. See Sáenz, *Quetzalcóatl.*

7. Fishkin, "Crossroads of Cultures," 20.

8. Henry Nash Smith, "Symbol and Idea in *Virgin Land*," in Bercovitch and Jehlen, *Ideology and Classic American Literature*, 21.

9. Ibid., 22.

10. Richard Slotkin, "Myth and the Production of History," in Bercovitch and Jehlen, *Ideology and Classic American Literature*, 70.

11. Rowe, introduction to *A Concise Companion to American Studies*, 2–3.

12. Belnap and Fernández, introduction to *José Martí's "Our America,"* 3–4.

13. Lomas, *Translating Empire*, 33.

14. Ibid., 2.

15. Ibid., 223. It should be noted, however, that Martí has served a very different cultural role in his native Cuba. There he has become central to the nation's founding mythology. See Guerra, *The Myth of José Martí.*

16. Cited in Conway, *The Cult of Bolívar in Latin American Literature*, epigraph.

17. Conway, *The Cult of Bolívar in Latin American Literature*, 3.

18. Paulmier and Schauffler, *Pan-American Day*, 69.

19. Ibid., 260.

20. Rowe, "Introduction: Bolívar's Influence in Its Larger International Aspects," 1188.

21. See Brickhouse, *Transamerican Literary Relations and the Nineteenth-Century Public Sphere*, 265n2.

22. Rowe, "Introduction: Bolívar's Influence in Its Larger International Aspects," 1188.

23. City of New York, Parks and Recreation, "Simon Bolivar Monument," http://www.nycgovparks.org/parks/centralpark/monuments/132.

24. "Text of President Harding's Speech to 'All Americas,'" *New York Times*, April 20, 1921.

25. Vasconcelos, *Bolivarismo y monroísmo*, 7. "Llamaremos bolivarismo al ideal hispanoamericano de crear una federación con todos los pueblos de cultura española. Llamaremos monroísmo al ideal anglosajón de incorporar las veinte naciones hispánicas al Imperio nórdico, mediante la política del panamericanismo."

26. McCarthy-Jones and Greig, "*Somos hijos de Sandino y Bolívar*," 233.

27. Sandino, "Plan de realización del supremo sueño de Bolívar," in *Augusto Cesar Sandino*, 218–19.

28. Carrera Damas, "Simón Bolívar, el Culto Heroico y la Nación," 109. See also Carrera Damas, *El culto a Bolívar*.

29. Hugo Chávez Frías, @chavezcandanga, https://twitter.com/chavezcandanga.

30. ALBA-TCP, "History of ALBA-TCP."

31. See Zermeño, "Between Anthropology and History," 318.

32. Ibid., 320.

33. Mignolo, *The Darker Side of the Renaissance*, 199.

34. Sahagún, *Florentine Codex*, 1: 59.

35. Ibid., 4: 55.

36. Sáenz, *Quetzalcóatl*, 56.

37. Lafaye, *Quetzalcóatl y Guadalupe*, 225.

38. Ibid., 230.

39. Orozco, *An Autobiography*, 104.

40. Brenner, *Idols behind Altars*, 13.

41. Lawrence, "America, Listen to Your Own," 69.

42. Lawrence, *The Symbolic Meaning*, 80–81.

43. Ibid., 81.

44. Vasconcelos, *The Cosmic Race / La raza cósmica*, 8.

45. Ibid., 16.

46. Marilyn Grace Miller has discussed at greater length Vasconcelos's relationship with the contemporary efforts at racial purity, revealing, as she puts it, "the affinity of Vasconcelos' thinking about race, even early in his career, with projects of eugenics and *blanqueamiento*, or whitening, in other parts of the hemisphere" (*Rise and Fall of the Cosmic Race*, 43–44).

47. Vasconcelos, *The Cosmic Race / La raza cósmica*, 26.

48. Siqueiros, "A New Direction for the New Generation of American Painters and Sculptors," in *Art and Revolution*, 22. This essay was originally published in the first and only number of the magazine *Vida Americana*, edited by Siqueiros in Barcelona.

49. Quoted in and translated by Anreus, "*Los Tres Grandes*," 38.

50. Orozco, "A Note from the Artist," n.p.

51. Paz, "The Concealment and Discovery of Orozco," 180.

52. Orozco, "New World, New Races, and New Art," xlv–xlvi.

53. Orozco, "A Note from the Artist," n.p.

54. Ibid.

55. Coffey, "An 'AMERICAN Idea,'" 27–28.

56. Orozco, *An Autobiography*, 158.

57. For instance, in her analysis of Orozco's mural at the Palace of Fine Arts in Mexico City, Coffey writes, "Orozco condemned the very civic project he had

been commissioned to ornament" (*How a Revolutionary Art Became Official Culture*, 33).

58. Ernest Hopkins, letter of May 31, 1932, in Elliott and Orozco, *Orozco!*, 54.

59. While living in the United States, Orozco often used this phrase in his letters home to Mexico. For an analysis of Orozco's years in the United States, see Anreus, *Orozco in Gringoland*.

60. As Drew Lopenzina notes, "Though Dartmouth was founded on money intended for the education of Indians and such a mission was written into its charter, only three Natives would graduate in the eighteenth century and only eight in the entire nineteenth" ("'The Whole Wilderness Shall Blossom as the Rose,'" 1143n37).

61. Paz, "The Concealment and Discovery of Orozco," 182.

62. Orozco, *An Autobiography*, 149–50.

63. Mignolo, *The Darker Side of the Renaissance*, 133.

3. Academic Discourse at Havana

1. González Echevarría, *Alejo Carpentier*, 64.

2. González Echevarría's *Alejo Carpentier: The Pilgrim at Home* is still the definitive English-language study of Carpentier's work, and it is one of the few critical studies to have devoted significant attention to *¡Écue-Yamba-Ó!* (34–96). While González Echevarría's reading of the novel is centered on its relation to Spengler's *Decline of the West*, the insightful connection he makes between Carpentier and the work of Fernando Ortiz has been the inspiration of my own study.

3. The fact that an English translation of *¡Écue-Yamba-Ó!* still does not exist merits some reflection, especially since Carpentier's other works have been available in English for so long. Knopf was an early promoter of Carpentier's novels in the 1950s, and his work continues to be easily available to readers of English through the University of Minnesota's reissue of many of his works in 2001 (though *Écue* was not included in this series.) One possible explanation for this is that *¡Écue-Yamba-Ó!* does not lend itself easily to translation since the original Spanish text makes extensive use of *ñáñigo* cant and Afro-Cuban vernacular. However, these obstacles did not prevent Gallimard from publishing a French translation in 1988. I am more inclined to think that there has been little eagerness to translate *¡Écue-Yamba-Ó!* into English because it does not fit easily into Anglophone readers' understanding of Carpentier's work. *¡Écue-Yamba-Ó!* disrupts the idea of Carpentier the magical realist, an identity that has been constructed around his later works, especially *Los pasos perdidos* (1953) and *El siglo de las luces* (1962). Perhaps Francophone readers, who did not experience the same aggressive marketing of Boom literature during the 1960s and 1970s as did Anglophone readers, are less invested in this version of Carpentier.

4. Anke Birkenmaier's *Alejo Carpentier y la cultura del surrealismo en América Latina* is the most exhaustive study of Carpentier's relationship with surrealism. She explores the novel as a product of his time in Paris, during which

his interest in the primitive and in ethnography would have been influenced by the journals he followed, such as Bataille's *Documents*, as well as visits to the Musée de l'Homme and the 1931 Exposition Coloniale Internationale. For her discussion of *¡Écue-Yamba-Ó!* in particular, see 53–79. See also Rogers, "Carpentier, Collecting, and *Lo Barroco Americano*."

5. Amy Fass Emery in *The Anthropological Imagination in Latin American Literature* has presented a thorough reading of *Écue* as an example of primitivism, though, like other critics, she bases her reading on the premise of the European avant-garde's influence on Carpentier's early writing. To understand the novel within a Cuban context, *negrismo* is the more relevant term. Although *Écue* is the only example of an Afro-Cuban novel, at the time the Cuban imagination was fascinated with the African elements within the island's culture. In addition to celebrating the achievements of the Afro-Cuban poet Nicolás Guillén, this *negrismo* movement was also manifested in the music and popular culture of the day. See Moore, *Nationalizing Blackness*.

6. Carpentier, *Écue-Yamba-Ó* (2002), 11. Subsequent references, including to the 1977 preface, are to the 2002 edition and are cited parenthetically in the text. Composed in 1927, the novel was originally published as *¡Écue-Yamba-Ó! Novela afrocubana* (1933). Translations are mine.

7. Miller, "Remoteness and Proximity," 5.

8. In *Sugar's Secrets*, Vera M. Kutzinski has explored at greater length the literary representation of the sugar industry in Cuba since the nineteenth century, noting the way the industry inscribed particular roles of race and gender into the Cuban national identity and also served as a literal and figurative representation of imperialism. Kutzinski has offered a thorough history of the economic changes in Cuba during the early twentieth century and, in her discussion of *¡Écue-Yamba-Ó!*, observes a downward turn in the fortunes of the Cué family similar to the one I have traced here. Significantly she also locates Carpentier's work within a larger Afro-Cubanist response to the sugar industry: "Carpentier was neither the first nor the only Cuban writer at the time who perceived Afro-Cuban secular and religious culture as a cultural alternative to North-Americanization and as a political vehicle for national integrity and survival. For many of the mostly white members of the Cuban intelligentsia, Afro-Cuban culture . . . was a talismanic presence that would somehow avert or transcend the dangers posed by Wall Street and the *central*" (142).

9. I take these terms from Mignolo, *Local Histories / Global Designs*.

10. For an account of Machado's political rise and fall, see Aguilar, *Cuba 1933*, especially 55–67.

11. For this translation as well as a discussion of the Minorista Group in Cuba, see Martínez, "Social and Political Commentary in Cuban Modernist Painting of the 1930s."

12. Foucault, *Security, Territory, Population*, 65.

13. See chapter 4 of this book for further discussion of these two building projects and for a broader analysis of U.S. representations of such material development in Latin America.

14. Machado y Morales, *Declaraciones del General Gerardo Machado y Morales*, 19–20, quoted in Bronfman, *Measures of Equality*, 109.

15. Bronfman, *Measures of Equality*, 110–11.

16. Ortiz, "Esta revista cubana," 5.

17. While Guillén's poem had already been published, this reprint treats the text more like an anthropological specimen than the avant-garde poem that it was. In his introduction to the poem, Ortiz suggests that Guillén's work is so enmeshed with folk music that "soon these verses will pass into the popular repertoire and it might be forgotten who the author was." See Ortiz, "Introduction to *Motivos del son*," 222.

18. As Pratt notes, Ortiz's use of the term appears in his 1940 study *Cuban Counterpoint: Tobacco and Sugar*. She explains transculturation as follows: "Ortiz proposed the term to replace the paired concepts of acculturation and deculturation that described the transference of culture in reductive fashion imagined from within the interests of the metropolis" (*Imperial Eyes*, 228n4). Pratt and a generation of scholars found this term useful in their own work, and one consequence of this has been that Fernando Ortiz is now synonymous with transculturation. This is, however, but one part of Ortiz's body of thought, what we might call late Ortiz. As with Carpentier (see n4 above), Ortiz's work is perceived very differently by Anglophone readers, who are less likely to be familiar with his decades of work as a criminologist. See Ortiz, *Cuban Counterpoint*, 97–103.

19. Birkenmaier, *Alejo Carpentier y la cultura del surrealismo en América Latina*, 65, my translation.

20. Ibid., 75, my translation.

21. Palmié, "The Cuban Republic and its Wizards," 75. Palmié's large body of work is indispensible to an understanding of Afro-Cuban religious practices and their relationship to the state. In addition to this article, see his book-length study, *Wizards and Scientists*.

22. Ortiz, *Proyecto de código criminal cubano*, 14.

23. Bronfman, "Poetry in the Presidio."

24. Ibid., 162.

25. Letter from Ramiro Cabrera, October 16, 1926, Biblioteca Nacional José Martí, quoted and translated in Bronfman, "Poetry in the Presidio," 162–63.

26. Ortiz, *Proyecto de código criminal cubano*, 50–51.

27. *Transactions of the First Pan American Conference on Eugenics and Homiculture of the American Republics*, 206. The minutes of the Eugenics conferences were published in the bilingual edition, yet the English half of the volume is filled with translation errors. In my quotations I have used the English half of the volume, relying on the Spanish text to correct obvious mistakes.

28. Ibid., 311–12.

29. Stepan, *"The Hour of Eugenics,"* 173. Laughlin continued to be a prominent figure in the Pan American eugenics movement, and in 1935 he lobbied successfully for the creation of the Laboratory for Pan American Population Research, which he went on to head.

30. *Transactions of the First Pan American Conference on Eugenics and Homiculture of the American Republics*, 232.

31. In addition to proliferating U.S. immigration policies throughout the Americas, U.S. scientists and public health workers made the hemisphere's inhabitants the subjects of unwilling scientific experiments. This can be seen in the recent revelation that between 1946 and 1948 U.S. doctors infected approximately seven hundred Guatemalans with syphilis in order to test penicillin treatments. This Tuskegee-like experiment suggests the vulnerability of bodies of color that lay within the purview of U.S. science. See Donald G. McNeil Jr., "U.S. Apologizes for Syphilis Experiments in Guatemala," *New York Times*, October 1, 2010, http://www.nytimes.com/2010/10/02/health/research/02infect.html.

32. Asturias, *Sociología Guatemalteca*.

33. *Transactions of the First Pan American Conference on Eugenics and Homiculture of the American Republics*, 217.

34. Ibid., 218.

35. Stepan, *"The Hour of Eugenics,"* 3–4.

36. For an account of the cocaine debate and Paz Soldán's role in it, see Gootenberg, *Cocaine*, 56–63.

37. *Transactions of the First Pan American Conference on Eugenics and Homiculture of the American Republics*, 249.

38. Ibid.

39. Ibid.

40. Ibid., 258.

41. Ibid., 270.

42. For an account of Castellanos's *La delincuencia feminine* as well as the *ficha-modelo* he employed in his anthropometric studies, see Bronfman, *Measures of Equality*, 129.

43. I would like to thank Elizabeth Maddock Dillon for suggesting this association.

4. Pan American Progress

1. Beals, "Red Clay in Alabama," 444.

2. Beals, *Pan America*, 101.

3. Cara A. Finnegan has written about the popular consumption of these sensationalized images of poverty during the 1930s. See her chapter "Spectacle of the Downtrodden Other" in *Picturing Poverty*, 168–219.

4. Although the term *underdevelopment* is a product of the post–World War II era, the concept of dividing regions according to their perceived industrial

progress or lack of progress can be extended much further back in the twentieth century. See Saldaña-Portillo, *The Revolutionary Imagination in the Americas and the Age of Development*. See also Escobar, *Encountering Development*.

5. Pratt, *Imperial Eyes*, 15.

6. "Pan American Airways," 80

7. Ibid., 82.

8. Ibid., iv.

9. See Brookover, "Cuba Completes Two Great National Tasks."

10. Noel, "Cuba—A Country on the Rise," 253.

11. Aguilar, *Cuba 1933*, 64.

12. See ibid., 58–60.

13. Beals, "The Crime of Cuba" pt. 1, 11. This issue of the magazine was promptly confiscated when it arrived in Havana, and those whom Beals indicted as supporters of the regime (among them U.S. Ambassador Harry Guggenheim) were scandalized. For a thorough account of Beals's experiences in Cuba and the publication of *The Crime of Cuba*, see Britton, *Carleton Beals*, 103–22.

14. Bourke-White's *Eyes on Russia* was in large part a celebration of the machine without any real consideration of life in Stalin's Russia. For a recent examination of her Russian photography, see Mickenberg, "The New Generation and the New Russia." To offer another sample from the left, Waldo Frank was more critical of the political developments in the Soviet Union during his travels, but he was nevertheless just as optimistic about the promise of mechanization in his *Dawn in Russia*: "The machine, it seems to me, inevitably leads—under whatever system—to the disappearance of physical want and to greater physical leisure for the masses" (268).

15. My formulation of the term *radical paternalism* is partly informed by what Renato Rosaldo describes as "imperialist nostalgia," in which the European observer mourns the loss of what he himself has had a hand in destroying. See Rosaldo, "Imperialist Nostalgia." In the twentieth century, however, writers like Beals deploy their politics of leftist advocacy as a more legitimate mood than nostalgia. But, nostalgia is still, in many ways, at the root of this critical posture since writers such as Stuart Chase continually praise the values of pre-industrial society.

16. For more on Stuart Chase's work, see Britton, *Revolution and Ideology*, 106–10.

17. Rubén Gallo, *Mexican Modernity* has written extensively about the role of new technologies in Mexican art and culture during this period.

18. See Redfield, *Tepoztlan, a Mexican Village*.

19. See Lynd, *Middletown*.

20. Chase, *Mexico*, 312.

21. Ibid., 324.

22. This brief biographical sketch is drawn from Britton, *Carleton Beals*.

23. Letter from Beals to his mother, October 1921, cited in Britton, *Carleton Beals*, 38.

24. See Britton, *Carleton Beals*, 87–90.

25. Mella, "Machado: Mussolini Tropical" (1925), in *J. A. Mella*, 169–70.

26. See Hughes's "The Little Old Spy," *Esquire*, September 1934; Hemingway's "One Trip Across" (1934) and "The Tradesman's Return" (1934), both of which became part of his novel *To Have and Have Not* (1937).

27. Beals, "The Crime of Cuba" pt. 1, 10.

28. Ibid., 112

29. Beals, *The Crime of Cuba*, 19, hereafter cited parenthetically.

30. David Luis-Brown has also had to contend with the contradictions of *The Crime of Cuba* and the way Beals's critique of U.S. imperial practices in Cuba is accompanied by his "sexist and racially essentialist language." Wrestling with the Fela passage in particular, Luis-Brown has concluded that "Beals's dominant primitivist discourse betrays his own participation within a sexualized tourist economy" (*Waves of Decolonization*, 168, 170).

31. Stott, *Documentary Expression and Thirties America*, 267.

32. Evans, *Walker Evans at Work*, 281.

33. Ibid., 82.

34. Ibid., 88.

35. Bear, "In the Morgue," 222. Bear has done excellent work in tracing Evans's use of anonymous photographs during his time in Cuba. Some of the grisly photos of murdered activists that Evans included in *The Crime of Cuba* were, as Bear points out, taken from an archive of photos unpublishable because of Machado's censors. An underlying principle of the documentary form is the representation of "truth" as political engagement, and so a case can be made that publishing these censored photographs influenced Evans's later efforts to document the face of poverty in Alabama. While Evans's inclusion of these gruesome photos in his Cuban portfolio is fascinating, my focus in the present chapter is his evolving attitude toward poverty and economic development in the Americas.

36. For background on GE's evolving role in Cuba's economy and its politics, see O'Brien, "The Revolutionary Mission."

37. Evans, "The Reappearance of Photography," 128, cited in Trachtenberg, "Signifying the Real," 10–11.

38. Mora, *Walker Evans*, 15–16.

39. Cited in Mellow, *Walker Evans*, 187.

40. For as discussion of the evolution of Evans's style and his move away from candid photography, see Stott, *Documentary Expression and Thirties America*, 268.

41. Stecopoulos, *Reconstructing the World*, 3.

42. Ibid., 3.

43. Beals, "Red Clay in Alabama," 445.

44. Beals, *Mexico: An Interpretation*, 204.
45. Ibid., 200.
46. Beals, *Mexican Maze*, 232.
47. Ibid., 238.
48. Beals and Plenn, "Louisiana's Black Utopia," 503.
49. Ibid., 503.
50. Beals, "Red Clay in Alabama," 445.
51. Ibid., 445.
52. Beals, *Mexican Maze*, 353.
53. Pratt, *Imperial Eyes*, 7.
54. Agee and Evans, *Let Us Now Praise Famous Men*, 10.
55. Cited in Stott, *Documentary Expression and Thirties America*, 223.
56. Stott traces the origins of documentary writing to the tradition of reportage. He invokes the definition that Joseph North and Matthew Josephson articulated in 1935 as "three-dimensional reporting" that "helps the reader *experience* the events recorded" (cited in Stott, *Documentary Expression and Thirties America*, 54).
57. Agee, "Six Days at Sea," 118.
58. Agee and Evans, *Let Us Now Praise Famous Men*, 5.
59. The University of Tennessee Libraries recently acquired several of Agee's notebooks, including two from his trip to Cuba. These will be published in *The Works of James Agee: Notebooks and Other Manuscripts*, forthcoming from the University of Tennessee Press.
60. Agee and Evans, *Let Us Now Praise Famous Men*, 42.
61. In another remarkable passage in *Famous Men*, Agee, on the porch in Alabama, observes the dawn and imagines the same sun touching points from Canada to the Andes (ibid., 77), an awareness Andrew Crooke has referred to as Agee's "hemispheric consciousness" ("A Continuous Center," 87).
62. Agee, "Six Days at Sea," 216.

5. Pan Americanism Revisited

1. See Adams, *Continental Divides*. Chapter 3, "Women of the South Bank: The Mexican Routes of American Modernism," explores the work of Anita Brenner, Katherine Anne Porter, and Tina Modotti within a transnational frame.
2. Threlkeld, "The Pan American Conference of Women, 1922," 804.
3. Cited in ibid., 815–16.
4. Moraga and Anzaldúa, *This Bridge Called My Back*, xxiii.
5. Sandoval, "U.S. Third World Feminism," 1.
6. Ibid., 5, 11.
7. Miller, *Latin American Women and the Search for Social Justice*, 176.
8. Ibid., 180.
9. Lee, "Correspondence," 294.

10. See *Poetry*, June 1925; *Anthology of Contemporary Latin-American Poetry*, edited by Dudley Fitts.

11. "Pan-American Literary Ties Urged on U.S," *New York Herald Tribune*, November 30, 1941, cited in Cohen, "Muna Lee: A Pan-American Life," in *A Pan-American Life*, 42. See also Lee's later essay on this topic, "Translating the Untranslatable."

12. See Cohen's biographical essay in *A Pan-American Life*, 3–74. For Lee's further ideas on hemispheric cultural exchange, see "Cultural Interchanges between the Americas." See also her book, coauthored with McMurry, *The Cultural Approach*.

13. Cited in Jiménez-Muñoz, "Deconstructing Colonialist Discourse," 19.

14. For a discussion of this case, see Kaplan, *The Anarchy of Empire in the Making of U.S. Culture*, 1–22.

15. Miller, *Latin American Women and the Search for Social Justice*, 82.

16. See ibid., 94.

17. Lee, "Correspondence," 295.

18. Lee, "In Behalf of Equal Rights Treaty before Unofficial Plenary Session." Havana, February 7, 1928, cited in Jiménez-Muñoz, "Deconstructing Colonialist Discourse," 18.

19. The biographical details that follow, unless otherwise stated, are drawn from Valle-Ferrer, *Luisa Capetillo*; Walker, introduction to Capetillo, *Absolute Equality*.

20. Capetillo, *Amor y anarquía*, 184, my translation.

21. Ibid., 185.

22. Ramos, introduction to Capetillo, *Amor y anarquía*, 27, my translation.

23. Sánchez González, *Boricua Literature*, 22–23.

24. Capetillo, *A Nation of Women*, 5.

25. Capetillo, *Absolute Equality*, 115–16, Walker translation.

26. Ibid., 60.

27. Ibid., 60–61.

28. Ibid., 61.

29. Castillo, *Massacre of the Dreamers*, 69, hereafter cited parenthetically.

30. Castillo, *The Mixquiahuala Letters*, 11, hereafter cited parenthetically.

31. Quintana, "Ana Castillo's *The Mixquiahuala Letters*," 79.

32. Ibid., 74.

33. Walker, *The Color Purple*.

34. Castillo taught this course in the Woman Studies Department at San Francisco State University for several years in the early 1980s. See Course Readers (Box 22) in the Ana Castillo Papers, California Ethnic and Multicultural Archives, Collection 2, Special Collections, University of California, Santa Barbara. The Castillo Papers also include a draft of an essay by the Hispanic literature scholar Carol Maier, dated July 1978, in which she states that Castillo "has been reading and writing about other women writers she admires—both Latina

and Anglo, Anaïs Nin and the Three Marías [*sic*]—, and she is very aware of how much their personal struggle as women, a struggle she herself is experiencing" (Box 11, Folder 5).

35. Barreno et al., *The Three Marias*, 1.

36. Ibid., 15.

37. See Alarcón, "The Sardonic Powers of the Erotic in the Work of Ana Castillo."

38. For biographical information on Fergusson, see Gish, *Beautiful Swift Fox*. Gish focuses almost exclusively on Fergusson's writing about the Southwest, though he does devote an appendix to "Fergusson's Latin American, Caribbean, and Hawaiian Travels."

39. Fergusson, *Mexico Revisited*, 5.

40. Ibid., 7.

41. Fergusson, *Fiesta in Mexico*, 36.

42. Fergusson, *Mexico Revisited*, 228.

43. Ibid., 184.

44. Ibid., 185.

45. Ibid., 185.

46. Throughout the novel, Castillo insists on using the lower-case "i" for Teresa. Her remarks at the beginning of *Massacre of the Dreamers* go a long way toward explaining her aversion to the capital letter: "Throughout the history of the United States 'I' as subject and object has been reserved for white authorship and readership . . . However, when I speak of women within these pages, I speak very specifically of the woman described above," that is, a "brown woman, from the Mexican side of town." *Massacre*, 1.

47. Squier, *Gringa*, 3.

48. It is interesting to note that very early drafts of *The Mixquiahuala Letters* were actually written in the third person. These earlier versions, composed in the late 1970s, bear little resemblance to the novel Castillo completed in 1984. The most recognizable section is probably a chapter titled "The Drought: California 1975–76, " which tells the story of two sisters, one of which is named "Alice." See the Ana Castillo Papers, Box 15, Folder 1.

49. Alarcón, "Chicana's Feminist Literature," in Moraga and Anzaldúa, *This Bridge Called My Back*, 182.

6. Decolonizing the Dance

1. Popularly spelled *voodoo*, this collection of cultural and religious practices has a number of alternative spellings used by scholars. The preferred spelling, though, is *Vodou*, which I use. However, Dunham consistently used *vaudun* in her texts and I have left this unchanged in quoted passages.

2. Dunham, *Island Possessed*, 106, hereafter cited parenthetically.

3. See Taylor, *The Archive and the Repertoire*, which I return to later in the chapter.

4. Mignolo, *The Darker Side of Western Modernity*, 122.

5. Polyné, *From Douglass to Duvalier*, 8.

6. Historians have occasionally marked the beginning of the Good Neighbor era with President Herbert Hoover's goodwill tour of 1928 or Roosevelt's inaugural address. However, the first material change of any significance came with the decision to remove U.S. troops from Haiti, which Roosevelt reaffirmed during his trip to Cap-Haïtien in July 1934.

7. John Martin, "The Dance: Dunham, Schoolmarm Turned Siren or Vice Versa; in 'Bal Nègre' at the Belasco," *New York Times*, November 17, 1946, in Clarke and Johnson, *Kaiso!*, 296. Since the late 1970s Vèvè Clarke's scholarship has recuperated Dunham's work and drawn critical attention to her significance to the fields of anthropology, performance studies, and African Diaspora studies. The anthology *Kaiso!* is an indispensible source for reprints of Dunham's original writings as well as critical and historical studies of her life and work. Several of the texts I cite in this chapter can be found in *Kaiso!*

8. Dunham, "Thesis Turned Broadway," *California Arts and Architecture*, August 1941, in Clarke and Johnson, *Kaiso!*, 214.

9. These biographical details are drawn from Aschenbrenner, *Katherine Dunham*.

10. For Dunham's discussion of her work in Martinique and her study of *l'ag'ya*, see her essay, written as Kaye Dunn, "L'ag'ya of Martinique," *Esquire* 12, no. 5 (1939), in Clarke and Johnson, *Kaiso!*, 201–7. See also Batiste's extended discussion of the ballet *L'Ag'ya* in *Darkening Mirrors*, 185–98.

11. For more on this aspect of *Stormy Weather*, for instance, see Batiste, *Darkening Mirrors*, 228–55. In addition to an extended analysis of the film in general, Batiste remarks that in her choreography for and performance in *Stormy Weather*, "shades of Dunham's ethnographic collection of indigenous black dance forms suffuse these movements" (249).

12. Though less often read than her book *Mules and Men* (1935), *Tell My Horse* makes an important contribution to the study of folklore. Arriving, as Dunham did, just after the occupation ended, Hurston's attitude toward U.S. intervention was more complicated. As J. Michael Dash has argued, "Hurston has the dubious distinction of being the only black writer who actually approved of the American Occupation" (*Haiti and the United States*, 58). However, John Carlos Rowe, "Opening the Gate to the Other America: The Afro-Cuban Politics of Hurston's *Mules and Men* and *Tell My Horse*," in *Literary Culture and U.S. Imperialism*, 253–91, has suggested that Hurston did not necessarily endorse U.S. imperial practices, but her politics were bound up with U.S. idealism, which led her to view the occupation as a stabilizing influence.

13. Cruz Banks, "Katherine Dunham," 122.

14. Dunham, "Dunham Technique: Prospectus," an unpublished paper, dated February 1963, in the Katherine Mary Dunham Papers, SIU Carbondale, in Clarke and Johnson, *Kaiso!*, 522.

15. "President Vincent Confers with President Roosevelt," 390.

16. Though Dash is careful to note that these literary accounts took various forms, overall he observes, "They provided images that were ultimately cherished as the rationale for America's imperialist designs on Haiti. Lurid accounts of savagery and cannibalism could not, perhaps, in themselves dictate national policy but under pressure of national and strategic interests they did reinforce the feelings that American intervention in Haiti was the only way of curbing the nation's barbarous instincts" (*Haiti and the United States*, 22–23).

17. Dunham points out how important it was to have been the first woman of color to conduct this kind of research on the island: "Being a 'first' on the scene helped. Seabrook with his *Magic Island* had been a great handicap because the élite were offended, not so much by the text, which, compared to much that has been written about Haiti, isn't so vilifying, but by the illustrations—grotesque impressions not only of the peasants, which wouldn't have mattered, but of the élite" (*Island Possessed*, 3–4).

18. Sylvain, "The Haitian Rural School at Work," 606.

19. Ibid., 608.

20. For a thorough account of Estimé's rise to power, see Smith, *Red and Black in Haiti*, 103–48.

21. Meredith Johns, "Haiti's 144th Independence Day Finds Her Fighting to Break U.S. Control," *Chicago Defender*, January 17, 1948, 13.

22. Renda, *Taking Haiti*, 285.

23. For more on Price-Mars and the Code Pénal, see Ramsey, *The Spirit and the Law*, 180.

24. Ibid., 218.

25. Ibid., 221.

26. See Ramsey, "Melville Herskovits, Katherine Dunham, and the Politics of African Diasporic Dance Anthropology": "One of the potentials of anthropology's 'modern scientific method,' as [Herskovits] termed it, was to authoritatively counter racist images of African and diasporic cultures that often fixated on dance and ritual forms" (202).

27. Ibid., 205.

28. Ibid., 203.

29. Later on, however, the avant-garde filmmaker and Dunham's protégée, Maya Deren, did manage to both film and participate in Vodou rituals. Having worked as a dancer in the Dunham Company and as Dunham's secretary, helping her edit her early fieldwork on Haiti, Deren was familiar with the rich interplay of ethnography and performance. In 1947 Deren traveled to Haiti on a Guggenheim Fellowship. The resulting book, *Divine Horsemen: The Living Gods of Haiti* (1953), was remembered by Dunham as "one of the classics of Haitian folk and religious customs" (excerpt from "Minefields," in Clarke and Johnson, *Kaiso!*, 134). Deren also recorded many hours of film on her trip, which was edited into a posthumous documentary, also titled *Divine Horsemen*.

30. Ramsey, "Melville Herskovits, Katherine Dunham, and the Politics of African Diasporic Dance Anthropology," 206.

31. Ibid.

32. Batiste, *Darkening Mirrors*, 177.

33. Dunham submitted her master's thesis, "Dances of Haiti: Their Social Organization, Classification, Form, and Function," to the University of Chicago in 1938. In 1947 a Spanish translation was published in Mexico as *Las danzas de Haiti*. An English-language version of *Dances of Haiti* was finally published in 1983 by UCLA's Center for Afro-American Studies.

34. Taylor, *The Archive and the Repertoire*, xvi.

35. Ibid., 19.

36. Ibid.

37. Ibid., 20.

38. Hill, "Katherine Dunham's 'Southland' Protest in the Face of Repression," 2.

39. Dunham, prologue to *Southland*, in Clarke and Johnson, *Kaiso!*, 341.

40. Hill, "Katherine Dunham's 'Southland' Protest in the Face of Repression," 2.

41. Von Eschen, *Satchmo Blows Up the World*. See also Prevots, *Dance for Export*.

42. This is an English translation of the Spanish prologue Dunham read, in Clarke and Johnson, *Kaiso!*, 341.

43. Ibid., 342.

44. Ibid.

45. Hill, "Katherine Dunham's 'Southland' Protest in the Face of Repression," 5.

46. Ibid., 6.

47. Estimé, *Dumarsais Estimé*, 136. "Dans New York, ville monstrueuse, aux multiples tentacules, nous arrivâmes comme des aveugles sans repères."

48. Ibid., 136–37. "En effet, au début des années 50, la ségrégation raciale était bel et bien une réalité à New York ou dans toute autre ville des États-Unis. Rien d'autre ne comptait pour ces propriétaires impitoyables: qu'on soit de culture française ou qu'on ait été Président d'un quelconque État . . . n'avait aucune importance à leurs yeux."

49. Beckford, *Katherine Dunham*, 61.

50. For a survey of Senghor's ideas on *négritude* and his state-sponsored arts program in Senegal, see Harny, *In Senghor's Shadow*.

51. Dunham, "The Performing Arts of Africa," 473.

52. Ibid., 476.

Epilogue

1. Mignolo, *Local Histories / Global Designs*, 23–38. For Mignolo's further treatment of cartography, see *The Darker Side of the Renaissance* and *The Idea of Latin America*.

2. Pease, "Introduction," 26.

3. Beals, *Pan America*, 397, hereafter cited parenthetically.

4. Cited in City College of San Francisco, The Diego Rivera Mural Project.

5. Lee, *Painting on the Left*, 211.

6. Diego Rivera, letter to Timothy Pflueger, April 15, 1940, Rivera Archive, City College of San Francisco, reprinted in City College of San Francisco, The Diego Rivera Mural Project.

7. Rodríguez, *A History of Mexican Mural Painting*, 272.

8. Ibid., 271.

9. Martí, "The Monetary Conference of the American Republics" (1891), in *José Martí: Selected Writings*, 307.

10. Mignolo, *Local Histories / Global Designs*, 143.

Bibliography

Adams, Rachel. *Continental Divides: Remapping the Cultures of North America*. Chicago: University of Chicago Press, 2009.

Agee, James. "Six Days at Sea." *Fortune*, September 1937, 117–20, 210, 212, 214, 216, 219–20.

Agee, James, and Walker Evans. *Let Us Now Praise Famous Men*. 1941. New York: Houghton Mifflin, 2001.

Aguilar, Luis E. *Cuba 1933: Prologue to Revolution*. New York: Norton, 1974.

Alarcón, Norma. "The Sardonic Powers of the Erotic in the Work of Ana Castillo." In *Breaking Boundaries: Latina Writing and Critical Readings*, edited by Asunción Horno-Delgado et al., 94–107. Amherst: University of Massachusetts Press, 1989.

ALBA-TCP. "History of ALBA-TCP." http://alba-tcp.org/en/contenido/history-alba-tcp.

Alofsin, Anthony. *Frank Lloyd Wright: The Lost Years, 1910–1922*. Chicago: University of Chicago Press, 1993.

Anreus, Alejandro. *Orozco in Gringoland: The Years in New York*. Albuquerque: University of New Mexico Press, 2001.

———. "*Los Tres Grandes*: Ideologies and Style." In *Mexican Muralism: A Critical History*, edited by Leonard Folgarait Anreus and Robin Adèle Greeley, 37–55. Berkeley: University of California Press, 2012.

Anreus, Alejandro, Diana L. Linden, and Jonathan Weinberg, eds. *The Social and the Real: Political Art of the 1930s in the Western Hemisphere*. University Park: Pennsylvania State University Press, 2006.

Aschenbrenner, Joyce. *Katherine Dunham: Dancing a Life*. Urbana: University of Illinois, 2002.

Asturias, Miguel Ángel. *Sociologia Guatemalteca: El problema social del indio / Guatemalan Sociology: The Social Problem of the Indian*. Translated by Maureen Ahern. Tempe: University of Arizona Press, 1977.

Barrenechea, Antonio. "Good Neighbor/Bad Neighbor: Boltonian American-ism and Hemispheric Studies." *Comparative Literature* 61, no. 3 (2009): 231–43.

Barreno, Maria Isabel, Maria Teresa Horta, and Maria Velho da Costa. *The Three Marias: New Portuguese Letters*. Translated by Helen R. Lane. New York: Doubleday, 1975.

Barrett, John. *Annual Report of the Director*. Washington, DC: Pan American Union, 1911.

Batiste, Stephanie Leigh. *Darkening Mirrors: Imperial Representation in Depression-Era African American Performance*. Durham, NC: Duke University Press, 2011.

Bauer, Ralph. "Hemispheric Studies." *PMLA* 124, no. 1 (2009): 234–50.

Beals, Carleton. "The Crime of Cuba." Pt. 1. *Common Sense*, December 29, 1932, 10–11, 30–32.

———. "The Crime of Cuba." Pt. 2. *Common Sense*, January 19,1933, 20–24.

———. "The Crime of Cuba." Pt. 3. *Common Sense*, February 1, 1933, 22–26.

———. *The Crime of Cuba*. Philadelphia: Lippincott, 1933.

———. *Mexican Maze*. Philadelphia: J. B. Lippincott, 1931.

———. *Mexico: An Interpretation*. New York: B. W. Huebsch, 1923.

———. *Pan America: A Program for the Western Hemisphere*. Boston: Houghton Mifflin, 1940.

———. "Red Clay in Alabama: 'Rehabilitation.'" *Nation*, April 8, 1936, 444–46.

———. *The Stones Awake: A Novel of Mexico*. Philadelphia: J. B. Lippincott, 1936.

Beals, Carleton, and Abel Plenn. "Louisiana's Black Utopia." *Nation*, October 30, 1935, 503–5.

Bear, Jordan. "In the Morgue: Censorship, Taste and the Politics of Visual Circulation in Walker Evans's Cuba Portfolio." *Visual Resources* 23, no. 3 (2007): 221–43.

Beckford, Ruth. *Katherine Dunham: A Biography*. New York: M. Dekker, 1979.

Belnap, Jeffrey, and Raúl Fernández, eds. *José Martí's "Our America": From National to Hemispheric Cultural Studies*. Durham, NC: Duke University Press, 1998.

Bercovitch, Sacvan, and Myra Jehlen, eds. *Ideology and Classic American Literature*. Cambridge, UK: Cambridge University Press, 1986.

Berger, Mark T. *Under Northern Eyes: Latin American Studies and U.S. Hegemony in the Americas 1898–1990*. Bloomington: University of Indiana Press, 1995.

Birkenmaier, Anke. *Alejo Carpentier y la cultura del surrealismo en América Latina*. Madrid: Iberoamericana, 2006.

Boas, Franz. "Scientists as Spies." *Nation*, December 20, 1919, 797.

Bolívar, Simón. "The Jamaica Letter: Response from a South American to a Gentleman of This Island (6 September 1815)." in *El Libertador: Writings of Simón Bolívar*, edited by David Bushnell, 12–30. Oxford: Oxford University Press, 2003.

Bourke-White, Margaret. *Eyes on Russia*. New York: Simon and Schuster, 1931.

Brading, David A. "Manuel Gamio and Official Indigenismo in Mexico." *Bulletin of Latin American Research* 17, no. 1 (1988): 75–89.

Braun, Barbara. *Pre-Columbian Art and the Post-Columbian World: Ancient American Sources of Modern Art*. New York: Harry N. Abrams, 1993.

Brenner, Anita. *Idols behind Altars*. New York: Harcourt Brace, 1929.

Brickhouse. Anna. "Scholarship and the State: Robert Greenhow and Transnational American Studies 1848–2008." *American Literary History* 20, no. 4 (2008): 695–722.

———. *Transamerican Literary Relations and the Nineteenth-Century Public Sphere*. Cambridge, UK: Cambridge University Press, 2004.

Britton, John A. *Carleton Beals: A Radical Journalist in Latin America*. Albuquerque: University of New Mexico Press, 1987.

———. *Revolution and Ideology: Images of the Mexican Revolution in the United States*. Lexington: University of Kentucky Press, 1995.

Bronfman, Alejandra. *Measures of Equality: Social Science, Citizenship, and Race in Cuba, 1902–1940*. Chapel Hill: University of North Carolina Press, 2004.

———. "Poetry in the Presidio: Toward a Study of *Proyecto de Código Criminal Cubano*." In *Cuban Counterpoints: The Legacy of Fernando Ortiz*, edited by Mauricio A. Font and Alfonso W. Quiroz, 157–68. Lanham, MD: Lexington Books, 2005.

Brookover, Lyle A. "Cuba Completes Two Great National Tasks." *Pan American Magazine*, April 1931, 279–87.

Capetillo, Luisa. *Absolute Equality: An Early Feminist Perspective / Influencias de las ideas modernas*. Edited and translated by Laura Walker. Houston: Arte Público Press, 2009.

———. *Amor y anarquía: Los escritos de Luisa Capetillo*. Edited by Julio Ramos. Río Piedras, Puerto Rico: Ediciones Huracán, 1992.

———. *A Nation of Women: An Early Feminist Speaks Out / Mi opinión sobre las libertades, derechos y deberes de la mujer*. Edited by Félix V. Matos Rodríguez. Houston, Arte Público Press, 2004.

Carpentier, Alejo. *Écue-Yamba-Ó*. Madrid: Alianza Editorial, 2002.

———. *¡Écue-Yamba-Ó! Novela afrocubana*. Madrid: Editorial España, 1933.

Carrera Damas, Germán. *El culto a Bolívar*. Caracas: Grijalbo, 1989.

———. "Simón Bolívar, el Culto Heroico y la Nación." *Hispanic American Historical Review* 63, no. 1 (1983): 107–45.

Castillo, Ana. *Massacre of the Dreamers: Essays on Xicanisma*. Albuquerque: University of New Mexico Press, 1994.

———. *The Mixquiahuala Letters*. Tempe, AZ: Bilingual Press/Editorial Bilingüe, 1986.

Césaire, Aimé. "Poetry and Knowledge." 1945. In *Refusal of the Shadow: Surrealism and the Caribbean*, edited by Michael Richardson. Translated by Richardson and Krzysztof Fijałowski, 134–46. London: Verso, 1996.

Chase, Stuart. *Mexico: A Study of Two Americas*. New York: Macmillan, 1931.

City College of San Francisco. The Diego Rivera Mural Project. http://www.riveramural.org.

Clarke, Vèvè, and Sarah E. Johnson, eds. *Kaiso! Writings by and about Katherine Dunham*. Madison: University of Wisconsin Press, 2005.

Coffey, Mary K. "An 'AMERICAN Idea': Myth, Indigeneity, and Violence in the Works of Orozco and Pollock." In *Men of Fire: José Clemente Orozco and Jackson Pollock*. Exhibition catalogue, Hood Museum, 21–36. Hanover, NH: University Press of New England, 2012.

———. *How a Revolutionary Art Became Official Culture: Murals, Museums, and the Mexican State*. Durham, NC: Duke University Press, 2012.

Cohen, Jonathan. *A Pan-American Life: Selected Poetry and Prose of Muna Lee*. Madison: University of Wisconsin Press, 2004.

Colby, Sasha. *Stratified Modernism: The Poetics of Excavation from Gautier to Olson*. Bern: Peter Lang, 2009.

Conrad, Bryce. *Reconfiguring America: A Study of William Carlos Williams' In the American Grain*. Urbana: University of Illinois Press, 1990.

Conway, Christopher. *The Cult of Bolívar in Latin American Literature*. Gainesville: University of Florida Press, 2003.

Crooke, Andrew. "A Continuous Center: Centripetal and Centrifugal Tendencies in *Let Us Now Praise Famous Men*." In *Agee at 100: Centennial Essays on the Works of James Agee*, edited by Michael Lofaro, 75–92. Knoxville: University of Tennessee Press, 2012.

Cruz Banks, Ojeya. "Katherine Dunham: Decolonizing Dance Education." In *Education as Freedom: African American Educational Thought and Activism*, edited by Noel S. Anderson and Haroon Kharem, 121–36. Lanham, MD: Lexington Books, 2009.

Darío, Rubén. *Songs of Life and Hope / Cantos de la vida y esperanza*. Durham, NC: Duke University Press, 2004.

Dash, J. Michael. *Haiti and the United States: National Stereotypes and the Literary Imagination*. New York: St. Martin's Press, 1997.

Deloria, Philip J. "American Indians, American Studies, and the ASA." *American Quarterly* 55, no. 4 (2003): 669–80.

Delpar, Helen. *The Enormous Vogue of Things Mexican: Cultural Relations between the United States and Mexico, 1920–1935*. Tuscaloosa: University of Alabama Press, 1992.

Dunham, Katherine. *Island Possessed*. 1969. Chicago: University of Chicago Press, 1994.

————. "The Performing Arts of Africa." In *Colloquium: Function and Significance of African Negro Art in the Life of the People and for the People (March 30—April 8, 1966)*, 473–80. Dakar: Editions Présence Africaine, 1968.

Elliott, David, and José Clemente Orozco. *Orozco! 1883–1949: An Exhibition Organised by the Ministry of Foreign Affairs and the Institute of Fine Arts, Mexico*. Oxford: Council of the Museum of Modern Art, 1980.

Emery, Amy Fass. *The Anthropological Imagination in Latin American Literature*. Columbia: University of Missouri Press, 1996.

Escobar, Arturo. *Encountering Development: The Making and Unmaking of the Third World*. Princeton, NJ: Princeton University Press, 1995.

Estimé, Lucienne H. *Dumarsais Estimé: Dialogue avec mes souvenirs*. Port-au-Prince: Éditions Mémoire, 2001.

Evans, R. Tripp. *Romancing the Maya: Mexican Antiquity in the American Imagination, 1820–1915*. Austin: University of Texas Press, 2004.

Evans, Walker. *American Photographs*. New York: Museum of Modern Art, 1938.

————. "The Reappearance of Photography." *Hound & Horn*, October–December 1931, 127–28.

————. *Walker Evans at Work*. New York: Harper & Row, 1982.

Fergusson, Erna. *Fiesta in Mexico*. New York: Knopf, 1934.

————. *Mexico Revisited*. New York: Knopf, 1955.

Finnegan, Cara A. *Picturing Poverty: Print Culture and FSA Photographs*. Washington, DC: Smithsonian Books, 2003.

Fishkin, Shelley Fisher. "Crossroads of Cultures: The Transnational Turn in American Studies. Presidential Address to the American Studies Association, November 12, 2004." *American Quarterly* 57, no. 1 (2005): 17–57.

Fitz, Earl, and Sophia McClennen, eds. *Comparative Cultural Studies and Latin America*. West Lafayette, IN: Purdue University Press, 2004.

Foucault, Michel. *The Archaeology of Knowledge*. Translated by A. M. Sheridan Smith. New York: Pantheon Books, 1972.

————. *Security, Territory, Population: Lectures at the Collège de France, 1977–78*. Edited by Michel Senellart. Translated by Graham Burchell. London: Palgrave Macmillan, 2007.

Fox, Claire F. "Commentary: The Transnational Turn and Hemispheric Return." *American Literary History* 18, vol. 3 (2006): 638–47.

————. *Making Art Panamerican: Cultural Policy and the Cold War*. Minneapolis: University of Minnesota Press, 2013.

Frank, Waldo. *Dawn in Russia: The Record of a Journey*. New York: Scribner, 1932.

Gallo, Rubén. *Mexican Modernity: The Avant-Garde and the Technological Revolution*. Cambridge, MA: MIT Press, 2005.

Gish, Robert Franklin. *Beautiful Swift Fox: Erna Fergusson and the Modern Southwest*. College Station: Texas A&M University Press, 1996.

González, Robert Alexander. *Designing Pan-America: U.S. Architectural Visions for the Hemisphere.* Austin: University of Texas Press, 2011.

González Echevarría, Roberto. *Alejo Carpentier: The Pilgrim at Home.* Ithaca, NY: Cornell University Press, 1977.

Gootenberg, Paul. *Cocaine: Global Histories.* London: Routledge, 1999.

Gruesz, Kirsten Silva. *Ambassadors of Culture: The Transamerican Origins of Latino Culture.* Princeton, NJ: Princeton University Press, 2002.

———. "The Occluded History of Transamerican Literature." In *Critical Latin American and Latino Studies,* edited by Juan Poblete, 121–37. Minneapolis: University of Minnesota Press, 2003.

Guerra, Lillian. *The Myth of José Martí: Conflicting Nationalisms in Early Twentieth-Century Cuba.* Chapel Hill: University of North Carolina Press, 2005.Hampton, Edward Lloyd. "Creating a New World Architecture." *Southern California Business,* April 1928, 16–17, 38, 45, 48.

Harny, Elizabeth. *In Senghor's Shadow: Art, Politics, and the Avant-Garde in Senegal, 1960–1995.* Durham, NC: Duke University Press, 2004.

Harris, Charles H., III, and Louis R. Sadler. *The Archaeologist Was a Spy: Sylvanus G. Morley and the Office of Naval Intelligence.* Albuquerque: University of New Mexico Press, 2003.

Herskovits, Melville J. *Life in a Haitian Valley.* New York: Knopf, 1937.

———. *The Myth of the Negro Past.* New York: Harper, 1941.

Hill, Constance Valis. "Katherine Dunham's 'Southland' Protest in the Face of Repression." *Dance Research Journal* 26, no. 2 (1994): 1–10.

Huang, Hsinya, Philip Deloria, Laura Furlan, and John Gambler. "Charting Transnational Native American Studies." *Journal of Transnational American Studies* 4, no. 1 (2012): 1–15.

Hudson, William Henry. *Idle Days in Patagonia.* 1883. New York: E. P. Dutton, 1917.

Ingle, Marjorie. *Mayan Revival Style.* Salt Lake City, UT: Peregrine Smith Books, 1984.

"The International Bureau and Its Building." *Bulletin of the Pan American Union,* May 1910, 714–30.

Jiménez-Muñoz, Gladys. "Deconstructing Colonialist Discourse: Links between the Women's Suffrage Movement in the United States and Puerto Rico." *Phoebe* 5, no. 1 (1993): 9–34.

Johnson, John J. *Simón Bolívar and Spanish American Independence, 1783–1830.* Princeton, NJ: Van Nostrand, 1968.

Kaplan, Amy. *The Anarchy of Empire in the Making of U.S. Culture.* Cambridge, MA: Harvard University Press, 2005.

Kaplan, Amy, and Donald E. Pease, eds. *Cultures of United States Imperialism.* Durham, NC: Duke University Press, 1993.

Kondritzer, Jeffrey. "*Broom*: An International Magazine of the Arts." PhD diss., Indiana University, 1984.

Kutzinski, Vera M. *Against the American Grain: Myth and History in William Carlos Williams, Jay Wright, and Nicolás Guillén*. Baltimore: Johns Hopkins University Press, 1987.

———. *Sugar's Secrets: Race and the Erotics of Cuban Nationalism*. Charlottesville: University of Virginia Press, 1993.

Lafaye, Jacques. *Quetzalcóatl y Guadalupe: La formación de la conciencia nacional de México*. 1974. Translated by Ida Vitale y Fulgencio López Vidarte. Mexico City: Fondo de Cultura Económica, 1999.

Lawrence, D. H. "America, Listen to Your Own." *New Republic*, December 15, 1920, 68–70.

———. *The Plumed Serpent*. New York: Knopf, 1926.

———. *The Symbolic Meaning: The Uncollected Versions of "Studies in Classic American Literature."* Edited by Armin Arnold. New York: Centaur, 1962.

"Laying of the Corner Stone of the International Bureau of the American Republics, Washington, May 11, 1908." *Bulletin of the International Bureau of the American Republics*, May 1908, xi–xxi.

Lee, Anthony W. *Painting on the Left: Diego Rivera, Radical Politics, and San Francisco's Public Murals*. Berkeley: University of California Press, 1999.

Lee, Muna. "Correspondence: Pan-American Women." *Nation*, March 14, 1928, 294–95.

———. "Cultural Interchanges between the Americas." *Pan American Magazine*, October 1929, 89–95.

———. "Translating the Untranslatable: Can Poetry Stand the Change?" *Américas* 6 (September 1954): 12–15.

Lee, Muna, and Ruth Emily McMurry. *The Cultural Approach: Another Way in International Relations*. Chapel Hill: University of North Carolina Press, 1947.

Lerner, Jesse. "A Fevered Dream of Maya: Robert Stacy-Judd." *La tortuga marina, historia en extinción*, May 2001. http://tortugamarina.tripod.com/articulos/lerner/stacy-judd.html.

———. *The Maya of Modernism: Art, Architecture, and Film*. Albuquerque: University of New Mexico Press, 2011.

Levander, Caroline F., and Robert S. Levine. "Introduction: Hemispheric American Literary History." *American Literary History* 18, vol. 3 (2006): 397–405.

Loevy, Steven Ross. "William Carlos Williams' *Rome*: Introduction." *Iowa Review* 9, no. 3 (1978): 1–11.

Lomas, Laura. *Translating Empire: José Martí, Migrant Latino Subjects, and American Modernities*. Durham, NC: Duke University Press, 2008.

Lopenzina, Drew. "'The Whole Wilderness Shall Blossom as the Rose': Samson Occom, Joseph Johnson, and the Question of Native Settlement on Cooper's Frontier." *American Quarterly* 58, no. 4 (2006): 1119–45.

Luis-Brown, David. *Waves of Decolonization: Discourses on Race and*

Hemispheric Citizenship in Cuba, Mexico, and the United States. Durham, NC: Duke University Press, 2008.

Lynd, Robert. *Middletown: A Study in American Culture*. New York: Harcourt Brace, 1929.

Machado y Morales, Gerardo. *Declaraciones del General Gerardo Machado y Morales*. Havana: Rambla y Bouza, 1928.

"Maize or Indian Corn: The Great Native Food Supply of America." *Bulletin of the International Bureau of the American Republics*, June 1909, 989–1002.

Mariani, Paul. *William Carlos Williams: A New World Naked*. New York: Norton, 1981.

Martí, José. "Our America" ["Nuestra América"]. 1891. In *José Martí: Selected Writings*. Translated by Esther Allen, 288–96. New York: Penguin, 2002.

———. "The Washington Pan-American Congress." 1889. In *Inside the Monster: Writings on the United States and American Imperialism by José Martí*, edited by Philip S. Foner, 339–41. New York: Monthly Review Press, 1975.

Martínez, Juan A. "Social and Political Commentary in Cuban Modernist Painting of the 1930s." In *The Social and the Real: Political Art of the 1930s in the Western Hemisphere*, edited by Alejandro Anreus, Diana L. Linden, and Jonathan Weinbert, 21–42. University Park: Pennsylvania State University Press, 2004.

Marzán, Julio. *The Spanish American Roots of William Carlos Williams*. Austin: University of Texas Press, 1994.

McCarthy-Jones, Anthea, and Alistair Greig. "*Somos hijos de Sandino y Bolívar*: Radical Pan-American Traditions in Historical and Cultural Context." *Journal of Iberian and Latin American Research* 17, no. 2 (2011): 231–48.

McClennen, Sophia. "Area Studies beyond Ontology: Notes on Latin American Studies, American Studies, and Inter-American Studies." *A contracorriente* 5, no. 1 (2007): 173–84.

———. "Inter-American Studies or Imperial American Studies?" *Comparative American Studies* 3, no. 4 (2005): 393–413.

Mella, Julio Antonio. *J. A. Mella: Documentos y Articulos*. Havana: Editorial de Ciencias, 1975.

Mellow, James R. *Walker Evans*. New York: Basic Books, 1999.

Mickenberg, Julia. "The New Generation and the New Russia: Modern Childhood as Collective Fantasy." *American Quarterly* 62, no. 1 (2010): 103–34.

Mignolo, Walter. *The Darker Side of the Renaissance: Literacy, Territoriality, and Colonization*. 2nd ed. Ann Arbor: University of Michigan Press, 2003.

———. *The Darker Side of Western Modernity: Global Futures, Decolonial Options*. Durham, NC: Duke University Press, 2011.

———. *The Idea of Latin America*. Oxford: Blackwell, 2005.

———. *Local Histories / Global Designs: Coloniality, Subaltern Knowledges, and Border Thinking*. Princeton, NJ: Princeton University Press, 2000.

Miller, Francesca. *Latin American Women and the Search for Social Justice.* Hanover, NH: University Press of New England, 1991.

Miller, Marilyn Grace. *Rise and Fall of the Cosmic Race: The Cult of* Mestizaje *in Latin America.* Austin: University of Texas Press, 2004.

Miller, Paul B. "Remoteness and Proximity: The Parallel Ethnographies of Alejo Carpentier and René Maran." *Symposium: A Quarterly Journal in Modern Literatures,* 66, no. 1 (2012): 1–15.

Moore, Robin D. *Nationalizing Blackness: Afrocubanismo and Artistic Revolution in Havana, 1920–1940.* Pittsburgh: University of Pittsburgh Press, 1997.

Mora, Giles. *Walker Evans: Havana 1933.* New York: Pantheon Books, 1989.

Moraga, Cherríe, and Gloria Anzaldúa, eds. *This Bridge Called My Back: Writings by Radical Women of Color.* Watertown, MA: Persephone Press, 1981.

Morley, Sylvanus Griswold. "The Foremost Intellectual Achievement of Ancient America: The Hieroglyphic Inscriptions on the Monuments in the Ruined Cities of Mexico, Guatemala, and Honduras Are Yielding the Secrets of the Maya Civilization." *National Geographic,* February 1922, 109–30.

Moya, Paula, and Ramón Saldívar, eds. "Fictions of the Trans-American Imaginary." Special issue, *Modern Fiction Studies* 49, no. 1 (2003).

Noel, John Vavasour. "Cuba—A Country on the Rise." *Pan-American Magazine* 42, no. 4 (1930): 249–55.

O'Brien, Thomas F. "The Revolutionary Mission: American Enterprise in Cuba." *American Historical Review,* 98, no. 3 (1993): 765–85.

Oles, James. *South of the Border: Mexico in the American Imagination, 1917–1947.* Washington, DC: Smithsonian Institution Press, 1993.

Orozco, José Clemente. *An Autobiography.* Translated by Robert C. Stephenson. Austin: University of Texas Press, 1962.

———. "New World, New Races, and New Art." *Creative Art,* January 1929, xlv–xlvi.

———. "A Note from the Artist." 1934. Orozco at Dartmouth. Hood Museum of Art, Dartmouth College. http://hoodmuseum.dartmouth.edu/collections/overview/americas/mesoamerica/murals/orozco.html.

Ortega y Medina, Juan. "Monroísmo arqueológico: Un intento de compensación de americanidad insuficiente." In *Ensayos, tareas y estudios históricos,* 37–86. Xalapa, Mexico: Universidad Veracruzana, 1962.

Ortiz, Fernando. *Cuban Counterpoint: Tobacco and Sugar.* Translated by Harriet de Onís. Durham, NC: Duke University Press, 1995.

———. "Esta revista cubana." *Archivos del Folklore Cubano* 1, no. 1 (1924): 5–8.

———. "Introduction to *Motivos del son.*" *Archivos del Folklore Cubano* 5, no. 3 (1930): 222–23.

———. *Proyecto de código criminal cubano (Libro primero o parte general).* Havana: Librería Cervantes, 1926.

Palmié, Stephan. "The Cuban Republic and Its Wizards." In *Permutations of Order: Religion and Law as Contested Sovereignties*, edited by Thomas G. Kirsch and Bertram Turner, 67–84. London: Ashgate, 2008.

———. *Wizards and Scientists: Explorations in Afro-Cuban Modernity and Tradition*. Durham, NC: Duke University Press, 2002.

"Pan American Airways." *Fortune*, April 1936, 78–91.

Paulmier, Hilah, and Robert Haven Schauffler, eds. *Pan-American Day*. New York: Dodd, Mead, 1943.

Paz, Octavio. "The Concealment and Discovery of Orozco." In *Essays on Mexican Art*. Translated by Helen Lane, 169–202. New York: Harcourt Brace, 1987.

Pease, Donald E. "Introduction: Re-mapping the Transnational Turn." In *Reframing the Transnational Turn in American Studies*, edited by Donald E. Pease, John Carolos Rowe, and Winfried Fluck, 1–48. Hanover, NH: Dartmouth College Press, 2011.

Pérez, Luis A., Jr. *Cuba in the American Imagination: Metaphor and Imperial Ethos*. Chapel Hill: University of North Carolina Press, 2008.

Pérez Firmat, Gustavo. *Do the Americas Have a Common Literature?* Durham, NC: Duke University Press, 1990.

Polyné, Millery. *From Douglass to Duvalier: U.S. African Americans, Haiti, and Pan Americanism, 1870–1964*. Gainesville: University of Florida Press, 2010.

Pratt, Mary Louise. *Imperial Eyes: Travel Writing and Transculturation*. London: Routledge, 1992.

"President Vincent Confers with President Roosevelt." *Bulletin of the Pan American Union* 68, no. 6 (1934): 389–92.

Prevots, Naima. *Dance for Export: Cultural Diplomacy and the Cold War*. Middletown, CT: Wesleyan University Press, 1998.

Prieto-Calixto, Alberto. "Rubén Darío and Literary Anti-Americanism/Anti-Imperialism." In *Beyond the Ideal: Pan Americanism in Inter-American Affairs*, edited by David Sheinin, 57–77. Westport, CT: Praeger, 2000.

Quintana, Alvina E. "Ana Castillo's *The Mixquiahuala Letters*: The Novelist as Ethnographer." In *Criticism in the Borderlands: Studies in Chicano Literature, Culture, and Ideology*, edited by Héctor Calderón and José David Saldívar, 72–83. Durham, NC: Duke University Press, 1991.

Ramsey, Kate. "Melville Herskovits, Katherine Dunham, and the Politics of African Diasporic Dance Anthropology." In *Dancing Bodies / Living Histories: New Writings about Dance and Culture*, edited by Lisa Doolittle and Anne Flynn, 196–216. Banff, Canada: Banff Centre Press, 2000.

———. *The Spirit and the Law: Vodou and Power in Haiti*. Chicago: University of Chicago Press, 2011.

Redfield, Robert. *Tepoztlan, a Mexican Village: A Study of Folk Life*. Chicago: University of Chicago Press, 1930.

Renda, Mary A. *Taking Haiti: Military Occupation and the Culture of U.S. Imperialism, 1915–1940*. Chapel Hill: University of North Carolina Press, 2001.

Rodríguez, Antonio. *A History of Mexican Mural Painting*. New York: G. P. Putnam's and Sons, 1969.

Rodríguez García, José María. "The Culture of Conversation and the Voice of the Indian in Williams Carlos Williams' 'Père Sebastian Rasles.'" *Neophilologus* 86 (2002): 477–92.

Rogers, Charlotte. "Carpentier, Collecting, and *Lo Barroco Americano*." *Hispania* 94, no. 2 (2011): 240–51.

Rosaldo, Renato. "Imperialist Nostalgia." *Representations* 26 (1989): 107–22.

Rowe, John Carlos, ed. *A Concise Companion to American Studies*. Oxford: Wiley-Blackwell, 2010.

———. *Literary Culture and U.S. Imperialism*. Oxford: Oxford University Press, 2000.

Rowe, Leo S. "Introduction: Bolívar's Influence in Its Larger International Aspects." *Bulletin of the Pan American Union*, December 1930, 1188–89.

Sacken, George. "Maya Art." *Broom* 4, no. 2 (1923): 86–88.

Sáenz, César A. *Quetzalcóatl*. Managua: Fundación Vida, 2002.

Sahagún, Fray Bernardino de. *Florentine Codex: General History of the Things of New Spain*. Translated and edited by Arthur J. O. Anderson and Charles E. Dibble. Salt Lake City: University of Utah Press, 1982.

Saldaña-Portillo, María Josefina. *The Revolutionary Imagination in the Americas and the Age of Development*. Durham, NC: Duke University Press 2003.

Salvatore, Ricardo D. "Libraries and Legibility of Hispanic America: Early Latin American Collections in the United States." In *Hybrid Americas: Contacts, Contrasts, and Confluences in New World Literatures and Cultures*, edited by Josef Raab and Martin Butler, 191–211. Tempe, AZ: LIT Bilingual Press/Editorial Bilingüe, 2008.

———. "Local versus Imperial Knowledge: Reflections on Hiram Bingham and the Yale Peruvian Expedition." *Nepantla* 4, no. 1 (2003): 67–80.

Sánchez González, Lisa. *Boricua Literature: A Literary History of the Puerto Rican Diaspora*. New York: New York University Press, 2001.

———. "Modernism and Boricua Literature: A Reconsideration of Arturo Schomburg and William Carlos Williams." *American Literary History* 13, no. 2 (2001): 243–64.

Sandino, Augusto. *Augusto Cesar Sandino: Pensamiento politico*. Edited by Sergio Ramírez. Caracas: Biblioteca Ayacucho, 1988.

Sandoval, Chela. "U.S. Third World Feminism: The Theory and Method of Oppositional Consciousness in the Postmodern World," *Genders* 10 (Spring 1991): 1–24.

Schmidt, Peter. "Descriptive List of Works from the Library of William Carlos Williams at Fairleigh Dickinson University." *William Carlos Williams Review* 10, no. 2 (1984): 30–53.

Schnapp, Jeffrey T., Michael Shanks, and Matthew Tiews. "Archaeology, Modernism, Modernity." *Modernism/Modernity* 11, no. 1 (2004): 1–16.

Siqueiros, David Alfaro. *Art and Revolution.* London: Lawrence and Wishart, 1975.

Smith, Matthew J. *Red and Black in Haiti: Radicalism, Conflict, and Political Change, 1934–1957.* Chapel Hill: University of North Carolina Press, 2009.

Sommer, Doris. *Proceed with Caution, When Engaged by Minority Writing in the Americas.* Cambridge, MA: Harvard University Press, 1999.

Squier, Emma-Lindsay. *Gringa: An American Woman in Mexico.* Boston: Houghton Mifflin, 1934.

Stacy-Judd, Robert. *The Ancient Mayas: Adventures in the Jungles of Yucatan.* Los Angeles: Murray & Gee, 1934.

Stecopoulos, Harilaos. *Reconstructing the World: Southern Fictions and U.S. Imperialisms, 1898–1976.* Ithaca, NY: Cornell University Press, 2008.

Stepan, Nancy. *"The Hour of Eugenics": Race, Gender, and Nation in Latin America.* Ithaca, NY: Cornell University Press, 1991.

Stott, William. *Documentary Expression and Thirties America.* Oxford: Oxford University Press, 1973.

Sylvain, Madeleine G. "The Haitian Rural School at Work." *Bulletin of the Pan American Union* 71 (July 1937): 606–17.

Taylor, Diana. *The Archive and the Repertoire: Performing Cultural Memory in the Americas.* Durham, NC: Duke University Press, 2003.

Threlkeld, Megan. "The Pan American Conference of Women, 1922: Successful Suffragists Turn to International Relations." *Diplomatic History* 31, no. 5 (2007): 801–28.

Totten, George Oakley. *Maya Architecture.* Washington, DC: Maya Press, 1926.

Trachtenberg, Alan. "Signifying the Real: Documentary Photography in the 1930s." In *The Social and the Real: Political Art of the 1930s in the Western Hemisphere,* edited by Alejandro Anreus, Diana L. Linden, and Jonathan Weinberg, 10–11. University Park: Pennsylvania State University Press, 2006.

Transactions of the First Pan American Conference on Eugenics and Homiculture of the American Republics. Havana: Government of Cuba, 1928.

Valle-Ferrer, Norma. *Luisa Capetillo, Pioneer Puerto Rican Feminist.* 1990. Translated by Gloria Waldman-Schwartz. New York: Peter Lang, 2006.

Vasconcelos, José. *Bolivarismo y Monroísmo: Temas Iberoamericanos.* 2nd ed. Santiago, Chile: Biblioteca América V, 1935.

———. *The Cosmic Race / La raza cósmica: A Bilingual Edition.* Translated by Didier T. Jaén. Baltimore: Johns Hopkins University Press, 1997.

Von Eschen, Penny. *Satchmo Blows Up the World: Jazz Ambassadors Play the Cold War.* Cambridge, MA: Harvard University Press, 2004.

Walker, Alice. *The Color Purple.* New York: Harcourt Brace, 1982.

Weaver, Mike. *William Carlos Williams: The American Background*. Cambridge, UK: Cambridge University Press, 1971.

Williams, William Carlos. *The Autobiography of William Carlos Williams*. New York: Random House, 1951.

———. *By Word of Mouth: Poems from the Spanish, 1916–1959*. New York: New Directions, 2011.

———. *I Wanted to Write a Poem: The Autobiography of the Works of a Poet*. New York: New Directions, 1958.

———. *Imaginations*. New York: New Directions, 1970.

———. *In the American Grain*. New York: New Directions, 1938.

———. "An Informal Discussion of Poetic Form." April 16, 1941. In *The First Inter-American Writers' Conference of the University of Puerto Rico, April 14–23, 1941*. San Juan: University of Puerto Rico, 1942.

———. *Paterson*. New York: New Directions, 1992.

———. "Rome." *Iowa Review* 9, no. 3 (1978): 12–65.

———. *Selected Essays of William Carlos Williams*. New York: Random House, 1954.

———. *Selected Letters of William Carlos Williams*. Edited by John C. Thirlwall. New York: McDowell, Oblensky, 1957.

———. *Something to Say: William Carlos Williams on Younger Poets*. Edited by James E. B. Breslin. New York: New Directions, 1985.

Woolf, Virginia. *Three Guineas*. New York: Harcourt, 1938.

Wright, Frank Lloyd. *Modern Architecture: Being the Kahn Lectures for 1930*. Princeton, NJ: Princeton University Press, 1931.

———. *A Testament*. New York: Horizon Press, 1957.

Zermeño, Guillermo. "Between Anthropology and History: Manuel Gamio and Mexican Anthropological Modernity, 1916–1935." *Nepantla: Views from the South* 3, no. 2 (2002): 315–31.

Index

RECENT BOOKS IN THE NEW WORLD STUDIES SERIES

Nick Nesbitt, *Universal Emancipation: The Haitian Revolution and the Radical Enlightenment*

Doris L. Garraway, editor, *Tree of Liberty: Cultural Legacies of the Haitian Revolution in the Atlantic World*

Dawn Fulton, *Signs of Dissent: Maryse Condé and Postcolonial Criticism*

Michael G. Malouf, *Transatlantic Solidarities: Irish Nationalism and Caribbean Poetics*

Maria Cristina Fumagalli, *Caribbean Perspectives on Modernity: Returning the Gaze*

Vivian Nun Halloran, *Exhibiting Slavery: The Caribbean Postmodern Novel as Museum*

Paul B. Miller, *Elusive Origins: The Enlightenment in the Modern Caribbean Historical Imagination*

Eduardo González, *Cuba and the Fall: Christian Text and Queer Narrative in the Fiction of José Lezama Lima and Reinaldo Arenas*

Jeff Karem, *The Purloined Islands: Caribbean-U.S. Crosscurrents in Literature and Culture, 1880–1959*

Faith Smith, editor, *Sex and the Citizen: Interrogating the Caribbean*

Mark D. Anderson, *Disaster Writing: The Cultural Politics of Catastrophe in Latin America*

Raphael Dalleo, *Caribbean Literature and the Public Sphere: From the Plantation to the Postcolonial*

Maite Conde, *Consuming Visions: Cinema, Writing, and Modernity in Rio de Janeiro*

Monika Kaup, *Neobaroque in the Americas: Alternative Modernities in Literature, Visual Art, and Film*

Marisel C. Moreno, *Family Matters: Puerto Rican Women Authors on the Island and the Mainland*

Supriya M. Nair, *Pathologies of Paradise: Caribbean Detours*